To Sister Helen Forshaw
With love from
the author

Alban Hood OSB.
20 February 2015

FROM REPATRIATION TO REVIVAL:

*CONTINUITY AND CHANGE IN THE
ENGLISH BENEDICTINE CONGREGATION,
1795-1850.*

Alban Hood OSB

All rights reserved. No part of this publication may be reproduced, stored in a retrieval system, or transmitted, in any form or by any means, electronic, mechanical, photocopying or otherwise, without the prior permission of the publisher, St Michael's Abbey Press.

© Alban Hood 2014

The author has asserted his rights, under the Copyright, Designs and Patents Act, 1988, to be identified as the author of this work.

British Library Cataloguing in Publication data

A catalogue record for this book is available from the British Library

ISBN 978-0-907077-66-4

First published in 2014 by St Michael's Abbey Press
Farnborough Abbey,
Farnborough, Hampshire GU14 7NQ

www.farnboroughabbey.org
www.theabbeyshop.com

St Michael's Abbey Press is a division of
St Michael's Abbey Press Ltd (reg. no. 326241)

Printed and bound in Slovakia

This book is dedicated to my parents, James Donald Hood and the late Barbara Joan Hood, whose love, generosity and Christian example continue to nourish and sustain me.

Alban Hood OSB

CONTENTS

List of Figures   vii
List of Illustrations   ix
Abbreviations   xi
Acknowledgements   xiii

    Introduction   1

1. Surveying the Landscape   3
2. The Monasteries, from Repatriation to Revival   25
3. Prayer and Devotion   61
4. Of Rabbits and Hedgehogs: Monks, Bishops and the English Mission   83
5. 'The Christian Instruction of the English People': Monks and their Missions   105
6. Monks, Learning and Books   137
7. 'Schools for the Lord's Service': English Benedictine Education   155
8. 'Sharing Treasures throughout a mighty Hemisphere': English Benedictines and the Empire   179
9. Conclusion   207

    Appendix 1   211
        List of Congregational officials and Superiors, 1795-1850

    Appendix 2   215
        List of Chapels, Chaplaincies and Missions served by the English Benedictines between 1795 and 1850

    Bibliography   219

    Index   241

LIST OF FIGURES

Figure 1	The Historical Development of the English Benedictine Congregation.	5
Figure 2	The structure of the English Benedictine Congregation until 1900.	6
Figure 3	The number of monks in the English Benedictine Congregation, 1789 – 1850	36
Figure 4	The number of monks resident in the monasteries of the English Benedictine Congregation, 1789-1850.	37
Figure 5	Map showing the geographical distribution of principal Chaplaincies and Missions served by the English Benedictines, 1795-1850	106
Figure 6	Monks working in Mauritius, 1819-1850	188
Figure 7	Monks working in Australia, 1833-1850	189

LIST OF ILLUSTRATIONS

1. Richard Marsh OSB - portrait by C. Mayer at Douai Abbey

2. Peter Augustine Baines OSB - portrait at Ampleforth Abbey

3. John Bede Polding OSB - portrait at Downside Abbey

4. William Bernard Ullathorne OSB – portrait of 1852 by Richard Burchett at Downside Abbey

5. William Bernard Allen Collier OSB – portrait by C. Mayer at Douai Abbey

6. Augustine Birdsall OSB - portrait at Downside Abbey

7. James Laurence Shepherd OSB

8. Watercolour of the buildings at Downside designed by H.E. Goodridge

9. Interior of the chapel at Ampleforth, c.1810 sketched by Maurus Powell OSB

ABBREVIATIONS

AA	Ampleforth Abbey Archives, Yorkshire.
AAW	Archives of the Archbishop of Westminster, London.
AB	A. ALLANSON, (eds. A. CRAMER and S. GOODWILL, *Biographies of the English Benedictines*, St Laurence Papers, Ampleforth 1999.
AH	Ampleforth Abbey, A. ALLANSON MS, "History of the English Benedictine Congregation".
AJ	*The Ampleforth Journal.*
AR	Ampleforth Abbey, ALLANSON MS, "Records of the English Benedictine Congregation".
BAA	Archives of the Archdiocese of Birmingham.
CDA	Clifton Diocesan Archives, Bristol.
CO	Colonial Office Papers, National Archives, Kew.
CRS (M)	Catholic Record Society (Monograph Series).
CRS (R)	Catholic Record Society (Records Series).
DA	Downside Abbey Archives, Stratton-on-the-Fosse, Bath, Somerset.
DAA	Douai Abbey Archives, Woolhampton, Reading, Berkshire.
DAB	Downside Abbey Archives, Birt papers.
DM	*The Douai Magazine.*
DR	*The Downside Review.*
EBHS	*English Benedictine History Symposium Papers*, privately printed, 1981-1999.

JEH	*Journal of Ecclesiastical History.*
LDA	Leeds Diocesan Archives.
LRO	Liverpool Record Office.
NA	National Archives, Kew, London.
NLW	National Library of Wales, Aberystwyth.
NWCH	*North West Catholic History.*
ODNB	*Oxford Dictionary of National Biography,* edited by H.C.G. MATTHEW and B. HARRISON, Oxford University Press, Oxford 2004.
RH	*Recusant History.*
RSRNC	Archive of Propaganda Fide, Rome, Scritture Riferite nei Congressi.
SAA	Stanbrook Abbey Archives.
TJ	*Tjurunga: An Australasian Benedictine Review.*
WRO	Warwick Record Office.

ACKNOWLEDGEMENTS

This book would never have seen the light of day without the assistance, support and encouragement of a whole host of people. First and foremost I acknowledge the support of Abbot Geoffrey Scott, who as friend, teacher, and religious superior first encouraged me to pursue academic research, and who has been a rich source of information, advice, sympathy and patience. I am also greatly indebted to my brother monks of Douai Abbey, in particular to Father Gabriel Wilson OSB for his assistance with the illustrations.

This present work began its life as a doctoral thesis, submitted in 2006 and I acknowledge the advice, support and patience of my supervisors, Dr Janet Hollinshead and Mr John Davies at Liverpool Hope University and Dr Pat Starkey at the University of Liverpool.

This book is substantially based on archival material kept in the various monasteries of the English Benedictine Congregation. Although a lot of material relating to the period up to the French Revolution was lost on the departure of monks and nuns from France, some important material is now to be found in various archives in France and Germany. Many of the archives of the Congregation are kept at Downside Abbey, near Bath, and I gratefully acknowledge the assistance and kindness of the former annalist of the Congregation, the late Dom Philip Jebb, the current annalist, Abbot Aidan Bellenger as well as the current keeper of the Downside Archives, Dr Simon Johnson. I am also grateful for the assistance and support provided by two of my colleagues on the English Benedictine History Commission: Dom Anselm Cramer, archivist of Ampleforth Abbey, and Dame Margaret Truran, former archivist of Stanbrook Abbey. I also gratefully acknowledge their communities for their hospitality and kindness.

Research for this book in various archives in Rome was kindly funded by awards from the Council of the Catholic Record Society, and I also gratefully acknowledge the generous financial support of the English Benedictine Trust, the St Mary's Priory, Fernham Residual Fund Trust and the Barbara Hood Trust for grants which funded the cost of publication. I thank His Eminence Crescenzio, Cardinal Sepe, Prefect of the Sacred Congregation for the Evangelisation of Peoples for allowing me access in 2005 to the Historical Archives of Propaganda Fide, and Don Luis Cuňa Ramos, the archivist, for his assistance and for microfilming various documents for me. I also thank Monsignor (now Bishop) Nicholas Hudson, who in 2005 as Rector of the English College in Rome allowed me access to the College archives, and Dom Bruno Marin, the Abbot President of the Subiaco Cassinese Benedictine Congregation for granting me access to the Congregational Archives at Sant'

Ambrogio in Rome. To my confrère Abbot Edmund Power and his community at the Abbey of St Paul outside-the-Walls, I owe a debt of gratitude for their hospitality and kindness, and I thank Abbot Paolo Lunardon for his assistance in the archives there.

I also acknowledge the help and guidance of the following diocesan archivists: the late Father Ian Dickie at Westminster, Father John Sharp at Birmingham, Father (now Canon) Anthony Harding at Clifton and Mr Robert Finnigan at Leeds. Drs Judith Champ and Paul Collins generously loaned me copies of letters and articles relating to the Australian ministry of Bishop Bernard Ullathorne, whilst Dr Michael Pearson assisted me in locating the papers of Bishop Thomas Joseph Brown at the National Library of Wales at Aberystwyth. Professor Maurice Whitehead and Dr Thomas Muir kindly shared with me some of their insights concerning the educational achievements of the Society of Jesus in the early nineteenth century.

I thank the Abbots and Trustees of Downside, Ampleforth and Douai for permission to reproduce portraits and illustrations in their keeping, and Mr Brian Farrimond of Ormskirk for creating the map in Chapter 5.

Last and not least, I acknowledge my gratitude to Abbot Cuthbert Brogan of Farnborough Abbey for accepting this volume for publication by St Michael's Abbey Press.

Alban Hood OSB
Douai Abbey,
Feast of the Abbey's patron, St Edmund King and Martyr,
20 November 2014.

INTRODUCTION

In the wake of the French Revolution, English Benedictine monks and nuns were forced to leave their monasteries in France and were repatriated in 1795 to England, over thirty years before emancipation was granted to Catholics. It took much of the following half century for them to settle into new houses and recover from the losses that had been sustained in terms of personnel, finance and property. This book explores thematically the continuities and changes in the fortunes of the English Benedictine Congregation during the early nineteenth century, a period that has tended to be neglected over the past century by historians of English Catholicism and dismissed by monastic commentators as a rather stagnant era for the English Benedictines: a time of hibernation until their monasteries and their grand buildings were revived later in the century. This work refutes such a view, and illustrates the richness and diversity of the Congregation's life at a time when its survival was under threat due to low numbers, scant resources, and challenges to its independence from the Vicars Apostolic.

In particular, the achievements of the English Benedictines in their missionary activity, both at home and abroad, will be highlighted, as well as their success in re-establishing monastic life despite their reduced circumstances in England. In demonstrating that continuity rather than change characterised English Benedictinism in the early nineteenth century this volume contends that, despite many achievements by 1850, with their conservative and entrenched mind-sets the English Benedictines were in danger of becoming "out of time, out of place."

Chapter 1

Surveying the Landscape

Introduction

In 1795 monks and nuns of the English Benedictine Congregation were among many of their fellow compatriots who arrived on English shores having escaped from revolution-torn France.[1] The courage of these monks and nuns in the face of the French Revolution has been well-documented but little has been written of the years that followed their repatriation.[2] This book aims to fill this gap, as well as to build upon the pioneering work on the English Benedictines by David Lunn and Geoffrey Scott.[3] In the main, the focus will be on the monks, but reference will also be made to the nuns, whose contemplative life provided a foil for the active, pastoral life of the monks.

The following chapters will provide a detailed picture of the resettlement of English monks and nuns from the time of their arrival in England until the re-establishment of the Catholic hierarchy in 1850. The early decades of the nineteenth century were important ones for the English Benedictines. New monasteries, churches and schools were built, new apostolates were begun, attempts were made to restore morale and recover property lost as a result of the French Revolution. Taking a thematic approach, this study will illustrate the richness and diversity of the life of the Congregation in its two operational modes, the monastic and the missionary. The traditional English Benedictine apostolates of education and pastoral work will be considered alongside developments in theology, spirituality and the new congregational apostolate of missionary work overseas. The achievements of the English Benedictines in the first half of the nineteenth century will be contrasted with their failure to respond to new challenges, especially those posed by the continental Benedictine revival, new Roman policies of ecclesiastical centralisation, and a new breed of English Catholic secular clergy, whose growth in professionalism and self-confidence increasingly threatened the independence of the monks.

---

[1] See A. BELLENGER (ed.), *The Great Return - The English Communities in Continental Europe and their Repatriation, 1793-4,* Downside Abbey 1994.
[2] STANBROOK ABBEY ARCHIVES, DAME A.T. PARTINGTON, *A Brief Narrative of the Benedictine Dames of Cambray, of their Sufferings while in the hands of the French Republicans, and of their arrival in England;* R. MARSH, *Fr Marsh's Escape from Dieulouard: His own account written in 1794,* St Laurence Papers, Ampleforth 1994.
[3] D. LUNN, *The English Benedictines, 1540-1688: From Reform to Revolution,* Burns and Oates, London 1980; G. SCOTT, *Gothic Rage Undone: English Monks in the Age of Enlightenment,* Downside Abbey, Bath 1992.

The early nineteenth century has tended to be neglected over the past century by historians of English Catholicism and dismissed by monastic commentators as a rather stagnant era for the English Benedictines: a time of hibernation until their monasteries and their grand buildings were revived later in the century. This work refutes such a view, and illustrates the richness and diversity of the Congregation's life at a time when its survival was under threat due to low numbers, scant resources, and challenges to its independence from the Vicars Apostolic.

1 The Development of the English Benedictine Congregation, 1619-1795

In 1795 the English Benedictine Congregation comprised four houses of monks and one of nuns.[4] The priory of St Gregory had been founded at Douai in 1606, that of St Laurence at Dieulouard in Lorraine in 1607. In 1615 a priory of monks was established in Paris under the patronage of St Edmund, King and Martyr and in 1643 the abbey of Saints Adrian and Denis at Lamspringe near Hildesheim was incorporated into the Congregation. A community of nuns under the patronage of Our Lady of Consolation was established at Cambrai in 1625.

Although the English Benedictine Congregation was re-established in 1619, it bore little resemblance to its medieval forebear, for the new Congregation was essentially a missionary body, with a centralised authority under a President General who presided over a loose federation of monastic houses on the continent mentioned above. These communities were usually small in size, for the majority of the professed monks throughout the seventeenth and eighteenth centuries were engaged in pastoral work in England, either as "riding missioners", covering a large area on horseback, or as private chaplains to wealthy lay patrons. During his time on the mission, the monk's immediate superior was either the Provincial of the North (or York) or the Provincial of the South (or Canterbury). All superiors were elected by the General Chapter every four years, and the membership of this body was almost exclusively composed of monks who were on the mission, as opposed to those resident in the monasteries. Although the papal bull *Plantata in agro Dominico veneranda Congregatio monachorum Anglorum* of 1633 attempted to stress the continuity between the old, pre-reformation English Benedictine Congregation and its seventeenth-century successor by granting the Congregation the use of ancient titles and privileges, it represented in the words of Geoffrey Scott, "a mirage of baroque extravagance". It bore little relation to reality, but provided the monks with ammunition when in the eighteenth century they needed to bolster their claims to independence from the Vicars Apostolic.

---

[4] See *Figure 1*.

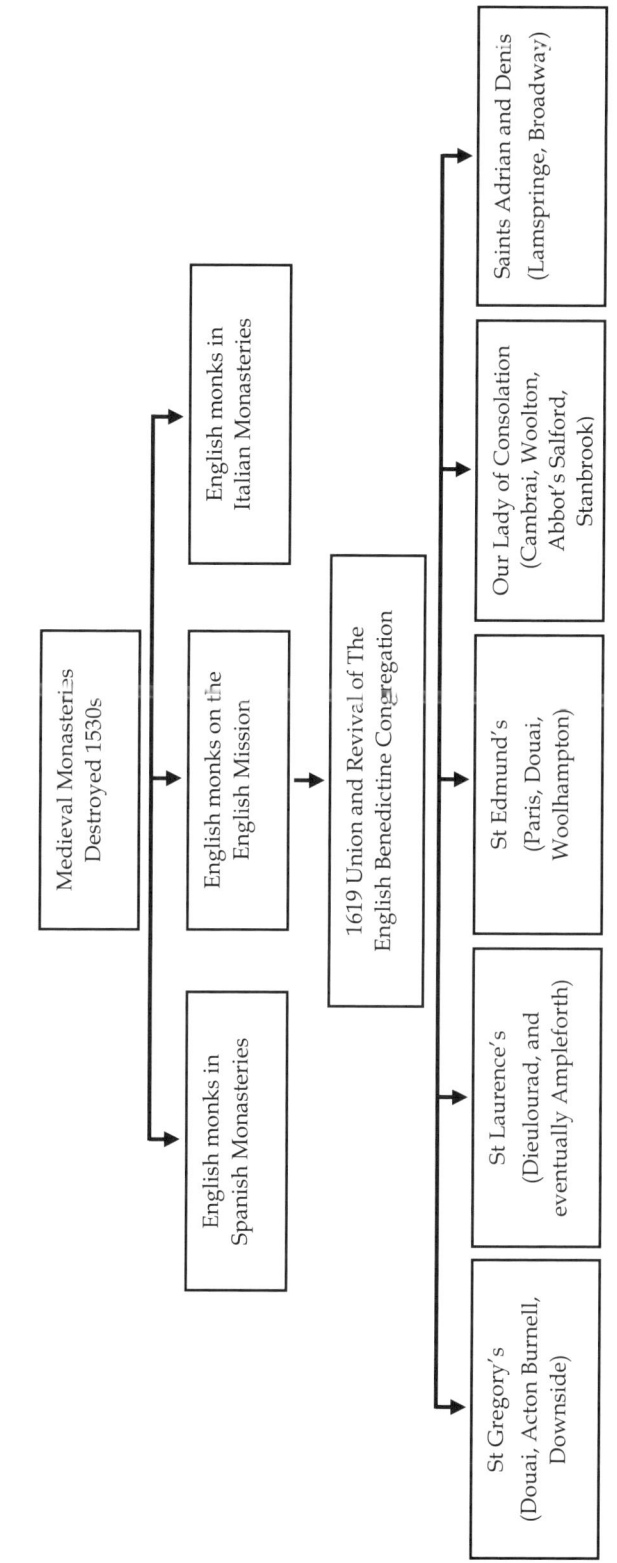

Figure 1 – THE HISTORICAL DEVELOPMENT OF THE ENGLISH BENEDICTINE CONGREGATION

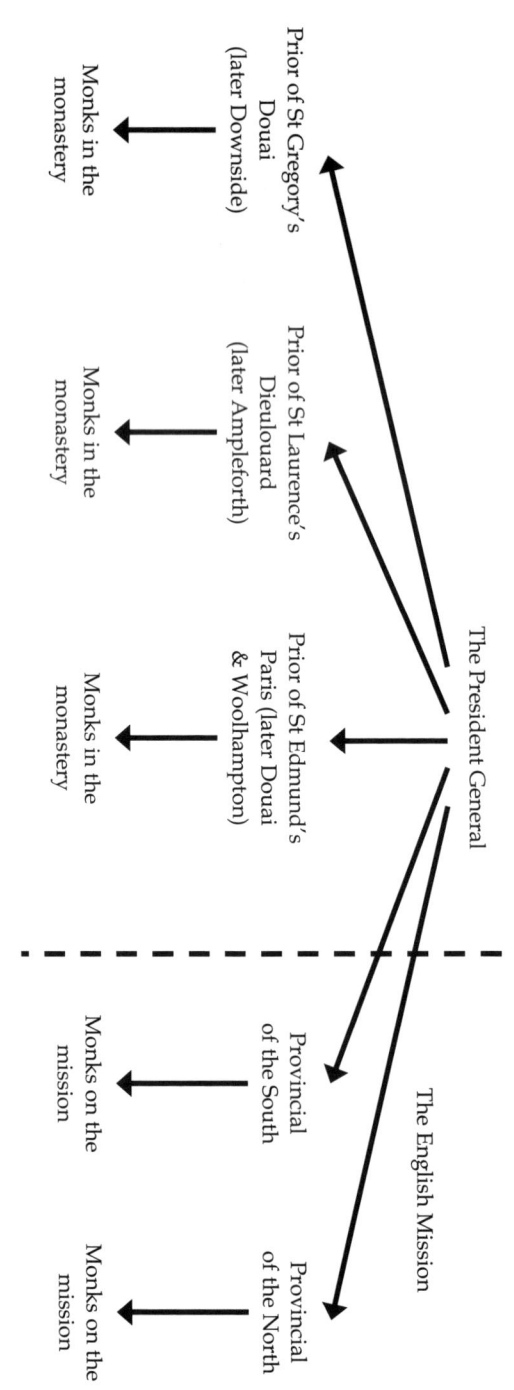

Figure 2 – THE STRUCTURE OF THE ENGLISH BENEDICTINE CONGREGATION UNTIL 1900

In his book *Gothic Rage Undone*, Scott has deftly sketched the diverse apostolates and interests of these eighteenth-century Benedictines against the wider canvas of the Enlightenment and its consequences. There can be no better opening for the present study than Scott's final paragraph, which declares:

> The two [English Benedictine] communities which had the good fortune to reach England appeared there just after the passing of the 1791 Relief Act, whose benefits they were to enjoy. Their homecoming brought together in close proximity, for the first time since the brief experiment of James II's reign, the two halves of the Congregation, the conventual and the missionary. This union ensured that the Congregation's history in the nineteenth century would be of quite a different character from what it has been under the *ancien régime*.[5]

The French Revolution brought an end to the continental exile of the English Benedictine monasteries, and focused the energies and attention of the monks on the missions in England, which provided sanctuaries for the refugees until permanent homes could be found for them.

2 Five Historiographical Traditions

The history of the English Benedictine Congregation between 1795 and 1850 clearly forms part of the narrative of an English Catholicism responding to major developments in church and society which is itself part of a wider landscape that requires some exploration. A context for the history of the English Benedictines in these years may be established by surveying that landscape and considering five historiographical traditions exemplifying five distinct epochs; the first on the period in general, the second on the principal features of early nineteenth-century European Catholicism, the third on the growth of English Catholicism, the fourth on the fortunes of the religious orders, both apostolic and monastic, and finally the corpus of material devoted specifically to the English Benedictines.

2.1 *The early Nineteenth Century Religious Revival*

George Kitson Clark has contended that in no other century, "except the seventeenth and perhaps the twelfth, did the claims of religion occupy so large a part of the nation's life, or did men speaking in the name of religion contrive to exercise so much power" as in the nineteenth century.[6] By the early decades of the century, a Protestant Evangelical Revival (which had

---

[5] Scott, *Gothic Rage Undone*, 218.
[6] G. Kitson Clark, *The Making of Victorian England*, London 1961, 20.

begun with the Methodist movement in the previous century) was in full swing, soon to be followed by a Catholic revival within the Church of England. The early decades of the nineteenth century also witnessed an expansion in population: Not only did the population of Britain almost double between the years 1801 and 1851, from nine to eighteen million, but the country also experienced social and economic effects produced by rapid industrialisation. Important constitutional changes took place in this period, such as the 1832 Great Reform Act and the reforming legislation of the 1830s. David Newsome has acknowledged that in the midst of various facets of change and transformation: "Religion never ceased to matter, whether as a cause of grief to the honest doubter, or as a rallying cry in denominational warfare".[7] The later eighteenth century saw a great development of missionary activity, especially in new colonial outposts, in which all the mainstream Christian churches had some involvement.[8] Among recent commentators on this phenomenon, Andrew Walls has traced the development of the missionary movement in the nineteenth century and shown it to be "the product of the concomitance of certain political, economic and religious conditions",[9] Economically, especially in Britain, the growth of missionary activity was assisted by the "Industrial Revolution", which provided the means of transport and communication that in turn assisted both the colonial and commercial expansion that opened up irresistible evangelical opportunities for all the churches, enabling them to claim their own share of "God's Empire...a house of many spiritual mansions".[10] The early decades of the nineteenth century also witnessed the popularisation of new scientific theories which began to disturb traditionally-held Christian beliefs.[11]

2.2 *European Catholicism, 1795-1850*

For the Catholic Church throughout Europe, the years 1795-1850 represented a period of recovery and rebuilding following the French Revolution.[12] It

---

[7] D. NEWSOME, *The Victorian World Picture*, John Murray, London 1998, 1-4.
[8] See H.M. CAREY, *God's Empire: Religion and Colonialism in the British World, c.1801-1908,* Cambridge University Press, Cambridge 2011.
[9] A.F. WALLS, "The Old Age of the Missionary Movement," in A.F. WALLS, *The Missionary Movement in Church History: Studies in the Transmission of Faith*, Orbis Books, New York 1996, 259.
[10] H.M. CAREY, *God's Empire*, 379.
[11] C.C. GILLESPIE, *Genesis and Geology: The Impact of Scientific Discoveries upon Religious Beliefs in the Decades before Darwin*, Harvard University Press, Harvard 1990; E. JAY, *Faith and Doubt in Victorian Britain*, Palgrave Macmillan, Basingstoke 1986.
[12] For a good summary see F. KNIGHT, *The Church in the Nineteenth Century*, I.B Tauris, London 2008, 53-72; also J.VIDEMAR, *The Catholic Church Through the Ages: A History*, Paulist Press, New York 2005, 266-286.

took time to reconstruct not only buildings that had been destroyed, but also the institutions to which these belonged: the universities, religious houses and seminaries, and the personnel that staffed them. The papacy was also a victim of the revolutionary upheavals of the early nineteenth century when its claim to temporal power was threatened. Nicholas Atkin and Frank Tallett characterise the first half of the nineteenth century as an era of religious revival, of which the return of the traditional orders such as the Benedictines was an important element, and also chart the Catholic Church's failure to respond positively to the revolutionary upheavals of the time as well as the papacy's rejection of modernity and its "retreat into a theological bunker", assisted "by the widespread Ultramontanism among both conservative and liberal Catholics, both lay and clerical". [13]

Atkin and Tallett also show that in this period, Catholicism "began to take on distinctive national characteristics within individual countries far more marked than in the eighteenth century". It is important also to acknowledge the importance of underground and popular religious piety, the significance of which in France we have come to appreciate through a clutch of books on the topic which has appeared over the last twenty years or so. Thomas Kselman has helped us to appreciate how prophecies and miraculous cures in nineteenth-century France were manifestations of popular religious fervour, which had their roots in popular folklore.[14] Judith Devlin's 1987 study examined the peasant culture of superstition and the occult and its relationship to the pressures and anxieties of nineteenth-century French society,[15] whilst Raymond Jonas' study of the cult of the Sacred Heart traced its origins, development and expression in popular and institutional French piety and underlined its importance for the development of nineteenth-century spirituality.[16] Vincent Viaene's study of papal-Belgian relations in the period 1831 to 1859 has challenged the traditional view that the demise of the Papal States in 1859-60 represented the beginning of the modern papacy, and focuses attention instead on a slower, less dramatic process of change that began much earlier in Rome in the first years of the papacy of Gregory XVI.[17] Each of these works has helped to establish the

---

[13] N. ATKIN and F. TALLETT, *Priests, Prelates and People: A History of European Catholicism since 1750*, Oxford University Press, Oxford 2003, 128.
[14] T.KSELMAN, *Miracles and Prophecies in Nineteenth-Century France*, Rutgers University Press, New Jersey 1983.
[15] J. DEVLIN, *The Superstitious Mind – French Peasants and the Supernatural in the Nineteenth Century*, Yale University Press, Yale 1987.
[16] R. JONAS, *France and the cult of the Sacred Heart – An Epic Tale for Modern Times*, University of California Press, Berkeley 2000.
[17] V. VIANE, *Belgium and the Holy See from Gregory XVI to Pius IX (1831-1859): Catholic revival, Society and Politics in 19th-century Europe*, Leuven University Press, Leuven 2001.

context for the issues of religious authority, piety and practice examined in this work.

2.3 *English Catholicism, 1795-1850*

For English Catholics, the period 1795-1850 marked several important watersheds. Toleration had already been granted to Catholics in the Relief Acts of 1778 and 1791, but the crucial legislation giving political emancipation to Catholics did not come until 1829. It was to be another twenty years before Rome considered that England was ready to have its hierarchy restored. The Catholic population swelled from about 80,000 in 1770 to an estimated 750,000 in 1851. Bearing these facts in mind it is surprising that so little has been published on English Catholicism in the early nineteenth century. Authors either tend to begin with the granting of Catholic emancipation in 1829, or, more usually, with the restoration of the hierarchy in 1850, leaving untouched the early decades which witnessed so much activity. The only two historians over the past thirty years to have paid any significant attention to this early period are John Bossy and John Hugh Aveling. Their ground-breaking studies of the Catholic community from the recusant period to the mid-nineteenth century successfully dispelled the traditional myth about the resurgence of English Catholicism in the nineteenth century resembling a "second spring" and remain unsurpassed. However important contributions have since been made in the study of English Cisalpinism by Eamon Duffy and Joseph Chinnici (although Chinnici's study is the more recent, and that was produced in 1980).[18]

The most thorough chronicle of the period is still Bernard Ward's seven-volume history, published almost a century ago, which begins in 1781 and ends in 1850.[19] One of the few weaknesses of Ward's survey, is, as Bossy has observed, its "almost exclusive attention...to what was going on in London and the South".[20] But given the fact that he had restricted access to archives and other manuscript collections, Ward's work is a remarkable

---

[18] J. BOSSY, *The English Catholic Community 1570-1850*, Darton, Longman and Todd, London 1975; J.C.H. AVELING, *The Handle and the Axe*, Blond and Briggs, London 1976; E. DUFFY, "Ecclesiastical Democracy Detected: I –1779-1787,"*Recusant History*, 10 (1970) 193-209; "Ecclesiastical Democracy Detected: II – 1787-1796,"*RH*, 10 (1970) 309-331; "Ecclesiastical Democracy Detected III – 1796-1803,", *RH*, 13 (1975) 123-148; J.P. CHINNICI, *The English Catholic Enlightenment, John Lingard and the Cisalpine Movement, 1780-1850*, Patmos Press, Shepherdstown 1980.

[19] B. WARD, *The Dawn of the Catholic Revival in England, 1781-1803* 2 volumes, Longmans, Green, London 1909; *The Eve of Catholic Emancipation: being the History of the English Catholics during the first 30 years of the 19th Century*, 3 volumes, Longmans, Green, London 1911-1912; *The Sequel to Catholic Emancipation*, 2 volumes, Longmans, Green, London 1915.

[20] BOSSY, *The English Catholic Community*, 351.

achievement for its time.[21] Edward Norman's 1984 survey, *The English Catholic Church in the Nineteenth Century*, also remains a reliable source. The author's lively prose is enhanced by substantial quotations from Roman archival material, as well as from the archives of the principal religious orders.[22] More recently, Peter Phillips has produced a biography of the priest historian John Lingard which provides an excellent survey of English Catholicism in the early nineteenth century.[23]

A pioneering addition to the literature on nineteenth-century English Catholicism has been Mary Heimann's *Catholic Devotion in Victorian England*, which is the first study to mine a particularly rich seam of English Catholic life, and in the words of a reviewer, Heimann "shows how a rich historical tapestry can be woven from hitherto neglected threads of evidence".[24] However the book fails to assess adequately the contribution made by the religious orders as a whole to English Catholic spirituality, especially in an age when they were at their most active and influential in missions throughout England and Wales. Heimann's book was also reviewed by the late liturgical scholar, J.D. Crichton, who asserted that the character of nineteenth-century English Catholic devotional life was rather more sophisticated than Heimann implies. Crichton's own short works, notably his *Worship in a Hidden Church,* provide an authoritative introduction to the subject in the centuries before Catholic emancipation.[25] A very useful addition to the literature on the history of spirituality has been the series written by Gordon Mursell, the last volume of which provides an excellent survey of the important Catholic works and writers in the late eighteenth and early nineteenth centuries.[26]

Many leading figures in early nineteenth-century English Catholicism lack full modern biographies, such as Vicars Apostolic William Poynter and John Milner. Poynter's diaries, which have now been published, help to shed light on this important figure, who as Vicar Apostolic of the London District was responsible for finding bishops for new British colonial sees.[27] Although Milner's importance as a Catholic apologist has been

---

[21] See S. FOSTER, "Bernard Ward: Edmundian and Historian,"in S. GILLEY (ed.), *Victorian Churches and Churchmen: Essays presented to Vincent Alan McClelland*, Catholic Record Society (Monographs), 7 , Trowbridge 2005, 163-182.
[22] E. NORMAN, *The English Catholic Church in the Nineteenth Century*, Oxford University Press, Oxford 1984.
[23] P. PHILLIPS, *John Lingard Priest and Historian*, Gracewing, Leominster 2008.
[24] M. HEIMANN, *Catholic Devotion in Victorian England*, Oxford University Press, Oxford 1995; J. WOLFE, "Heimann, *Catholic Devotion in Victorian England,"Journal of Ecclesiastical History*, 48 (1997) 593.
[25] J.D. CRICHTON, "Popular devotion in Victorian England,"*The Month*, 257 (1996) 322-327; J.D. CRICHTON, *Worship in a Hidden Church*, Columba Press, Blackrock 1998.
[26] G. MURSELL, *English Spirituality from 1700 to the Present Day*, SPCK, London 2001.
[27] P.PHILLIPS (ed.), *The Diaries of Bishop William Poynter, V.A., (1815-1824)*, Catholic Record Society (Records), 179, (2006).

highlighted by Peter Nockles, a short but informative pamphlet by Archbishop Maurice Couve de Murville is all the recent scholarship we have on the life of the controversial Vicar Apostolic of the Midland District who has been dubbed "the English Athanasius".[28] Biographies, however, have been published of two important Benedictine Vicars Apostolic whose activities will be highlighted in the following chapters, namely Peter Augustine Baines and William Bernard Ullathorne.[29] Joseph Gillow's 1885 *Literary and Biographical History or Bibliographical Dictionary of the English Catholics* is still a useful and reliable source.[30] The *Oxford Dictionary of National Biography* contains some new and revised articles on a number of early-nineteenth-century Catholic figures such as Bishops Milner, Walsh and Poynter.[31]

Monographs produced by the Catholic Record Society are a useful source of information, together with the many volumes containing transcripts of parish registers, as well as contemporary diaries and letters.[32] The Society's journal, *Recusant History*, has published a number of important articles over the past thirty years relating to the early nineteenth century, some of which, like the one by Nockles on Milner, have already been noted. Helpful and incisive work has also continued to be produced relating to English Catholicism over the past thirty years by local historians, much of which has been published in regional Catholic history journals such as *North West Catholic History* and *Northern Catholic History*. This present work has been greatly aided by the work focussing on Liverpool and Lancashire by Janet Hollinshead, John Davies, and David Pope.[33]

---

[28] P.B. NOCKLES, "'The Difficulties of Protestantism": Bishop Milner, John Fletcher and Catholic Apologetic against the Church of England in the era from the First Relief Act to Emancipation,"*RH*, 24 (1998) 193-236; M.N.L. COUVE DE MURVILLE, *John Milner 1752-1826*, Archdiocese of Birmingham Historical Commission, Birmingham 1986.
[29] P. GILBERT, *The Restless Prelate, Bishop Baines (1786-1843)*, Gracewing, Leominster 2006; J. CHAMP, *A Different Kind of Monk, William Ullathorne (1806-1889)*, Gracewing, Leominster 2006.
[30] J. GILLOW, *A Literary and Biographical History or Bibliographical Dictionary of the English Catholics*, 5 volumes, Burns and Oates, London 1885.
[31] J. CHAMP, "Milner, John, (1752-1826),"*Oxford Dictionary of National Biography*, Oxford University Press, Oxford 2004, <http://www.oxforddnb.com/view/article/18791> {accessed 19 February 2013]; J.P. CHINNICI, ' Poynter, William (1762-1827),'*ODNB*, <http://www.oxforddnb.com/view/article/22688> [accessed 19 February 2013]; R.J. SCHIEFEN, 'Walsh, Thomas (1776-1849,)' *ODNB*, <http://www.oxforddnb.com/view/article/48858> [accessed 19 February 2013].
[32] Of particular interest to this study has been the two volume work produced by J.A Williams on Bath, containing the registers for the early nineteenth century, as well as the diary kept by Augustine Baines: J.A. WILLIAMS, *Post-Reformation Catholicism in Bath, Catholic Record Society (Records)* 65 & 66, 1975 & 1976.
[33] J.E. HOLLINSHEAD, "Return of Papists for the Parish of Childwall in the Diocese of Chester, October 1706," *North West Catholic History*, 26 (1999) 21-27; "Hall to House:

2.4 Revival of Religious Life in the early Nineteenth Century

As on the continent, Britain witnessed a significant revival of religious life during the nineteenth century, not only in the growth of the traditional orders such as the Benedictines and the Jesuits, but also in the foundation of newer congregations dedicated to education and nursing. Francis Edwards has charted the progress of the English Jesuits in his 1985 study, which includes two lively chapters focussing on their struggles and fortunes from their suppression in 1778 to the mid-nineteenth century. He is particularly eloquent in describing the battles of the Society with the English Vicars Apostolic, and outlining the richness of the Jesuit contribution to English Catholic life in the middle decades of the nineteenth century.[34] The celebration of the bicentenary of the restoration of the English Jesuits prompted the publication of a collection of essays and documents, including an important article by Maurice Whitehead, who has recently undertaken a research project funded by the Spencer Foundation on the educational achievement of the English Jesuits.[35] Whitehead has also written extensively on various aspects of nineteenth-century Jesuit history.[36]

The Women's History movement has done a tremendous service in re-awakening interest in the female religious orders, about whom several studies have appeared in recent years, beginning with Walter Arnstein's 1982

The Catholic Mission in Woolton during the Eighteenth Century,"*NWCH,* 32 (2005) 5-20; J. DAVIES, "Liverpool Libraries: Sources for Catholic History,"*NWCH,* 27 (2000) 107-109; "The D'Andria Collection, Liverpool Record Office,"*NWCH,* 24 (1997) 51-57; D.J. POPE, "Liverpool's Catholic Mercantile and Maritime Business Community in the second half of the Eighteenth century,"*RH,* 27 (2004) 244-279, 383-414.

[34] F. EDWARDS, *The Jesuits in England from 1580 to the present day,* Burns and Oates, Tunbridge Wells 1985.

[35] M. WHITEHEAD, '"A Prolific Nursery of Piety and Learning": Educational Development and Corporate Identity at the *Académie Anglaise,* Liège and Stonyhurst,' in T. MCCOOG, *Promising Hope – Essays on the Suppression and Restoration of the English Province of the Society of Jesus,* Institutum Historicum Societatis Iesu, London 2003, 127-150.

[36] Among these should be noted, M. WHITEHEAD, unpublished Ph.D. thesis, *The contribution of the Society of Jesus to secondary education in Liverpool: the history of the development of St Francis Xavier's College c.1840-1902,* University of Hull 1984; "The English Jesuits and Episcopal Authority: The Liverpool Test Case, 1840-43,"*RH,* 18 (1986) 197-219; "The Jesuit Contribution to Scientific and Technical Education in Late-Nineteenth-Century Liverpool,"*Annals of Science,* 43 (1986) 353-368; '"In the Sincerest Intentions of Studying": The Educational Legacy of Thomas Weld (1750-1810), Founder of Stonyhurst College,'*RH,* 26 (2002) 169-193; '"Education and correct conduct": Randal Lythgoe and the Work of the Society of Jesus in Early Victorian England and Wales,' in S. GILLEY (ed.), *Victorian Churches and Churchmen: Essays presented to Vincent Alan McClelland, Catholic Record Society Monographs, 7,* Trowbridge 2005, 75-93.

trail-blazing study on mid- Victorian attitudes to nuns.[37] Aidan Bellenger has provided an incisive essay on female religious from the Reformation to the First World War.[38] However, the first to examine in any significant detail the collective importance of female religious in England as a distinct group was Susan O'Brien, who in 1988 observed that "the ways in which these women governed one another, trained one another, related to one another and to the laity and the men of the church ought to be a rich and promising subject for further research".[39] O'Brien's prediction that "in the near future we should begin to see the results of doctoral research" has proved true;[40] the most recent offering being that by Barbara Walsh, who, disappointingly for the purposes of this study, makes few references to Benedictine nuns,[41] and fails to make any mention at all in her detailed geographical study of convents of the presence of the largest community of English Benedictine nuns, that of Our Lady of Consolation, whose arrival in Woolton near Liverpool in 1795, as Janet Hollinshead observes, "provided the first experience in Lancashire" of a female contemplative community. Hollinshead also astutely observes that whilst "the experiences of the English communities expelled from the continent have been the subject of some examination, their interaction with their new English neighbours has attracted little attention".[42] New interest in English nuns has been stimulated by a 2008 research project entitled 'Who were the Nuns,'which has made a comprehensive study of English convents

---

[37] W.L. ARNSTEIN, *Protestant versus Catholic in Mid-Victorian England: Mr Newdegate and the Nuns,* University of Missouri Press, Columbia, Missouri 1982.

[38] A. BELLENGER, "France and England: The English Female Religious from Reformation to World War,"in F. TALLETT and N. ATKIN (eds), *Catholicism in Britain and France since 1789,* Hambleden Continuum, London 1996, 3-12; R. KOLLAR, *A Foreign and Wicked Institution? The Campaign against Convents in Victorian England,* James Clarke, Oregon 2011.

[39] S. O'BRIEN, "Terra Incognita: The Nun in nineteenth-century England," *Past and Present,* 121 (1988) 110-140. Other important contributions by O'Brien include the following: "Nuns: Working in Convent Archives," *Journal of Catholic Archives,* 9 (1989) 27-33; "Lay Sisters and Good Mothers: Working-class Women in English Convents, 1840-1910," in W. SHEILS and D.WOOD (eds), *Women in the Church: Studies in Church History,* 27, Basil Blackwell, Oxford 1990, 453-466; "Making Catholic Spaces: Women, Décor and Devotion in the English Catholic Church, 1840-1900," in D. WOOD (ed.), *The Church and the Arts: Studies in Church History,* 28, Basil Blackwell Oxford, 1992, 449-466; "French nuns in Nineteenth-century England," *Past and Present,* 154 (1997) 142-180; "Religious Life for women," in V.A. MCCLELLAND and M. HODGETTS (eds), *From Without the Flaminian Gate: 150 years of Roman Catholicism in England and Wales,* Darton, Longman and Todd, London 1999, 108-141.

[40] O'BRIEN, "Terra Incognita," 117.

[41] B. WALSH, *Roman Catholic Nuns in England and Wales 1800-1937: A Social History,* Irish Academic Press, Dublin 2002.

[42] J.E. HOLLINSHEAD, "From Cambrai to Woolton: Lancashire's First Female Religious House,"*RH,* 25 (2001) 462.

on the Continent from the sixteenth century down to the year 1800.[43] Perhaps the comparative neglect of female contemplatives in recent research is unsurprising, given that a distinctive feature of the nineteenth-century religious revival was the introduction of new active apostolates for female religious. Nevertheless, the contribution of the nuns was an important part of English Benedictine life, and will be highlighted in this work.

2.5 *Revival of Monasticism*

Until recently, post-reformation monasticism has received little attention by English scholars, an omission recently addressed by the publication of two books by Derek Beales and Ulrich Lehner.[44] In *Prosperity and Plunder: European Catholic Monasteries in the Age of Revolution, 1650-1815,* Beales draws attention to the importance of the monasteries for the development of learning in western European society, and emphasises the extent of their ownership of land in Western Europe. In a work of such impressive scholarship, it is unfortunate that, whilst Beales highlights the significant contribution made by the Jesuits to the Enlightenment, he describes them incorrectly as a "monastic body",[45] and at times places Capuchins and Dominicans in the same category. However, a pleasing inclusion in Beales' treatment of "the great monasteries of the German Catholic lands", is the often overlooked English Benedictine monastery of Lamspringe near Hildesheim (1643- 1803).[46] Lehner's book shows how German eighteenth-century Benedictines represented a remarkable subculture of enlightened, even revolutionary, religious who challenged the traditional ways of life in the Benedictine Order. Sadly, for the purposes of this present study, Lehner, unlike Beales, fails to mention the English Benedictine monastery of Lamspringe, near Hildesheim. The European monastic revival of the nineteenth century has been chronicled in a number of recent books, notably the first volume of Dom Giovanni Lunardi's history of the Subiaco Congregation which is devoted to the life and work of reformer Abbot Pietro Casaretto. French monastic revival under Abbot Prosper Guéranger has been competently chronicled by a Benedictine nun of St Cecilia's Abbey, Ryde, and is followed by a useful collection of Guéranger's writings. The publication of the first English translation of Abbot Guéranger's unfinished autobiography gives some insight into his links with the English Benedictine

---

[43] "Who were the Nuns? A Prosopographical Study of the English Convents in Exile in the Seventeenth and Eighteenth Centuries,"
<http://wwtn.history.qmul.ac.uk/index.html> [accessed 19 February 2013].
[44] D. BEALES, *Prosperity and Plunder: European Catholic Monasteries in the Age of Revolution, 1650-1815*, Cambridge University Press, Cambridge 2003; U.L. LEHNER, *Enlightened Monks: The German Benedictines,* Oxford University Press, Oxford 2011.
[45] BEALES, 18.
[46] BEALES, 74-76.

Congregation, particularly with Dom Laurence Shepherd, whose importance in transmitting Guéranger's liturgical teaching will be highlighted in a later chapter of this book.[47] Another welcome addition to the literature on monasticism has been a volume on the Irish Benedictines, which includes a useful chapter by Aidan Bellenger on "the Post-Reformation English Benedictines and Ireland."[48]

2.6 The English Benedictine Congregation

Despite the absence of detailed histories of the English Benedictines in the nineteenth century, a number of important studies have appeared over the past thirty years. Bernard Green's highly readable survey of the history of the Congregation, published in 1980, remains the only published overview.[49] There has been a clutch of significant articles relating to the period by a number of authors, of whom Abbot Aidan Bellenger of Downside is the most prolific. His pioneering work on the contribution of the French émigré clergy to English Catholicism enabled him to gain an informed perspective on the wide canvas of popular belief and practice from the 1790s to the middle of the nineteenth century.[50] His 1997 essay entitled "Revolution and Emancipation" provides a concise but informative survey of the main themes of contemporary English Benedictinism which, according to Bellenger, can be characterised as "a subtle blend of the home and colonial with a strong dose

---

[47] G. LUNARDI OSB, *La Congregazione Sublancense OSB: L'abate Casaretto e gli inizi (1810-1878)*, La Scala, Noci 2004; M.D. TOTAH OSB (ed.), *The Spirit of Solesmes*, Burns and Oates, Tunbridge Wells 1997; D. HAYES and H. DEFOS DU RAU (eds), *In a Great and Noble Tradition: The Autobiography of Dom Prosper Guéranger*, Gracewing, Leominster 2009.

[48] M. BROWNE OSB and C. Ó CLABAIGH OSB, *The Irish Benedictines: A History*, Columba Press, Blackrock 2005.

[49] B. GREEN, *The English Benedictine Congregation*, Catholic Truth Society, London 1980.

[50] See in particular: "The Exiled Clergy and Religious of the French Revolution and the English Benedictines," *English Benedictine History Symposium Papers* (privately printed, 1985, 14-30; *The French Exiled Clergy in the British Isles after 1789*, Downside Abbey, Bath 1986; *The Great Return-The English Communities in Continental Europe and their Repatriation, 1793-4*, Downside Abbey 1994; "Benedictine Responses to Enlightenment," in N. ASTON (ed.), *Religious Change n Europe: Essays for John McManners*, Oxford University Press, Oxford 1997, 149-160; "Revolution and Emancipation", in D. REES (ed.), *Monks of England: The Benedictines in England from Augustine to the Present Day*, SPCK, London 1997, 199-212; "The Normal State of the Church: William Bernard Ullathorne, first Bishop of Birmingham," *RH*, 25 (2000) 325-334; "Religious Life for Men," in V. MCCLELLAND and M. HODGETTS (eds), *From Without the Flaminian Gate*, 142-166; "The English Benedictines and the British Empire," in S. GILLEY (ed.), *Victorian Churches and their Churchmen: Essays presented to Vincent Alan McClelland*, Catholic Record Society Monographs, 7, 94-109; A. BELLENGER (ed.), *Downside Abbey: An Architectural History*, Merrell, London 2011.

of Euro-scepticism".[51] He effectively demonstrates that the essential English Benedictine temperament at this time was activist, rather than contemplative. But in a later article he balances these earlier judgments with the observation that although the Benedictines had survived the dislocation brought about by the French Revolution, they afterwards resembled "distressed gentlefolk determined not to disappear from view but looking for a new role".[52] It is also important to mention "Plantata," the website of the English Benedictine History Commission which is a rich source documents and papers on the history of the Congregation.[53]

As John Aveling observed, from its earliest days, the restored English Benedictine Congregation has resembled "a minutely-documented family and institution",[54] not only through its archival deposits, but also its house journals, *The Downside Review, The Ampleforth Journal* and *The Douai Magazine*, all of which contain important documents from archives and articles on many aspects of nineteenth-century English Benedictine history. Over the past few decades, sterling work has been done by the English Benedictine History Commission to promote awareness of the Congregation's heritage, and papers from its annual symposia have covered several aspects of nineteenth-century history. Another useful resource for the nineteenth-century Benedictine historian is the Australian Benedictine journal *Tjurunga*, which has published a number of important articles on the English Benedictines who provided the first two Archbishops of Sydney. Australian Catholics are proud of their history, and over the past 30 years a number of important studies have been produced relating to the Benedictine founders of the Australian Catholic church. These include a biography of Bede Polding, together with published editions of his personal and pastoral letters.[55]

Histories of the four oldest English Benedictine houses (Downside, Ampleforth, Douai and Stanbrook[56]) are in good supply: H.N. Birt's *Downside*

---

[51] A. BELLENGER, "Revolution and Emancipation," in D. REES (ed.), *Monks of England*, 206.

[52] A. BELLENGER, "Religious Life for Men," in V.A. MCCLELLAND and M. HODGETTS, (eds), *From Without the Flaminian Gate*, 144.

[53] <http://www.plantata.org.uk/> [accessed 19 February 2013].

[54] J. AVELING, "Some aspects of the eighteenth century EBC," *EBHS*, privately printed, 1984, 3.

[55] G. HAINES, M.G. FORSTER, F. BROPHY, *The Eye of Faith: The Pastoral Letters of John Bede Polding*, Lowden, Kilmore 1978; F. O'DONOGHUE, *The Bishop of Botany Bay: The Life of John Bede Polding, Australia's First Catholic Bishop*, Angus & Robertson, Sydney 1982; J.B. POLDING, The *Life and Letters of John Bede Polding*, 2 volumes, Glebe, Australia 1994-1996.

[56] The houses of St Gregory (Douai, Acton Burnell, Downside), St Laurence (Dieulouard, Acton Burnell, Vernon Hall, Brindle, Tranmere, Parbold, Ampleforth), St Edmund (Paris, Douai, Woolhampton), Our Lady of Consolation (Cambrai, Woolton, Abbot's Salford, Callow End and Wass.) See *Figure 1*.

remains the most detailed history of the community of St Gregory.[57] There have been several histories over the past century of the Ampleforth community, the most recent being those written by Anselm Cramer and Anthony Marrett-Crosby.[58] The 2003 celebrations of the Douai community's centenary at Woolhampton in Berkshire prompted the publication of *Douai 1903 - Woolhampton 2003: A Centenary History* which helpfully included a CD-ROM containing lists of the monastic community, its missions, and its pupils at both Douai, France and Woolhampton.[59] The story of the nuns of Cambrai, later at Stanbrook, is chronicled in the elegant study *In a Great Tradition*.[60] A symposium was held at Ampleforth Abbey in 2003 to mark the bicentenary of the suppression of the monastery at Lamspringe, which was revived briefly in the 1830s at Broadway. The papers from that symposium have been published, and are an important source of reference for the history of that community.[61]

Two dominant figures in early nineteenth-century English Benedictinism have left us important autobiographical studies: William Bernard Ullathorne's autobiography was discovered in manuscript by Sir Shane Leslie in 1939 and published by him two years later under the title *From Cabin Boy to Archbishop*. The volume certainly communicates the first half of Ullathorne's fascinating life from a cabin boy to missionary in Australia, missioner in the English Midlands and, finally, architect of the new English and Welsh hierarchy, but Leslie's work is "peppered with errors" and a new edition was produced by Leo Madigan in 1995 under the title *The Devil is a Jackass* and it is this edition which is quoted in this study, the major weakness of which is its lack (unlike its predecessor) of an index.[62] A very different style of autobiographical account to have been published is the *Reminiscences* of Richard Marsh, the last Prior of St Laurence's Dieulouard, and later President General of the English Benedictines. This document is of tremendous interest to the historian of the early nineteenth century because Marsh vividly narrates his varied experience, including his escape from

---

[57] H.N. BIRT, *Downside: A History of Downside School,* Kegan Paul, Trench, Trubner, London 1902.
[58] A. CRAMER, *Ampleforth: The Story of St Laurence's Abbey and College,* St Laurence Papers, Ampleforth 2001; A. MARRETT-CROSBY, *A School for the Lord's Service: A History of Ampleforth,* James & James, London 2002.
[59] G. SCOTT (ed.), *Douai 1903- Woolhampton 2003: A Centenary History,* Stanbrook Abbey Press, Worcester 2003.
[60] THE BENEDICTINES OF STANBROOK, *In a Great Tradition: Tribute to Dame Laurentia McLachlan,* John Murray, London 1956.
[61] A. CRAMER (ed.), *Lamspringe: An English Abbey in Germany,* St Laurence Papers, Ampleforth 2004.
[62] *From Cabin-Boy to Archbishop: The Autobiography of Archbishop Ullathorne with an Introduction by Shane Leslie,* Hollis and Carter London 1941; *The Devil is a Jackass: Being the dying words of the autobiographer William Bernard Ullathorne* edited by Leo Madigan, Downside Abbey, Bath 1995.

revolutionary France and his success in recovering English Benedictine property there after the revolutionary wars, as well as the re-founding, despite significant opposition from his brethren, of the community of St Edmund at Douai in 1818. Both Marsh's *Reminiscences* and his dramatic account of his escape from Dieulouard in 1794 have been made accessible to a wider readership through their publication by the Ampleforth archivist, Anselm Cramer.[63]

This study has made extensive use of the rich archival material extant in the monasteries of the English Benedictine Congregation, principally the thirteen heavy manuscript volumes which comprise the *History, Biographies and Records of the English Benedictine Congregation* compiled by the nineteenth-century congregational annalist, Athanasius Allanson (1804-1876) and the artificial collection of letters and documents made by the Downside monk, Henry Norbert Birt (1861-1919). Both of these collections merit some introduction and comment. The significance of the work Allanson has been better appreciated in recent years, thanks to the publication of the eight hundred or so *Biographies of the English Benedictines* written by Allanson, dating from 1585 to 1850.[64] Of even greater assistance to the historian are the five volumes of *Records,* comprising contemporary letters and documents dating from the same period collected by Allanson, many of which he comments upon in the three volumes of his *History* of the Congregation[65]. Allanson's judgments need to be approached with caution. Although in places he is diffident about passing judgment on some of his recent contemporaries (such as the extravagant Northern Provincial Anselm Brewer) he is not so reluctant to do so upon others, for instance, Bernard Barber, President General from 1842 until 1850, whom Allanson judged to be apathetic and "culpably passive".[66] Although it has been said that Allanson "never asserts anything for which he has not got precise evidence",[67] it is important to appreciate the background and sympathies of the author, who, as his obituarist observes,

> had a solid conservative outlook and was firmly attached to the old traditions and methods of the Congregation…he was out of sympathy with the ecclesiastical developments of nineteenth-century England, and not

---

[63] R. MARSH, *Reminiscences 1794-1830,* St Laurence Papers, Ampleforth 1995; *Fr Marsh's Escape from Dieulouard,* St Laurence Papers, Ampleforth 1994.
[64] A. ALLANSON, *Biographies of the English Benedictines,* St Laurence Papers, Ampleforth 1999.
[65] Allanson's "History" will henceforth be cited as AH, the "Records" as AR and the *Biographies* as AB.
[66] AH, 3:409.
[67] AMPLEFORTH ABBEY ARCHIVES (henceforth cited as AA), Aberford box, 9 November 1944, Justin McCann to Abbot Herbert Byrne.

infrequently appears in the character of a 'die-hard', sternly stemming the tide of unwelcome change.[68]

Although such characteristics are occasionally evident in Allanson's work they do not greatly devalue its significance as a detailed and largely sober record of the history of the Congregation. Indeed, there is evidence that despite his prejudices, Allanson strove to be fair. One such example is his inclusion of letters and documents written by those who chose to defect from Ampleforth to join Augustine Baines in his new seminary at Prior Park.[69]

The English Benedictine historian has cause also to be grateful to Henry Norbert Birt, monk of Downside, who not only produced the *Obit Book of the English Benedictines 1600-1912*, a useful work of reference in checking names and dates, but also who collected an array of original and copied letters and other documents dating from the twelfth to the mid-nineteenth centuries which are stored in the Congregational archives at Downside in seventy box files. Birt himself wrote an abstract for each document, and the collection has been made more accessible in recent years by the creation of an index of names and places. The collection contains a variety of documents, from letters and printed circulars to maps and plans and is a rich treasure-trove for the monastic historian. Birt's achievements as a magpie-collector are beyond doubt, but his capabilities as an annalist and historian have been called into question. His *Obit Book* suffers from inaccuracies and omissions, and needs to be supplemented by other sources, whilst his two-volume history of the foundation of the Australian church has also been found wanting, Birt being castigated for his "sins of omission" and for "bowdlerising" the correspondence of Archbishop Bede Polding.[70] Extensive use has also been made of original material deposited in the Congregational archives at Downside and in the abbeys of Ampleforth, Douai and Stanbrook. [71] Use has also been made of other archival deposits,

---

[68] "Athanasius Allanson 1804-76," in "Ampleforth Obituaries,"<http://www.archive.zenwebhosting.com/sites/obits/willson/allanson_a.htm > [accessed 7 August 2014].
See also A. CRAMER, "Peter Athanasius Allanson, Monk, Missioner, Historian," *Northern Catholic History*, 40 (1999) 35-46.
[69] AR, 3, 31-77, 79-82, 85-87, 91-96, 98-167, 167 bis –213, 216-444.
[70] DOWNSIDE ABBEY ARCHIVES (DA), VIII.A, H.N. BIRT, *Benedictine Pioneers in Australia*, 2 volumes, Herbert and Daniel, London 1911; *Obit Book of the English Benedictines 1600-1912*, privately published, London 1970. For Birt's obituary see *Downside Review*, 37 (1919) 118-119; see also A.E. CUNNINGHAM, "Henry Norbert Birt's Sins of Omission, The Polding Correspondence. A partial appraisal,"in *Tjurunga*, 46 (1994) 43-56 and the response to this in T. KAVANAGH OSB, "The Polding Correspondence: Norbert Birt's 'Sins' revisited," *TJ*, 47 (1994) 45-62.
[71] An overview of the English Benedictine archives at Downside has been provided by Dom Philip Jebb in two articles in *DR*, 93 (1975) 208-225 and *DR*, 113 (1995) 284-288. Ampleforth archivist Anselm Cramer has set up a useful website which includes a

both in England at the diocesan archives of Birmingham, Clifton, Leeds and Westminster, which contain correspondence from leading English Benedictines in the early nineteenth century, as well as in Rome, at the archives of *Propaganda Fide*, the Venerable English College, and the Abbey of St Paul outside-the-Walls.[72]

John Aveling was probably thinking of both Allanson and Birt when he declared that "the great classical monk-historians" of the Congregation viewed the seventeenth-century Congregation as "their ideal, the eighteenth century as a disgraceful mess only redeemed by a thin golden thread of highly observant monks" and, presumably because of its many disputes, the history of the nineteenth-century Congregation as "far too recent and explosive material to be allowed out of locked monastic cupboards of archives…into print".[73] A reform of the Congregation took place at the end of the nineteenth century, which did away with the Provincial system and put the English missions under the newly-created abbeys of Downside, Ampleforth and Douai. These developments have often been regarded as sounding the death knell of the "old" Congregation, and the birth of the "new" Congregation, which now took a similar shape in structure and organisation as its counterparts elsewhere in the world. From the absence of detailed studies of the Congregation in the early part of the nineteenth century, one gets the impression that the century following the French Revolution has tended to be regarded, in the words of Geoffrey Scott, as "an intertestamental age when the monasteries were at their lowest ebb, suspended in a time-warp until their revival began later in the century".[74]

Cuthbert Butler, the second abbot of Downside, has to claim responsibility for much of the perpetuation of such a view. He was one of the leading lights of the so-called "Downside Movement" of the last decades of the nineteenth century that inspired the impetus to reform the English Benedictine Congregation. Butler believed that the early nineteenth-century Congregation was in a "transitional stage", and criticised the traditional practice of sending monks on the Mission where they did "the work of the

---

number of documents from the archives and library there, including a set of monastic obituaries from 1850 to the present. Its URL is <http://www.monlib.org.uk>.
[72] Many documents from the archives of the archdiocese of Birmingham can be accessed via the website <http//www.a2a.org.uk>. A description of the archives of *Propaganda Fide* is given in N. KOWALSKY OMI and J. METZLER OMI, *Inventory of the Historical Archives,* Pontificia Universitatas Urbania, Rome 1983. Descriptions of the archives of the Venerable English College, Rome have been provided in Appendix 1. of M. WILLIAMS, *The Venerable English College Rome: A History, 1579-1979,* 2nd edition, Gracewing, Leominster 2008 and in C. BRIGGS and B. WHELAN,"The Archives of the Venerable English College in Rome," *Catholic Archives,* 7 (1987) 3-11.
[73] AVELING, "Some aspects of the eighteenth century EBC,"3.
[74] G. SCOTT, "The English Benedictine Mission and Missions," in D.H. FARMER (ed.), *Benedict's Disciples,* 2nd edition, Gracewing, Leominster 1995, 312.

secular clergy and under conditions undistinguishable from those of the secular clergy".[75] It is notable that whilst Butler's record of the first century of the community of St Gregory contains detailed chapters on the monastic buildings and the scholarship of the community, the Mission is given only a short paragraph.[76] It was, however, in perhaps his best-known work, *Benedictine Monachism*, published in 1919, that Butler gave free rein to his views. In sketching the lines of the "ideal twentieth century monastery", he contended that there was no place for monastic work away from it.[77] Aveling's contention about the idealisation of the seventeenth-century English Benedictine Congregation seems to be borne out even at the present day. It is striking that the short history of the Congregation included in the annual *Benedictine Yearbook*, contains quite a detailed account of its seventeenth-century revival, but the nineteenth century is allotted only four lines, and then the only events considered worthy of mention are the establishment of the purpose-built Gothic monastery at Belmont in 1859, and the raising of status to abbeys in 1899 of the monasteries of Downside, Ampleforth and Douai.[78]

Conclusion

Just as the history of the nineteenth-century English Catholic community has undergone revision, thanks to John Bossy and others, so the same is true of the English Benedictines in the same period. Yet this present work is the first to respond in any detail to the contention of Geoffrey Scott in 1995 that "to concentrate only on the plight of the monasteries in the nineteenth century", as Butler and others have done, "fails to do justice to the great vitality generated in the missions during these years".[79] This study aims to highlight this vitality, through tracing the continuities and changes in the English Benedictine Congregation in the first half-century after the repatriation of its monks and nuns.

---

[75] D. KNOWLES, "Edward Cuthbert Butler: 1858-1934," in D. KNOWLES, *The Historian and Character and other essays,* Cambridge University Press, Cambridge 1963, 276.
[76] E.C. BUTLER, "Record of the Century," *DR,* 33 (1914) 85. On the personality and career of Butler see D. KNOWLES, "Abbot Cuthbert Butler: 1858-1934," in KNOWLES, *The Historian and Character,*264- 362; R. YEO and L. MAIDLOW DAVIS, "Abbot Cuthbert Butler, 1858-1934," in J. GRIBOMONT (ed.), *Commentaria in S Regulam I,* Sant' Anselmo, Roma, 1982, 91-108; for Butler's contribution to the Downside Movement, see A. BELLENGER, "The Downside Stirs: Personalities, principles, documentation," *EBHS,* privately printed, 1986, 11-66; A. BELLENGER, "Vingt ans après: Downside from Ford to Knowles," *EBHS,* privately printed, 1987, 2-37.
[77] C. BUTLER, *Benedictine Monachism: Studies in Benedictine Life and Rule,* Longmans, Green, London 1919, 328-331, 374.
[78] *The Benedictine and Cistercian Monastic Yearbook 2013,* 19.
[79] SCOTT, "The English Benedictine Mission and missions", 312.

A brief overview of the contents of the following study can now be sketched. The following chapter will consider the plight of the monasteries, which took time to be transplanted from long-established centres on the continent to new homes in England. This chapter will highlight the energy expended by the English Benedictines in the early nineteenth century, despite the scarcity of monks and nuns and the material losses sustained as a result of the French Revolution. It will show that the Congregation not only adapted to changed circumstances and surroundings, but also attempted to maintain old traditions of community life and worship long practised during their continental exile. This flows naturally into the third chapter with its consideration of the piety and devotional life of the early-nineteenth-century English Benedictines, which reflected both the sober spirituality bequeathed by previous generations, and also the slow infiltration of new devotions into England from continental Europe. Chapter Four will trace the strong thread of continuity in English Benedictine ecclesiology in this period expressed in its approach to local episcopal authority and will thus provide a context for the following chapter which, in contrast emphasises the expansion and vitality of the English Benedictine Mission. The next pair of chapters will be devoted to the theme of education and will consider the developments in monastic learning and scholarship and then the educational apostolate exercised by early nineteenth-century monks and nuns. Finally an assessment will be made of the English Benedictine involvement in Catholic missions overseas, a new challenge for the monks that turned out merely to provide a new setting for traditional structures and attitudes. Although the history of the English Benedictine Congregation in the early nineteenth century certainly proved to be of quite a different character to what it had been in the *ancien régime*, continuity rather than change proved to be the order of the day.

CHAPTER 2

The Monasteries, from Repatriation to Revival

Monastic Life in Europe after 1789

In 1789 a decree of the revolutionary government in France put church property "at the disposal of the nation" and the following year a further decree ordered the merger and closure of religious houses. Initially educational and charitable establishments were exempt from this legislation but it became increasingly impossible for religious houses to function as a result of restrictions placed upon them as the policy of dechristianisation of the country began in earnest. The government's attack on the English Benedictine Congregation came after the declaration of war on England in 1793. By 1795 countless thousands of priests, and members of religious orders had been killed or dispersed. Aspects of this policy spread to other countries of Europe, although the manifestation in other countries tended to be less violent than in France.

Derek Beales has suggested that in 1750 there were 25,000 monasteries in Europe and 350,000 monks and nuns living in them. Although he correctly asserts that distinctions between different types of vowed religious have tended to be blurred, in his book *Prosperity and Plunder*, Beales uses the terms "monasteries, monks and nuns" generically to include all religious and religious houses, whether monastic or not, so it would seem more correct to assume that his statistics refer to all religious houses and those who lived in them. According to Beales, the year 1750 witnessed the peak of monastic growth since the crisis of the Reformation' and the following decades saw a dramatic reduction, especially in the number of monks, due to the reforms in France instigated by the *commission des réguliers* and the various religious suppressions elsewhere.[1]

Although the English Benedictine Congregation experienced just such a numerical decline towards the end of the century, nevertheless it proved to be one of the very few Benedictine Congregations to survive the ravages of the French Revolution, which directly and indirectly resulted in the closure of some 1500 monasteries in Europe.[2] The early nineteenth century witnessed the beginnings of a monastic restoration in Europe, and it is in this context that the continuities and discontinuities in English Benedictine monasticism in this period will be considered, from the repatriation of English monks and nuns in 1795 and their ultimate survival, to the revival of their communities which only really began half a century

---

[1] BEALES, *Prosperity and Plunder*, 17-22, 291-292.
[2] SCOTT, *Gothic Rage Undone*, 17-19.

later.[3] This study is the first to consider in any significant detail their struggles during the first half of the nineteenth century, and to shed some light on their achievements during a period that has been regarded as 'an intertestamental age'.[4]

The losses sustained by European monks and nuns as a result of the French Revolution were colossal, both in terms of wealth and property and of personnel, for of the 1500 monasteries that existed in 1789, only 50 survived. The confiscation of monastic property across Europe between 1789 and 1815 led to the virtual extinction of the monastic life, although in Spain and Austria-Hungary, and in the part of Poland annexed by Russia, some monasteries survived because French legislation was not enforced or did not reach there.

However, it is important to emphasise that religious, especially women religious, did not disappear entirely from the European ecclesiastical landscape for, particularly in France, teaching and nursing sisters were tolerated on an official level by Napoleon, who even placed them under the general protection of his mother, Madame Laetitia. The Jesuits were revived by Pope Pius VII (Pope from 1800 to 1823) in 1814, but, as Roger Aubert has noted, the revival of the Society and of the mendicant orders such as the Franciscans and Dominicans was facilitated by the fact that they had the advantage of strong central authority, which the Benedictine Order as a whole lacked.[5] Whilst these mendicant orders were able to establish small communities that earned their own living through their active apostolates, this was not a predominant feature of European monasticism which relied upon large buildings and landed revenues on which monks and nuns could live. Yet after Napoleon's banishment to St Helena, a monastic revival began to take place, although it was hampered, especially in Belgium and France, by governments which were generally unfavourable to monasticism. The problem for the monasteries in France was that, unlike the centralised orders, they were directly tied into the government through the "commende" system. Thus, because of the secular government established by the Revolution, there was no place for them in the new France governed by a secular constitution, although Napoleon tolerated Catholicism.

Revival took two main forms; firstly the revival of a style of monastic life that had existed before the French Revolution (this was easier for the Trappist branch of the Cistercians for instance, who earned their living from the land, and were able to develop fairly rapidly after the fall of Napoleon

---

[3] See BEALES, *Prosperity and Plunder*, 231ff; R. AUBERT, "XIXth Century Monastic Restoration in Western Europe," *TJ*, 8 (1974) 7; D. REES, "The Benedictine Revival in the Nineteenth Century," in D.H. FARMER (ed.), *Benedict's Disciples*, 324-349. For the repatriation in England of other religious orders and congregations see BELLENGER, *The Great Return*, 51-67.
[4] SCOTT, "The English Benedictine Mission and missions," 312.
[5] AUBERT, "XIXth Century Monastic Restoration in Western Europe," 9.

when they were able to purchase land) and secondly a re-creation of monastic life, which proved to be the predominant model for the Benedictines whose abbeys had mostly disappeared during the Revolution. Aubert's point about the advantages of centralised authority seems to be especially pertinent to monasticism in Italy and to a lesser extent, in England, for the subsequent survival of the twelve Benedictine monasteries re-established in Italy after 1815 was assisted by their incorporation into a revived Cassinese Congregation and the centralised authority structure of the English Benedictine Congregation assisted the re-establishment of the three houses of St Gregory, St Laurence and St Edmund. [6] For the most part, however, the nineteenth-century Benedictine revival was largely brought about as a result of personal initiatives, made principally by individual diocesan priests such as Prosper Guéranger, a French priest who founded a monastery at Solesmes near Le Mans, the Wolter brothers, who established a monastery at Beuron in Germany, and Jean-Baptiste Muard (1809-54), who founded the French Province of the Cassinese Congregation of the Primitive Observance. It is also important to note the re-founding of old monasteries and the establishment of new monasteries by various European monarchs such as Emperor Francis I of Austria and King Ludwig I of Bavaria.[7]

The European monastic renaissance was greatly assisted by the papacy in the first half of the nineteenth century. Pius VII had been a Benedictine monk at Cesena, and he restored the Benedictine abbeys in the Papal States. Two of these, St Paul outside-the-Walls in Rome and the monastery at Subiaco were to become important sources of monastic revival, not just in Italy, but throughout the world, for it was these monasteries that provided the monks for new foundations as far away as Australia.[8] He also formally recognised the re-establishment of the monasteries of the English Benedictine Congregation.[9] Gregory XVI (1765-1846) had been a Camaldolese monk and his monastic background ensured that support was given to the work of both Guéranger and to Pietro Casaretto, the Italian who was responsible for the revival of the Italian Cassinese Congregation. Gregory's previous work as head of the Roman Congregation of *Propaganda Fide* also gave him some insight into the plight of the English Benedictine Congregation, whose superiors appealed to the then Cardinal Cappellari for his support in their disputes with the English Vicars Apostolic, notably with

---

[6] In 1792, the Cassinese Congregation comprised 900 monks in 60 houses. In 1821 there were 250 monks in 24 houses: G. PENCO, *Storia del Monachesimo in Italia: nell' apoca moderna*, Edizioni Paoline, Roma 1968, 2: 159-181.

[7] See the helpful series of articles on the early nineteenth-century monastic revival: ANON, "Succisa Virescit," *DR*, 1 (1880) 17-24, (1881) 113-119, 197-211, 271-278;

[8] See especially G.RUSSO, *Lord Abbot of the Wilderness: The Life and Times of Bishop Salvado*, Polding Press, Melbourne 1980; G. TURBESSI, "Vita monastica dell'Abbazia di San Paolo nel secolo XIX," *Revue Bénédictine*, 83 (1973) 49-118.

[9] AR, 3: 14.

the Benedictine, Peter Augustine Baines.[10] In contrast, Pius IX (1792-1878) had no first-hand experience of monasticism, but within a year of succeeding to the Papacy he declared the monastery to be "the bulwark and ornament of the Christian republic, as well as of civil society".[11] The work of both Gregory XVI and Pius IX in transforming the Catholic Church into a centralised body also indirectly benefited the Benedictines, for they were able to take a share in the worldwide missionary apostolate which flourished as a result of this.[12]

It is against this background that continuities and changes in English Benedictine monasticism need to be considered. It should be appreciated that the English Benedictine Congregation was rather different from other monastic institutes. Firstly, it had a centralised authority structure under a President General, and secondly, it had two beneficial features. The first consisted of the monasteries of monks and nuns, three of which transplanted to England after 1795, and the second component was a missionary one, with monks serving chapels and chaplaincies in England. It could be argued that because of these differences the English Benedictine Congregation was better placed to recover from the ravages of the French Revolution. Survival rather than revival marked the tone of English Benedictine monasticism until the middle of the nineteenth century. In 1795 the superiors of the Congregation were not at all optimistic about the future. Prior James Sharrock of St Gregory's mused in a letter to his opposite number at St Laurence's, Richard Marsh:

> Will England really admit of a proper Religious establishment? The laws at least are clearly against us...Prejudices are still very strong...England is yet an intolerant country...Is not the Religious Institute a plant of Catholic growth that requires a Catholic soil? Will it bear being transplanted into an heretical country?

There were, however, hints of optimism in the lines that followed: "I suppose we could make a tolerably comfortable settlement in England", Sharrock contended, "but could we wear the monastic habit; could we have any solemn office; could we very easily shut out the world?"[13]

The monks and nuns who arrived at Dover in 1795 were not returning to an entirely hostile country. They certainly benefited from a wave of sympathy prevalent at the time for the victims of the French Revolution.

---

[10] The future Pope also became personally acquainted with the English Benedictines through Thomas Joseph Brown, whilst the latter was in Rome to present the Benedictines' case against Baines. For the detail on this incident see DR, 33 (1914) 107-108.
[11] Encyclical letter of 17 June 1847 quoted in C. MONTALEMBERT, *The Monks of the West*, W Blackwood, London 1861, dedication.
[12] See R. AUBERT, P.J. CORISH and R. LILL, *The Church between Revolution and Restoration*, Herder & Herder, London 1981, 189-205.
[13] AR, 2: 364, 367.

Popular perceptions of Catholics had also become more favourable as a result of the growth of indifferentism towards them among the upper class, and also as a result of contact with French émigré clergy, thousands of whom had arrived in England in 1792 to escape the Revolution. Apart from a few isolated instances of hostility, the exiles had been met, on the whole, with sympathy and relief, although as Aidan Bellenger has observed, their presence led to traditional anti-Catholicism being concealed rather than forgotten.[14] The arrival of Trappist monks at Lulworth, Dorset, in 1794, at the invitation of Thomas Weld certainly tested English Protestant sensibilities. The monks' determination to cling to their ascetic practices and display their monasticism so openly led to suspicion and hostility from the locals,[15] an experience not shared by any of the transplanted English Benedictine communities, who mainly lived a quiet rural existence. At Downside the presence of monks initially aroused the suspicions of the locals but in time they became satisfied

> that they resembled other men without horns or appendages, were affable and kind, gave daily relief to the poor, employed labour, spent money in their shops and made good landlords; moreover many villagers had adopted their creed and attended their church.[16]

Such local perceptions of Catholic religious orders were undoubtedly important, but it took time for the national image of them to change and, according to Bernard Aspinwall, signs of such a change were not evident until 1850 when "against a background of general European social and political unrest", religious communities emphasised stability and order in an age when 'various attempts to deal with the social problem seemed discredited".[17] Yet it could be argued that already by 1850, a significant shift had taken place in popular culture through the Romantic movement and especially, the Gothic Revival, which idealised monasteries as the highest expression not only of artistic and architectural aesthetics but also of the Christian life, where prayer and learning were combined with practical

---

[14] D.A. BELLENGER, *The French Exiled Clergy in the British Isles after 1789*, Downside Abbey, Bath 1986, 43.

[15] BELLENGER, *The French Exiled Clergy*, 87-90. See also BELLENGER, "A Standing Miracle: La Trappe at Lulworth 1794-1817," in W. SHEILS (ed.), *Monks, Hermits and the Ascetic Tradition, Studies in Church History*, 22, Wiley-Blackwell, Oxford 1985, 343-350. Local prejudice was also experienced by the Cistercian monks at Mount Saint Bernard in Leicestershire in the 1830s. See A. LACEY, *The Second Spring in Charnwood Forest*, East Midlands Studies Unit, Loughborough 1985.

[16] B. SNOW, *Sketches of Old Downside*, Sands & Co, London 1902, 46.

[17] B. ASPINWALL, "Changing Images of Roman Catholic Religious Orders in the Nineteenth Century." in SHEILS, (ed.), *Monks, Hermits and the Ascetic Tradition*, 352-353.

charity, hospitality and benevolence.[18] Of importance in popularising such a view was William Cobbett's *A History of the Protestant Reformation in England and Ireland* which emphasised the important role played by monasteries in society as sources of social relief.[19] Yet Cobbett's romanticised view of a Merrie England of large Gothic monasteries with plentiful resources did not reflect the reality of the small and unpretentious English Benedictine houses at Downside, Ampleforth and Abbot's Salford. It was not until the late nineteenth century that these communities were able to build the large Gothic monasteries pictured by Cobbett and others. The only Gothic monastery in existence by 1850 was the Cistercian abbey of Mount Saint Bernard, near Coalville in Leicestershire, designed by Augustus Welby Pugin and paid for by a wealthy benefactor, Ambrose Phillips de Lisle. The only evidence of an English Benedictine interest in Gothic buildings in the period before 1840 is to be found in the 1828 edition of the *Benedictine Church Directory*, the frontispiece of which contains two prints of ruined English Gothic monasteries.[20]

Immediately after their repatriation, English monks and nuns were evidently too busily engaged in the business of survival to have time to plan the building of Gothic monasteries or to be concerned with elaborate liturgy or ritual. Although the French Revolution had brought the two halves of the Congregation much closer together, the conventual and the missionary, the essential dynamic of English Benedictine monasticism in the early nineteenth century was active, rather than contemplative, as monks and nuns struggled to establish new monasteries at a time when their numbers and finances were severely depleted. An appreciation of just how serious was their predicament can be gained from considering the circumstances of the repatriation of these monks and nuns in 1795, and their dalliance with nostalgia, in the first two decades after their arrival on English soil.

Repatriation

By the summer of 1795, three English Benedictine communities had arrived in England from France, having been ejected from their monasteries there. Six monks of St Gregory had been imprisoned at Doullens in northern France,[21] and the nuns of Cambrai at Compiègne, where they had narrowly

---

[18] On the Gothic Revival see R.J. SMITH, *The Gothic Bequest: Medieval Institutions in British Thought, 1688-1863*, Cambridge University Press, Cambridge 1987.
[19] W. COBBETT, *A History of the Protestant Reformation in England and Ireland*, James Duffy, Dublin 1824.
[20] *The Benedictine Church Directory for the Laity and Catholic Lady's and Gentleman's Annual Remembrance for the Year 1828*, privately printed, London 1827.
[21] BIRT, *Downside*, 108-118.

escaped the guillotine.[22] Some had died in prison, including the President of the Congregation, Augustine Walker. The Prior of St Laurence's, Dieulouard, Richard Marsh made a dramatic escape to avoid imprisonment, which involved swimming across the River Moselle.[23] Back in England, it took time for the communities to settle. For a time both St Gregory's and St Laurence's were invited to shelter under one roof at Acton Burnell in Shropshire as guests of Sir Edward Smythe who had been educated by the monks at Douai.[24] The monks of St Gregory's stayed there for nearly twenty years before moving to Downside in Somerset, but those of St Laurence settled at various places in Lancashire and Cheshire before finally moving to Ampleforth in Yorkshire in 1802 to the house built by Lady Ann Fairfax for her Benedictine chaplain, Anselm Bolton.[25] The Cambrai nuns were invited to Woolton near Liverpool by the future President, Bede Brewer, where they stayed until 1807 before moving to Salford Hall near Evesham, and then, in 1838, to Stanbrook Hall near Worcester.[26] Only two of the communities remained on the continent: the Paris community of St Edmund, King and Martyr[27] and the Abbey of Saints Adrian and Denis at Lamspringe, near Hildesheim in Hanover, whose situation is considered below.

Despite the cramped conditions and the uncertainty of what the future might bring them, monks and nuns of the Congregation seemed resigned at first to remaining in England and not returning to France. In 1800 Prior Sharrock of St Gregory's confidently declared: "France, I am convinced, will never again serve as a refuge".[28] Yet by 1814, with the signing of the Treaty of Paris which provided for the restoration of confiscated British property, there were hopes not merely of restoration, but of return.[29] Some English Benedictines began to yearn nostalgically for their old homes in France. Bernard Ryding, one of the few surviving monks of St Edmund's, by now on the mission in the north of England at Warwick Bridge, wished he could end his days in "the happy retreat and place of delights" of La Celle, the country house belonging to the St Edmund community near Meaux. Although he declared he would like his community to return to France he conceded "it is the old France I speak of; of the new France I know not".[30]

---

[22] STANBROOK ABBEY ARCHIVES, DAME A.T. PARTINGTON, *A Brief Narrative of the Benedictine Dames of Cambray, of their Sufferings while in the hands of the French Republicans, and of their arrival in England.*
[23] R. MARSH, *Fr Marsh's Escape from Dieulouard: His own account written in 1794*
[24] AR, 2: 287, 361.
[25] CRAMER, *Ampleforth,* 23-40.
[26] BENEDICTINES OF STANBROOK, *In a Great Tradition* 35-54.
[27] G. SCOTT, "Paris, 1677-1818," in SCOTT (ed.), *Douai 1903 –Woolhampton 2003,* 56-60.
[28] DOWNSIDE ABBEY ARCHIVES, BIRT COLLECTION, B369, 1800, Sharrock to Marsh.
[29] The Treaty of Paris, 30 May 1814, Additional article IV.
[30] DOUAI ABBEY ARCHIVES, VII.A.1.1, Parker letters 82, 22 July 1816, Ryding to Parker; letter 84, 10 April 1817, Ryding to Parker.

Henry Parker, the Prior of St Edmund, Paris, who remained in the city throughout the Revolution, frequently had to temper the enthusiasm of the monks and nuns in England who rushed to write to him to gain his assistance in claiming their properties, and remind them that the France of 1815 was not the same country they had known in 1789.[31]

But the desire to return to France was not simply nostalgia: post-war England was austere. Bernard Ryding wrote: "the country is exhausted, utterly drained of money. Agriculture is brought to nothing...trade is dead, commerce languishes, and manufacturers stop their work: the labouring poor are starving".[32] Just before the signing of the Paris peace treaty, the monks of St Gregory had moved to their new home at Downside near Bath, but their new Prior, Augustine Lawson, was less than impressed with the accommodation there.[33] He wrote to a confrère: "It is impossible to go on in the manner we are here as a religious community, and I am disgusted with the house in which proper discipline cannot be carried out as it ought".[34] Another monk wrote: "Downside does not at all please me. We are sadly off for room. I sleep in the calefactory".[35] The Bath missioner Augustine Baines spoke of the place "in the most contemptible manner, calling it a dog-hole".[36] Furthermore there was always the fear of prejudice. Even before the signing of the Paris treaty, President Brewer had expressed the view that in France the monks of the Congregation would "succeed better as religious than in any place in England".[37] The nuns also favoured a "return as speedily as possible to Cambrai, seeing that England afforded little facility and but poor hopes for the restoration of their much-loved strict enclosure and consequent monastic practices".[38]

Two not-unrelated issues lay at the heart of the movement to return to France: the hope of financial compensation for losses sustained at the Revolution, and the recovery of property, including buildings. Thus the nuns agitated, unsuccessfully, to recover precious books and manuscripts left behind at Cambrai,[39] and the monks fought to be awarded rents for their properties at Dieulouard and Paris. Recovering English Benedictine

---

[31] See the remarkable collection of letters written to Parker in this period, DAA, VII.A.1.1. Parker lived at the Irish College in Paris and from there supervised the *Fondations Britanniques*. See L. SWORDS, *The Green Cockade: The Irish in the French Revolution, 1789-1815*, Glendale, Sandycove 1989.
[32] DAA, letter 80, 4 December 1816, Ryding to Parker.
[33] L. GRAHAM, "The Migration to Downside," *DR*, 189 (1944) 119-135.
[34] DAB, D367, 28 July 1815, Lawson to Lorymer.
[35] DAB, D388, 13 February 1815, Morris to Lorymer.
[36] DA, E.321, 26 April 1820, Barber to Lorymer.
[37] DAA, Parker letter 15, Acton Burnell, 20 April 1814, Brewer to Parker.
[38] SAA, Annals, 1, 507-508.
[39] DAA, Parker letters 178, Salford Hall, 5 November 1815, Abbess Shepherd to Prior Parker.

buildings in France proved a more difficult problem. Both the conventual buildings at Dieulouard and Cambrai were sold and demolished during the Revolution; only the houses at Paris and Douai remained standing. The property belonging to the St Edmund community in Paris was leased out, and thus the buildings at Douai represented the monks' only hope of returning to France. The nuns tried and failed to return to Cambrai, despite support from friends there.[40] For a time it seemed that the monks of St Gregory would return to their old home, but bureaucratic delays and the poor state of the property led Prior Lawson to conclude that "France is in a wretched state and it would be unwise to take steps to establish ourselves there. Everything is against us as the law exists at the present moment and …the difficulties are likely to remain for a considerable time".[41]

Not all monks favoured a return to France. The question evoked a fierce debate at Downside between those who wished to go back to the monastery they had known in France, those who had known nothing of Douai and who wished to develop the new house at Downside or move to an alternative property in England.[42] The debate was a forerunner of another, more intense controversy later in the nineteenth century between those who wished to reform the Congregation by abolishing the two missionary provinces of Canterbury and York and establish autonomous monasteries, and those who wished to preserve the *status quo*.[43] In fact the whole issue of repatriation and the question of a return to France highlighted a change of mindset in the Congregation. Before the Revolution, loyalty to the individual houses, and rivalries between them, had not been too apparent. Whilst the French Revolution had united the Congregation against a common foe, once Napoleon had been defeated, warfare within its ranks soon broke out. The communities of St Gregory and St Laurence did not co-exist happily under the same roof at Acton Burnell, largely because the Laurentian monks outnumbered the Gregorians. Yet, their host, Sir Edward Smythe had originally invited the Gregorians and had only offered his house as a temporary shelter to the Laurentians.[44] It soon became clear that the monks

---

[40] SAA, Annals, 1: 541-546.
[41] DAA, Parker letters, letter 62, 8 December 1816, Lawson to Parker.
[42] In 1819 Prior Bernard Barber was in London concerning "the prospective purchase of property in place of Downside," DAB, E 206, 29 November 1819, Brewer to Lorymer.
[43] See A. CLARK, "The Return to the Monasteries," in REES, (ed.), *Monks of England*, 213-234.
[44] DAB, B 73, Acton Burnell, 12 March 1795, Smythe to Bennet. The friction between the two communities is chronicled in AR, 2: 287, 361, 364-8. The friction continued even after the departure of the Laurentian monks and concerned finances, see CDA, Bishops' Letter-books, 1796 no.3, 5 January 1796, J. Sharrock to Bishop W. Sharrock. Allanson comments: "The baneful effects of jealousy and rivalry had been glaringly perceptible ever since the two communities had been under the necessity of separating at Acton Burnell on account of their mutual animosities," AH, 3: 10.

of St Laurence would have to find somewhere else to lodge and this unhappy episode fanned the embers of rivalry and did much to cement house loyalties and jealousies that were to re-appear throughout the following century, especially in the early years after repatriation, and again, later, when various schemes for amalgamating the houses were discussed.[45] In 1826, Augustine Birdsall complained that in opposing the revival of the community of St Edmund at Douai, Ampleforth sought "to reduce the Congregation to two houses by...swallowing up in its own belly our dear Lamspringe, upon which they have set their voluptuous appetite".[46] In that same year, Prior Burgess at Ampleforth responded to an appeal for funds by the nuns at Salford, insisting that "though we have not half the means of our brethren at Downside, yet we will endeavour to make our subscription equal to theirs".[47]

The decision of Richard Marsh to re-found the Paris community at Douai in 1818 proved to be particularly contentious, bringing inter-house rivalries to the fore. Henry Parker had hoped to see the revival of his community at Douai, but he had died in 1817, leaving Marsh, his heir and executor, to bring the project to fruition. In doing so, Marsh not only had to fight the French authorities who opposed the proposal, but his own community at Ampleforth, who claimed that in re-founding St Edmund's, Marsh had used money that belonged by right to the community of St Laurence.[48] There were even those at Ampleforth who claimed that Marsh's "zeal for re-establishing St Edmund's was only a screen behind which to pay his debts in private". They were contemptuous of the new French establishment and its new community, which was described as "a colony of Lancashire Blacksmiths and Joiners".[49]

In the event, Marsh succeeded in getting papal approval for his actions, and to use antipathies between Downside and Ampleforth at the General Chapter of 1826 to his own advantage in gaining Congregational approval for the re-establishment of the community of St Edmund at Douai.[50] It could be argued that such rivalries and mutual hostilities at the start of the nineteenth century signalled the end of the Congregation's *ancien régime* a century earlier than has traditionally been thought, so that it was the French Revolution, and not the monastic reforms of the 1890s that significantly changed the Congregation. Although the expansion in the number of monks and nuns resident in the monasteries, the grandeur of conventual buildings, and improvements in monastic observance, liturgy and ceremonial came in

---

[45] Following "prevailing disagreements and uneasings" between the two communities at Acton Burnell it was proposed to unite the three houses of St Gregory, St Laurence and St Edmund, a plan which came to nothing. See AR, 2: 361.
[46] DAB, F 358, 16 July 1826, Birdsall to Kenyon.
[47] SAA, 1: 563.
[48] AH, 3: 3-13.
[49] DAB, F 369, 8 August 1826, Burgess to Turner.
[50] AH, 3: 34-48.

the second half of the century, much of the work to prepare for this was completed in the period before 1850. Whilst the English Benedictines lacked both human and material resources to live the full monastic life in this period, they had plenty of determination and grit to ensure that many of their monastic traditions and rituals continued, as their new circumstances permitted. Statistics provide some indication of this monastic life in England.

Numbers of monks and nuns

Numerically, it took the Congregation half a century to recover from the French Revolution. In 1789 there were 118 monks, a figure not reached again until 1842.[51] A downward trend in numbers, however, had commenced long before the French Revolution.[52] In 1961 Aveling provided figures for the period 1621-1818.[53] The table in *Figure 3*, compiled from Allanson's *History*, extends the figures up to 1850 and gives a fair indication of the man-power situation in the Congregation. Throughout the eighteenth century the majority of the monks had continued to reside on the mission rather than in the monasteries, so that the numbers of conventuals was always relatively small. Thus of the 118 monks in 1789, only 66 were conventuals.[54] The smallest fluctuation in the numbers of conventuals in the period 1795-1850 was to be found at St Gregory's, which, unlike the other two male houses, never fell to less than ten conventuals in the first half of the century. The suppression of Lamspringe in 1803 drastically affected the figures, for in 1806, (not counting the former conventuals of Lamspringe) there were only twenty-one conventuals in the three male houses of the Congregation. By 1850 the total number of male conventuals had risen to 51, but was still short of the 1789 figure of 66. A recurring complaint in contemporary correspondence was the shortage of numbers in the houses. In 1823 Prior Burgess at Ampleforth complained: "the houses are thinned of priests much too soon, but what can be done?"[55] Prior Francis Appleton at Douai contended that the "evils" of manpower shortages "will not cease until the monasteries are more attended to".[56]

---

[51] See *Figures* 3 and 4.
[52] SCOTT, *Gothic Rage Undone*, 17-18.
[53] H. AVELING, "The Education of Eighteenth-century English Monks," *DR*, 79 (1961) 136.
[54] These figures taken from AH, 2: 314, seem to be in conflict with those provided a year later, by President Walker, noted in SCOTT, *Gothic Rage Undone*, 18.
[55] DAB, F 59, 16 June 1823, Burgess to Lorymer.
[56] DAB, J 392, 15 April 1837, Appleton to Heptonstall.

Figure 3 -

NUMBER OF MONKS IN THE ENGLISH BENEDICTINE CONGREGATION, 1789-1850

DATE	TOTAL	ON THE MISSION
1789	118	52
1794	106	*
1798	101	58
1802	92	51
1806	99	53
1810	81	41
1814	82	42
1818	80	43
1822	88	54
1826	97	60
1830	97	66
1834	101	64
1838	106	59
1842	118	73
1846	125	80
1850	125	74

* The exact figures are difficult to calculate as monks were scattered to different locations due to the French Revolution.

Figure 4 -

NUMBER OF MONKS RESIDENT IN THE MONASTERIES OF
THE ENGLISH BENEDICTINE CONGREGATION, 1789-1850

DATE	St Gregory's	St Laurence's	St Edmund's	Ss. Adrian & Denis
1789	15	14	16	23
1794	*	*	*	23
1798	9	8	4	22
1802	11	5	~	20
1806	10	7	~	15**
1810	14	12	1	12**
1814	17	13	1	9**
1818	20	10	-	7**
1822	15	13	-	6**
1826	15	15	7	
1830	12	12	7	-
1834	17	9	8	3***
1838	12	16	13	6***
1842	19	11	15	-
1846	18	13	14	-
1850	17	16	18	-

*=   The exact figures are difficult to calculate as monks were scattered to different locations due to the French Revolution.

~ =   precise places of residence of the Paris monks, apart from Prior Henry Parker, are unknown.

**=   Although the monastery at Lamspringe was suppressed in 1803, Allanson continues to give the numbers of its former conventuals until 1822.

***=   The community of Saints Adrian and Denis was briefly revived at Broadway.

All the houses had laybrothers and laysisters in this period, several of whom made significant contributions to the work of the houses at a time when their numbers were severely depleted. Some of these were trained craftsmen, such as Brother Joseph Binnell of Douai, who contributed much to the building and decoration of the Pugin chapel there.[57] Brother Benet McEntee at Ampleforth turned his hand to a variety of tasks but it was as infirmarian that he was principally remembered, his ministrations earning him the affectionate sobriquet of "old quack".[58] The continuity of the laybrother tradition in the Congregation was exemplified by James Minns, who became a laybrother at St Edmund, Paris and managed to return to England in 1802. After a brief period with the St Laurence community at Parbold, he went to assist the Cambrai nuns at Woolton and moved with them to Salford Hall near Evesham where he died in 1828.[59]

The numbers of the nuns remained fairly steady in this period. By the time of the Revolution, there were about 20 in the community at Cambrai, and 16 arrived in Woolton from France in 1795. 19 nuns went to Abbot's Salford 1807, and 30 years later 23 moved to Stanbrook, where until the 1860s the numbers hovered around the mid to high twenties.[60] Analysing information given by Allanson and Birt shows that both male and female Benedictine vocations in the period 1795-1850 came principally from the north of England, especially from Lancashire.

Some consideration needs to be given to the average age of the monks residing in the monasteries. In France, a royal edict of 1768 had forbidden religious professions before the age of 21, but after the communities returned to England the former practice of making profession between the ages of 16 and 20 was revived. In the early years of settlement in England, there were concerns in the Congregation about whether religious profession would be possible at all in Protestant England, despite the two recent Catholic relief acts. A significant danger posed in this period was the 1829 Catholic Emancipation Act, which outlawed religious orders. Allanson noted that the Act "made it necessary for superiors to take time to consider what would be the best mode of arranging professions in future lest they should expose themselves and their subjects to the penalty of transportation".[61] The Act certainly delayed professions in some of the houses, notably at Ampleforth,[62] but the protestations of President General

---

[57] *Douai Magazine*, 2 (1894) 80.
[58] "Ampleforth Obituaries by Willson," <http://www.monlib.org.uk/obits/willson/willson5.htm> [accessed 27 August 2004].
[59] *AB*, 309.
[60] HOLLINSHEAD, "From Cambrai to Woolton: Lancashire's First Female Religious House," 461, 480; information from D Margaret Truran, 17 June 2004.
[61] AH, 3: 198.
[62] Allanson cites the case of Augustine Lowe in 1829, AR, 3: 198-199.

Birdsall to Sir Robert Peel, seeking to gain exemption for the Benedictines from the clauses of the Act, proved to be unnecessary as the clauses were soon recognised as being a dead letter.[63]

At least in the three houses of St Gregory, St Laurence and St Edmund the average age of conventuals was low, the average age being early to mid-twenties. The senior Fathers were based on the Mission, whilst the monasteries comprised mainly the young who were preparing for ordination and were also engaged in teaching in the schools attached to the monasteries. For instance, in 1841 the community at Downside consisted of thirteen professed and four novices. Of the twelve active professed members, the Prior was 40, the Subprior 35, the Procurator 45, and the remainder all under 30. Occasionally, profession had to be delayed, such as the profession of the future bishop, Thomas Joseph Brown, who had been clothed at the age of 15. When the novitiate year ended, it was found he was not old enough to take vows with his fellows.[64] It was not uncommon for novices to be clothed at 15, but there was no tradition in the Congregation for younger candidates being admitted, although the monastery founded by Bede Polding in Sydney, Australia, in 1848 adopted the practice of receiving boy postulants, as young as nine or ten. This had never been a feature of revived English Benedictinism. Polding seems to have been so desperate to find monks for Sydney that he encountered a young boy at the dockside in Liverpool in 1847 and took him baggage-less to Australia.[65] Of the nuns who arrived in Woolton in 1795, four of the 16 were over 60 years of age, eight over 50. Only the nuns and, until its suppression in 1803, the monastery at Lamspringe, had the benefit of a full spread of ages in the community, something which was not to become the norm in the other houses until much later.

Monastery and Mission

The estrangement between the monasteries and the missions prevalent in the eighteenth century, continued into the nineteenth century, despite the closer distance geographically between the two. In already small monastic communities, priors resented their monasteries being "drained to supply the mission",[66] a complaint made as late as the 1840s, despite the increased number of conventuals. Prior Prest at Ampleforth wrote to the President in

---

[63] On the Catholic Emancipation Act see NORMAN, *The English Catholic Church in the Nineteenth Century,* 65-68. There are a number of letters extant on this subject: DAA, EX 1120, 16 March 1829; Birdsall to Peel. DAB, G 331, 30 March 1829; Peel to Birdsall, Ibid., G 352, 17 March 1829; Birdsall to Marsh. SAA, Presidents' letters, 9 June 1829, Marsh to Abbess Chare.
[64] *DR*, 1 (1880) 5.
[65] T. KAVENAGH, "Romanticism and Recrimination: The Boy Postulants at St.Mary's, Sydney," *TJ*, 46 (1994) 21-42; DAB, M 5, 17 October, 1847, Moore to Morrall.
[66] DAB, G 157, 1827, memo of Prior Joseph Brown.

November 1846 begging for help, pointing out that the community, including a novice, numbered just ten people.[67] Resentment was also felt by missioners who were recalled to their monasteries of profession, where their presence was not always a blessing. The presence of disaffected missioners in the already small monastic communities could be damaging. This seems to have been a particular problem at Douai, where difficult characters were often sent, so much so that Bishop Bernard Collier recalled that Douai was often called "the Botany Bay of monks, for unruly and dissatisfied monks were sent there: they gave no end of trouble".[68]

As in the eighteenth century, the Mission continued to be a place of temptation and slack discipline for some monks. Bede Rigby, monk of Lamspringe, although "an amiable and good natured little man, was unable to keep a restraint upon himself in the use of spirituous liquors and was sent back to conventual life and never more trusted on the mission".[69]

Bernard Hawarden of Downside, on the Mission at Bonham, caused "great scandal... by the manner in which his household was conducted". In 1822, Hawarden seduced a young woman in the area who subsequently became pregnant. The couple were married in secret and Hawarden's superiors visited him whereupon he admitted "his own fall which he attributed to having in the first place neglected his meditations and spiritual reading". Hawarden later repented, but subsequently fell away again.[70] At Ampleforth, the "instability of mind and great irregularity of habits" of Basil Bretherton "totally disqualified him for missionary life", and he was sent back to the monastery where his behaviour led him to be permanently expelled and pensioned off in France.[71]

As in the eighteenth century, monasteries experienced a number of scandals: Ampleforth suffered from the machinations of one of its own former subjects, Peter Augustine Baines, the Vicar Apostolic of the Western District. In 1830 Baines persuaded the prior, Laurence Burgess, as well as the subprior and the procurator, to move to Baines' new college at Prior Park, near Bath, and to bring with them three of Ampleforth's four novices, the art master and up to 30 of the boys in the school. It was alleged, but never proved, that Burgess also left Ampleforth with a considerable amount of its financial capital, to say nothing of a large number of its herd of cows.[72] Beyond the problems of the Baines affair, Prior Adrian Towers proved to be "unfit to assume the government of others", who "being of a suspicious and jealous turn of mind, stooped to any dishonourable act to thwart and crush

---

[67] AA, MS 240, no.26.
[68] DAA, VII.A.3.F. 5 May 1887, Collier to O'Gorman.
[69] *AB*, 337.
[70] *AB*, 441-444.
[71] *AB*, 337-338.
[72] AH, 3: 195ff; C. ALMOND, *History of Ampleforth Abbey*, R & T. Washbourne, London 1903, 319-321.

those whom he believed to be his opponents". Towers' behaviour led "serious charges to be brought by the Community against him" at the visitation of 1833. One such charge concerned the theft by Towers of a diary of one of the brethren, whom he suspected to be hostile to his authority.[73] In all the various aspects of their daily life and worship, monks and nuns had to balance these and other practical problems and circumstances with their desire to revive the traditions of the past.

Cistercian aspirations

Just as in the eighteenth century certain members of the Congregation had found themselves drawn to La Trappe, so in the early nineteenth century a number of monks and nuns found their way to Lulworth and Stapehill, where French Cistercian exiles had settled in 1795 and 1802. Joseph Barber had been professed at Douai in 1792.[74] After spending two years in a French prison he went to Acton Burnell in Shropshire to join other members of his community before entering the monastery at Lulworth in 1805. His novitiate there is described in a letter preserved at Downside which reveals how strong was his resolution to lead a true Cistercian life. Indeed, the prior at Lulworth described him as one of the best monks they had ever had.[75] The young Bernard Ullathorne as a novice at Downside dreamed of becoming a Trappist monk,[76] whilst Jerome Digby, another monk of St Gregory had what his superiors regarded as "Trappist fever" in 1813.[77] Henry Stonor, who had been clothed as a novice at Downside in 1820 and had provided the majority of the funds for the 1822 chapel, entered La Trappe in Switzerland in 1832. Two nuns from Abbot's Salford gained permission to join the Cistercian nuns at Stapehill in Dorset. Dame Louisa Bridge returned to Abbot's Salford after twelve months, but Dame Bernarda Barnewall, who had left Abbot's Salford for Stapehill in 1825, persevered, dying there ten years later. Writing to inform her old community of her death, the superior at Stapehill commented rather acidly that "she was very charitable and edifying, but she could not be made to keep silent".[78] At least two students educated by the English Benedictines chose to enter other, stricter monastic houses: James Heaney, who left Ampleforth in 1831, subsequently entered the new Trappist monastery of Mount Saint Bernard in Leicestershire, and although he did not persevere, his letters to the Ampleforth monk Jerome Hampson provide a

---

[73] AH, 3: 199-200.
[74] On Barber see D.A. BELLENGER, *Opening the Scrolls: Essays in honour of Godfrey Anstruther*, Downside Abbey, Bath 1987, 160-163
[75] DAB, C 236, December 1805- June 1806.
[76] *The Devil is a Jackass*, 40-41.
[77] DAA, Parker Letters, C1R (A), 23 February 1813, President Brewer to Prior Parker.
[78] SAA, Box 4 no 24 bis.

snapshot of the austere, demanding lifestyle of a Trappist monk.[79] In 1849, sixteen year-old Edward O'Gorman, the future President General Anselm O'Gorman left St Edmund's College, Douai for Italy, abandoning his plans to join the community at Douai to embrace the more rigorous monastic life at Subiaco, where he fancied "he would speedily become a saint". O'Gorman later returned to Douai, disillusioned by his experience of Italian monasticism.[80] It is important also to note here that it was not uncommon for monks who belonged to other Congregations to enter communities of the English Congregation. Two monks who had hitherto belonged to the French Maurist Congregation (which was suppressed during the French Revolution) joined the community of St Gregory's, bringing with them their distinctive traditions of scholarship and liturgical observance.[81]

The suppression of the English Benedictine monastery at Lamspringe

In 1803 the English Benedictine monastery at Lamspringe was suppressed.[82] It had the distinction of being the only English Benedictine house in the eighteenth century to be ruled by a life abbot, as opposed to a prior, elected by the General Chapter. It was also the only German house in the Congregation and was somewhat isolated geographically from the other houses in France. Lamspringe's buildings were the finest in the Congregation; indeed the long frontage of the monastery "with its twin carriage entrances and double flight of steps rivalled the great monasteries of Austria and Bavaria".[83] It also had the largest resident community among the houses of the Congregation, 23 in number in 1798 and appeared to have maintained a fuller conventual life than the others. In 1795, unscarred by revolution unlike the other houses, the abbey at Lamspringe, in the opinion of one of its monks, Joseph Crook, seemed "likely to survive alone", for "little can be expected from those houses in England".[84] Yet by 1803 the ripples of the French Revolution reached Lamspringe as Napoleon succeeded in expanding French territory and in re-drawing the map of Europe. The mini-state of Hildesheim, in which Lamspringe was situated, was given to Prussia as partial compensation for the land taken by Napoleon, and soon the

---

[79] AA, MS 262, no.6. Mount Saint Bernard Abbey, 21 June 1838, Heaney to Hampson.
[80] *DM*, 24 (1902) 4.
[81] One of these monks was Dom Martin Leveaux (1745-1828), later Novice master and Subprior at Acton Burnell and Downside, a former Maurist scholar and prolific writer, see P. LENAIN, *Histoire Littéraire des Bénédictins de Saint-Maur*, 4 (Brepols, Turnhout 2014, 487-489.
[82] Lamspringe was the only English Benedictine house at this time to be ruled by an abbot: the other male monasteries were priories, under a prior.
[83] D. AGIUS, "The Lambspring Council Book, 1715-1802,"*DR*, 104 (1986) 159.
[84] DA, MS 386, A. BIRDSALL, "The Contest between the Abbot of the EBC monastery of Lamspringe and the President of the EBC, 1801-02," 3.

Prussians passed an edict that declared that not only would church and monastic property be confiscated, but that religious professions and the election of superiors were outlawed.

Internal problems at Lamspringe also threatened its survival, problems that had been festering for some time. The house had become increasingly aloof from the Congregation. The Abbot did not usually attend General Chapter personally, but sent a delegate. Moreover, the Constitutions of the Congregation were never accepted at Lamspringe, and even the revision of these in 1784 did not ensure their enforcement there. The abbot, Maurus Heatley argued that as a German house, Lamspringe could not accept Constitutions framed to accord with French law.[85] Nevertheless, the Constitutions were passed and published, but the Abbot of Lamspringe refused to recognise them, inserting in all old and new copies a paragraph which declared them to be incompatible with abbatial government and not binding at Lamspringe. The onset of the French Revolution appeared to encourage the abbot to disassociate his abbey even further from the Congregation, for in 1794 he sent neither accounts nor delegate to the General Chapter.

This was the background to the visitation of the monastery by the English Benedictine President, Gregory Cowley in 1797, in which he failed to challenge the abbot on a number of matters, not least on his treatment of one of the monks, Maurus Chaplin whom he had imprisoned for "scandalous misdemeanours" nine years before, something specifically prohibited by the 1784 Constitutions.[86] The abbot's response to the President's policy of appeasement was to make a unilateral declaration of independence, which was resented by a group of younger monks in the community. Divisions soon sprang up, with those who supported the Abbot pitched against the malcontents.[87] It took the determined President Bede Brewer to challenge Heatley at the 1801 visitation, a colourful account of which was written by the future President, Augustine Birdsall.[88]

Alongside almost comic descriptions of the tussle for pre-eminence between Brewer and Heatley (each of whom rushed to the church each day in order to command the abbatial throne), the account chronicles the President's release of Maurus Chaplin and his severe reminder to the abbot, in the Acts of Visitation (which Brewer instructed to be read in the refectory) that he "had no other authority over his religious than what be derived from the President and General Chapter".[89] The visitation over, Brewer returned to England, but the following year he was back in Germany, Heatley having

---

[85] See SCOTT, *Gothic Rage Undone,* 31-32.
[86] Maurus Chaplin had threatened Heatley with a cricket bat and slashed his portrait; see *AB,* 257-258, 286.
[87] B. GREEN, "The Fall of Abbot Heatley", *DR,* 97 (1979) 81-98.
[88] DA, MS 386, 19-33.
[89] DA, MS 386, 24-28.

refused to comply with two Presidential orders since the visitation. Returning to Lamspringe in May 1802, Brewer determined to bring the Abbot to heel and appointed Placid Harsnep as temporary superior. Heatley died soon afterwards and within a few months came the order from the Prussians for the monastery to be suppressed. The Prussian government was generous with pensions for the community and allowed the monks to remain in Lamspringe or the surrounding area. Bishop Douglass, Vicar of the London District noted in his diary:

> On the third of this month the Abbey of Lamspringe, which in the partition of Germany called *Indemnities* had been given away to the King of Prussia was dissolved by orders from Berlin. A layman was appointed to reside in the monastery and take care of the lands. The English monks are permitted to remain in their cells and to keep choir, and are allowed an annual pension, each monk, amount £50, more or less in English money. O tempora! O mores! Thus has this Abbey, belonging to the English Benedictine monks, been lost![90]

Although a succession of superiors was appointed until the 1820s, and the monastery was briefly revived at Broadway under Augustine Birdsall, the last monk of the community, Anselm Kenyon, died in 1850, and the monastery of Saints Adrian and Denis was never formally revived. Its funds were given to the newly-founded monastery of Fort Augustus in 1875. The suppression of Lamspringe was to leave significant legacies for the English Benedictine Congregation, not only its library and other treasures, but its pupils, who were sent to Ampleforth at a crucial time for that community's recruitment and survival. A number of these pupils went on to distinguish themselves, such as Peter Baines (1786-1843), who later became Vicar Apostolic of the Western district, and John Molyneux (1783-1860), who was to become President of the English Benedictines. These legacies will be considered separately in later chapters.

Conventual buildings

It took time for the transplanted communities to build conventual buildings on anywhere near the scale of Lamspringe or the other buildings they had left behind on the continent. The buildings initially occupied by the monks and nuns after 1795 were essentially large domestic houses where the emphasis was on functionalism rather than aesthetics. Characteristically the flamboyant future bishop, Augustine Baines, put his own stamp on the additions to Ampleforth Lodge in 1815, adorning the ceiling of the dining hall with Grecian plasterwork and ensuring it was supported by two rows of

---

[90] ARCHIVES OF THE ARCHBISHOP OF WESTMINSTER, MS *Diaries of Bishop John Douglass*, 3 January 1803.

Greek Doric columns.[91] The only purpose-built monastery in the Congregation in this period was St Mary, Sydney, Australia, but despite the grand vision of Polding, the building that housed the monastic community was a disappointment. Although the monastery had a private enclosure, its effectiveness was subverted by the close proximity of the school and other offices.[92]

As we have seen, the first resting places of the repatriated monks and nuns were temporary. The monks of St Gregory were the house guests of Sir Edward Smythe until 1814, when Downside was purchased, at a cost of over £7,000, to which friends of the community made "handsome donations".[93] Ampleforth Lodge in 1802 was already the home of Anselm Bolton, chaplain to Lady Ann Fairfax of Gilling, who at her death in 1793 had bequeathed the house for the endowment of a permanent mission at Ampleforth. President Bede Brewer persuaded Bolton to move out and allow the Lodge to become the new home for the Laurentian monks and purchased the property for £1,000. Brewer also provided Bolton with a life-annuity of £50.[94] For the community of St Edmund, the issue of ownership of their monastic buildings in Douai was always to be a vexed question, long before their expulsion from France in 1903. Officially the property belonged to the *Bureau des Fondations Anglaises*, and was not owned by the monks themselves.[95] The nuns, unlike the monks of St Gregory at Acton Burnell, paid rent to President Brewer, for their occupancy of his property in Woolton, which by the year 1800 amounted to over £57.[96] At Abbot's Salford the nuns did not pay rent to the owner of Salford Hall, Mary Stanford, but were responsible for paying for alterations to the house and repairs inside the house, whilst the owner undertook to take care of external repairs.[97] In 1838 they moved to Stanbrook Hall, in the village of Callow End, near Worcester, which they were able to purchase with the £8,000 left to one of the nuns, the future abbess, Scholastica Gregson, by her grandfather.[98]

The most ambitious building schemes of this period were at Downside, where in 1823 the construction of a new chapel and college

---

[91] B. LITTLE, *Catholic Churches since 1623*, Robert Hale, London, 1966, 62.
[92] See T.J. KAVENAGH, "Polding and 19th century monasticism," *TJ*, 8 (1974) 16; R.F. KEAN, "The Monastic Buildings of Old St Mary's, 1835-50," *TJ*, 37 (1989) 51.
[93] BIRT, *Downside*, 15.
[94] AR, 2: 463; CRAMER, *Ampleforth*, 43-47; ALMOND, *The History of Ampleforth Abbey*, 274-278.
[95] I am grateful to Father Peter Harris, archivist of the Royal English College, Valladolid, for sending me a copy of a document outlining the financial details of British properties in France drawn up by Abbot David Hurley of Douai Abbey in the early twentieth century.
[96] HOLLINSHEAD, "From Cambrai to Woolton," 473.
[97] E. EDWARDS, "'Salford Hall' or "The Nunnery,"' *Worcestershire Recusant*, 27 (1976) 6.
[98] Information provided by D Margaret Truran, 27 February 2006.

building enabled the monks to retain the original house as the monastery. Henry Stonor, clothed at Downside in 1820, donated £2,800 of the cost, estimated at £3,000 in 1820".[99] Various classical architectural designs were considered, but "the monks remembered their Gothic church at Douay, and were not unmindful of the beauty of the ancient abbeys of England".[100] The architect appointed was H.E. Goodridge, a protégé of Augustine Baines, who produced a building that has been described as epitomizing "a new approach to monasticism, attempting with its Gothic atmosphere to recapture the still-elusive spirit of medieval monasticism and to bring monasticism into the open".[101] Another commentator has described it as "something of a fantasy…apparently the nave and transept of a large English church in elevation", but in fact a building where "part of the transept is given over to a church and on a first floor at that".[102] It was the most significant new monastic building to have been constructed in England since the Reformation."[103]

Here again, the emphasis was on functionalism, for even though the monastic building was in a simple early Gothic style, it was L shaped, quite unlike a medieval quadrangle, containing classrooms and dormitory in one wing, and a vaulted chapel above a library and refectory in the other.[104] However the chapel did have some features of which the Gothic architect Pugin would have approved, such as an apse, in the style of Pershore Abbey, "for the Benedictines…were faithful to their old traditions".[105] The completed chapel was greatly admired, and many entering it were

> surprised to find so large, so lofty and so perfect a church with such massive stone pillars, not on the ground but upstairs…the sanctuary a semi-hexagon of unequal sides, finished by an apse, all parts of a church are there and are clearly defined; there is the nave for the people, and the choir for the students and monks raised one step above it, and the transepts are still more strongly marked by the special arrangement of the seats and stalls; the presbyterium, or sanctuary is raised three steps above the presbyterium, by three other steps with a large predella.[106]

---

[99] R. O'DONNELL, "Benedictine building in the Nineteenth Century," *EBHS*, privately printed, 1983, 43.
[100] BIRT, *Downside*, 183.
[101] A. BELLENGER, "Models of Monasticism," in BELLENGER (ed.), *Downside Abbey: An Architectural History*, 16.
[102] R. O'DONNELL, "Benedictine building in the Nineteenth Century," 43.
[103] A. FROST, "Henry Edmund Goodridge and the first buildings at Downside," in BELLENGER (ed.), *Downside Abbey: An Architectural History*, 85.
[104] LITTLE, *Catholic Churches since 1623*, 62; A. FROST, "Henry Edmund Goodridge and the first buildings at Downside," 65-85.
[105] G. DOLAN, "The Apse in English Architecture," *DR*, 19 (1900) 73.
[106] *DR*, 9 (1890) 145.

Two decades later further expansion made more new building necessary and "it was felt that there was a need of producing at Downside something more like the Benedictine Monasteries of Old England than was possible in the Old House". The prior of the time, Thomas Joseph Brown was believed to be

> a man able to throw himself into the aspirations of the time, and so it is easy to understand how the vision of a great monastery floated through the minds of Prior Brown and his monks, and how they turned to the man of the hour, Augustus Welby Pugin, to plan a building that should express the natural position of a Benedictine monastery in the Church life of the country.[107]

Goodridge's scheme in 1823 had contained no quadrangles, but Pugin's had four, one for each of community, boys, guests and laybrothers and servants. Publication of the ambitious plans in the *Dublin Review* of February 1842 gave the false impression that the plans had been officially accepted by the community and provoked one old Gregorian to note with dismay that Pugin's plan would sweep away all that had been built already.[108] In the event, Pugin's plans were never executed, the projected cost, as well as the architect's "megalomania and impracticability" being cited as official reasons, but as Roderick O'Donnell points out, the proposal was too ambitious psychologically, as well as financially. Whilst other religious communities enthusiastically embraced Pugin's Gothic vision, it was not shared by Downside, with the result that stones cut for the building of his monastery were used for farm buildings.[109]

Pugin's only executed commission for the English Benedictines in this period was at Douai in France, where he designed the chapel and refectory for the community of St Edmund.[110] Although the Edmundian monks inherited the grand façade of the Benedictine College built by Prior Augustine Moore in the late eighteenth century, the Gothic church fondly remembered by the Gregorian monks had been badly damaged during the Revolution and was demolished in 1832, and the interior of the old monastery of St Gregory had for a time been taken over by a local chemist who made beetroot sugar on the premises; for decades afterwards the flooring was saturated with beetroot syrup.[111] The Pugin chapel was begun in 1840, but only completed a decade later.

---

[107] *DR,* 33 (1914) 46.
[108] *Dublin Review,* 12 (1842) 135-37; see also R. O'Donnell, "Benedictine Building in the Nineteenth Century," 43-44; "The Abbey Church as first imagined and first built: From Pugin to Dunn and Hansom," in Bellenger (ed.), *Downside Abbey: An Architectural History,* 87-115 and DAB, L 107, 6 December 1841, Pugin to Prior Wilson.
[109] *DR,* 33 (1914) 150.
[110] R. O'Donnell, "Pugin in France: Designs for St Edmund's College, Douai (Nord), 1840," *Burlington Magazine,* 125 (1983), 607-611.
[111] *DM,* 8 (1898) 82.

At Ampleforth, there were many alterations during the nineteenth century to the original house, Ampleforth Lodge, but apart from temporary ancillary buildings, no major new buildings were erected until the 1860s, when a new church and new college building were built to the designs of Charles and Joseph Hansom.[112]

A detailed picture of the cramped monastic quarters of the former Cambrai nuns' house at Woolton near Liverpool is given by Janet Hollinshead, whilst an extract from a contemporary letter gives a description of their second home at Abbot's Salford near Evesham: "There are nine lodging rooms, a kitchen, small servants' hall, larder, dairy, butler's pantry, and a large brew-house". A chapel was created out of the drawing room, which was then enlarged. According to the account of the first official visitation of the house in 1809 by President Brewer, it was decreed that "all the upper part of the house from the bottom of the staircases is to be considered as forming a strict enclosure; no secular person is to go up stairs without an express leave in writing".[113] In 1838 the nuns moved to Stanbrook Hall, near Worcester where one of their early visitors was Sir Charles Throckmorton from nearby Coughton Court. He recorded in his diary: "the shell of the house is good, well-built and uniform, but the rooms are small and scarce two on a level." He continued: "the chapel, refectory, work-room and dormitory are exceptions".[114]

At Broadway in Worcestershire, where in 1834 President Augustine Birdsall attempted to revive the monastic community of Saints Adrian and Denis of Lamspringe a quarter-of-a-century after its expulsion, Birdsall built "a perfectly common sort of house, with no pretence at orthodox conventual arrangement…a plain sort of place, characteristic of the man and of his aims".[115]

Daily life and worship

The daily life and worship of each of the monasteries was regulated by the Constitutions of the Congregation, which had been revised in 1784. In addition, there were adaptations and customaries made by each house. The 1784 Constitutions stipulated that in monasteries having more than ten monks, there should be a morning office at 4 am. This seems to have lapsed at the Revolution, for the General Chapter of 1814 reinforced the requirement that this should be the case at Downside and Ampleforth, but Allanson records that this did not occur after the Chapter of 1842, presumably because

---

[112] See CRAMER, *Ampleforth*, 65-67, 73-74.
[113] HOLLINSHEAD, "From Cambrai to Woolton," 468-472; EDWARDS, "Salford Hall," 2-20.
[114] WARWICK RECORD OFFICE, CR 1998/CD/Drawer 8, no. 10 1st series, 1 July 1838.
[115] G. DOLAN, "Broadway," *DR*, 25 (1906) 68.

then each house had begun to develop its own timetable.[116] Vespers in most of the communities was at 5.30 pm. To begin with, daily life and worship in the transplanted communities must have been difficult, but few concessions seem to have been given for the privations the communities must have suffered. The Cambrai nuns who settled at Woolton in 1795 quickly established an horarium for both summer and winter. The summer horarium reads:

> 5am Rise. 5.30 Meditation. 6.30 Workroom until 8; At 8 breakfast in common; 8.30 Mass or private prayer. 9-11 Work; 11. Say hours in oratory; 11.30 dine and recreation until 1.30. Make spiritual reading until 2. 2-5 Work, 5pm Vespers and Compline and meditate for 15 minutes. Supper at 6 and recreation until 7.30. 7.30 Say Matins and Lauds for the following day. 9pm Retire.[117]

Even the Divine Office was not allowed to lapse during the process of moving from Salford Hall to Stanbrook in June 1838. Matins and Lauds were said at Salford before their departure, Compline was said *en route* at the church of St George in Worcester, and Prime was celebrated the following morning at Stanbrook.[118] Similarly the Gregorian monks from Acton Burnell arrived at their new home at Downside in April 1814 to find "scarcely a table or chair to make use of...and they have no sufficient supply of fuel to warm their empty house". Dom Leveaux, their temporary superior, "was a strict disciplinarian, and did not recognise in these circumstances any sufficient reason to depart from the usual routine" of monastic duties. Their office was recited under great difficulties...They were told to study, yet no books had arrived and they had no tables to sit at".[119]

At Ampleforth, despite the early example of Bede Brewer's fidelity to the times of the daily office, by the early 1830s the liturgical life of the house was at a low ebb. When he arrived there from Downside in 1831, Bernard Ullathorne found "the choir almost deserted in the morning, the Holy Communion forlorne (sic) and it was a common thing to see a snuff box handed to each other in chapel, and to see religious men with their heads together talking during a sermon".[120] At Douai, attempts were made to keep the community together, for in 1829 the community annalist recorded that "all the brethren were to go out for a walk together on Thursdays, except the

---

[116] AH, 2: 489.
[117] SAA, Annals, 1: 491.
[118] G. OLIVER, *Collections illustrating the History of the Catholic Religion in the Counties of Cornwall, Devon, Wiltshire, Somerset and Gloucester,* Charles Dolman, London 1857, 354; E. EDWARDS, *Home at Last,* Stanbrook Abbey Press, Worcester 1999, 10.
[119] *DR,* 1 (1880) 5-6; on Leveaux see BELLENGER, "An Anti-monastic Incident, 1794," *Worcestershire Recusant* 39 (1982) 32-35. Also, "The Benedictines at Acton Burnell, a further note," *Worcestershire Recusant* 40 (1982) 37-39
[120] DA, Abbot's Archives, Ampleforth, 11 May 1831, Ullathorne to Birdsall.

sick". It was also resolved that on Tuesday evenings between 5 pm and 6 pm "there should be a pious exhortation in the chapel".[121]

The *horarium* at Broadway in the revived community of Lambspring has been described as "simple and Spartan enough for the most exacting." Besides the hours of the Divine Office, the first of which being celebrated at 5am, whilst the time of Vespers varied between 3pm and 6pm, "the after-dinner recreation took the form of good healthy occupation in the garden." The superior, Augustine Birdsall, evidently ran a tight ship and warned his monks to expect a frugal fare, saying "Christmas Day will be as Good Friday with you."[122]

Habits were not worn in the monasteries for most of the early nineteenth century, such a practice having been specifically banned by the terms of the 1791 Catholic Relief Act.[123] The nuns had been forced to abandon their habits in the prison at Compiègne in 1794 and arrived in England dressed in the secular clothes left behind by the Carmelite nuns who had briefly shared their prison at Compiègne before being executed.[124] At Woolton the nuns had to concoct a new religious garb. The Stanbrook Abbey Annals record that "for the habit they wore gowns of a black material called wild boar, white muslin neckerchiefs and hoods, black worsted stockings and brown tick pockets, blue cloth cloaks, small purple shawls and black silk bonnets".[125] It was 1823 before the habit, cowl and veil, as worn at Cambrai, were worn once again,[126] the pattern for the garments having been obtained from another community of Benedictine nuns, who had also settled at Princethorpe after being imprisoned in France, but, unlike the Cambrai community, had been able to retain or retrieve their religious habits.[127] However, when the nuns moved to Stanbrook Hall, they resolved at first not to wear their habits for fear of upsetting the inhabitants of the village of Callow End.[128]

The monks were not so fortunate, the pattern for their habits having been lost at the Revolution. The monks of St Gregory seem to have worn the cowl (the outer, ceremonial garment) in the chapel at Acton Burnell.[129] Once the new chapel at Downside was opened in 1823, the cowl was abandoned in

---

[121] DAA, VII.A.2¹, 'Material for the annals of St Edmund's from its restoration in 1818', 25 March 1829.
[122] DOLAN, "Broadway," 72-73.
[123] For a detailed survey of this and other measures see C. BUTLER, *A Memoir of the Catholic Relief Bill Passed in 1829,* privately printed, Lincoln's Inn, London 1829.
[124] SAA, PARTINGTON, *A Brief Narrative,* 30 -31.
[125] SAA, Annals, 1: 502.
[126] THE BENEDICTINES OF STANBROOK, *In a Great Tradition,* 49.
[127] This is the community now settled at Colwich Abbey, near Stafford.
[128] EDWARDS, *Home at Last,* 10.
[129] Downside folklore suggests that there was only one cowl, used for the professions of novices.

favour of a gown (perhaps out of fear of unfavourable publicity, as the new chapel, unlike its predecessor in the house, was accessible to the general public). It was 1846 before the full habit was worn at Downside, and the cowl was re-instated in 1850. The Downside council book records that "on the feast of All Monks that year the cowl was resumed and was to be worn always in choir, at chapter acts, and at Mass when the Brothers go to Holy Communion".[130] It was 1852 before this practice was followed at Douai, but a living relic of the former fashion was Charles Fairclough, an Ampleforth monk and regular visitor:

> He dressed in a garb which the clergy must have worn in the days of the four Vicars-Apostolic – a swallow-tailed coat with collar reaching almost to the ears, a broad white neck-cloth, trousers straight up and down without any pretence to elegance, and the head crowned with a tall silk hat.[131]

An illustration, pre-dating the building of the Pugin chapel of the 1840s, shows monks at Douai wearing birettas and capes. At Ampleforth, according to the diary kept by schoolboy Robert Nihell, in June 1816: "the Religious began to wear cassocks".[132] On the mission, Bernard Ullathorne began wearing his monastic habit in his church and house at Coventry in 1844, but it was an innovation that was not universally welcomed, not even by his monastic brethren. Ullathorne recalled that he was asked to

> ... preach at the opening of the church of St Edmund (sic) in Liverpool. I replied that, as a Benedictine, I always preached in the habit of the Order, I received a reply from the venerable Father at the head of that church that 'another preacher would be provided.[133]

In his new monastery at St Mary, Sydney, Australia, Bede Polding consciously chose to establish a very different tradition in this regard than the one then observed in English Benedictine monasteries. He observed to a correspondent in 1845 that "the religious habit is worn with as much publicity as in the home itself whenever the novices visit the hospitals and asylums".[134] Polding directed that the monastery of Benedictine nuns nearby, founded by a nun of Stanbrook and a nun of Princethorpe, near Rugby, should follow the French religious dress code and customs of Princethorpe,

---

[130] O. SUMNER, "The English Benedictine Habit – Part Three," *DR,* 61 (1944) 77-78.
[131] F.C. DOYLE OSB, "St Edmund's in Douai" in F.C. DOYLE, (ed.), *Tercentenary of St Edmund's Monastery* R & T Washbourne, London 1917, 45.
[132] AA, EX01-10.
[133] *The Devil is a Jackass,* 272.
[134] O. THORPE, *The First Mission to the Australian Aborigines,* Pellegrini, Sydney 1950, 193.

rather than English customs of Stanbrook.[135] Polding's authority over the nuns even extended to decreeing the colour of their handkerchiefs.[136]

It has already been emphasised that in the rural communities around the new English Benedictine houses, locals came to accept gradually the presence of their new monastic neighbours. Nevertheless, anti-Catholic bigotry was a constant factor that had to be faced, especially after Catholic emancipation in 1829, and confronting it brought some English Benedictines to the forefront of public attention, one such was Thomas Joseph Brown, who gained national notoriety by debating with Protestant orators in a series of debates at Downside in early 1834. These debates, which were later published, enabled Downside to become better known.[137] At Ampleforth, Adrian Towers showed himself to be skilled in both oral and written controversy. He published a number of pamphlets and gained local notoriety in North Yorkshire by debating with a parson in the open air from a wheelbarrow.[138] At Douai in France, the monks enjoyed good relations with the local inhabitants. The future Cardinal Desprez, Archbishop of Toulouse, remembered the kindness of Prior Richard Marsh, who endeared himself to the local community.[139] Locally born laybrother, Didace Six became a well-known figure in the town from the 1840s until his death in 1896.[140] Bernard Gore died at Douai in September 1844 at the early age of 26. At his funeral, a large number of the townspeople joined the members of the community and pupils, thus demonstrating the "affection and piety" Father Bernard had inspired in the hearts of the locals.[141] The Cambrai nuns during their stay at Woolton seem to have received practical support from the local Catholic community, but no record exists of their relations with the local community at Abbot's Salford.[142]

The cramped conditions in temporary accommodation in the early years after their arrival in England must have made the celebration of the liturgy difficult for monks and nuns, but it is striking to observe how concerned they were to continue the liturgical traditions of their former houses in France. Thus, despite shortage of space at Acton Burnell, and in the

---

[135] M.G. FORSTER, "Magdalen le Clerc," *TJ*, 8 (1974) 272-273.
[136] FORSTER, "Magdalen le Clerc," 274.
[137] E. TOTTENHAM, *The Authenticated Report of the discussion...in the chapel of the Roman Catholic College of Downside near Bath on the 25th, 26th, 27th of February and the 5th, 6th and 7th of March 1834. Subjects 'The Rule of Faith' and 'the Sacrifice of the Mass', Protestant Speakers: Rev Edward Tottenham, Rev John Lyons. Roman Catholic Speakers: Rev T.J. Brown etc. Rev. T.M. Macdonnell...Rev Francis Edgeworth*, J & F Rivington, J. Booker, London 1836.
[138] For Towers, see *AJ*, 17 (1912) 417 and R. TOWERS, *A Second Letter to the Rev. Thos. Comber...in reply to his and other charges*, privately printed, York 1833.
[139] DOYLE, (ed.), *Tercentenary of St Edmund's Monastery*, 49.
[140] A. HOOD, "Douai 1818-1903," in SCOTT (ed.), *Douai 1903-Woolhampton 2003*, 67.
[141] E. HUGHES, *British en Douai, 1800-1850*, unpublished paper, no date, 48.
[142] HOLLINSHEAD, "From Cambrai to Woolton," 472-474.

early years at Downside, the community of St Gregory tried to be as faithful as possible to the spiritual and liturgical practices it had followed at Douai. The Smythe family had not only provided shelter for the Gregorian monks, but had also added a wing to Acton Burnell Hall for them and built a chapel. A later commentator on this period noted that "if Downside's flair for dignified ceremonial comes down to us from Douay, Arras and Compostella, it does so through the sacristy door of the Smythes' domestic chapel".[143] On 3 July 1809, Prior Peter Kendal wrote to procurator Anselm Lorymer, requesting "two thuribles for the chapel, that our ceremonies of the divine service be carried on as much as possible as at Douai. The chains must not be too long that our thurifers may use them at their full length as at Douai".[144] The conditions of the chapel were certainly not adequate for ceremonial, for in 1801 Benedict Pembridge wrote to President Bede Brewer to bring to his attention the matter of slackness regarding ceremonial there, especially when professions were celebrated. "One omission of ceremonies which struck and affected me with surprise and sorrow", commented Pembridge, "was at the profession of the last professed, whereat I was the celebrant. Not a single ceremony was observed, except the essential one- their vows at the altar". He complained that there was "no prostrating…the scapular and cowl might have been put on throughout the day".[145]

Yet as early as 1799 thought was being given to the subject of music for the new chapel. The 1784 Constitutions had stipulated that the organ should be used in the liturgy "to increase dignity". Furthermore, 'much less should musical instruments be used, especially when they do not accord with the monastic choir".[146] However, in 1799, Anselm Lorymer wrote to Prior Sharrock to say that he was endeavouring to obtain suitable instruments for use in the liturgy. Here too was concern to preserve the musical traditions of Douai, for old account books of the eighteenth century give instances of the purchase and repair of various wind and stringed instruments.[147] The organ was not forgotten, for a year later Prior Sharrock informed his brother, who was Vicar Apostolic of the Western District, "a good organ is ordered. It is thought it will be ready for July".[148] There was also concern for continuity in the style of the music itself used at Douai. Joseph Eldridge responded rather disparagingly to a letter from Lorymer

---

[143] H. VAN ZELLER, *Downside by and Large*, Sheed and Ward, London 1954, 25; A description of the monks' chapel at Acton Burnell is given in D. REES, "Reduced Circumstances," *The Raven*, 63 (1973) 24

[144] DAB, C 481, 3 July 1809, Kendal to Lorymer.

[145] DAB, B 377, 20 January 1801, Pembridge to Brewer.

[146] *Constitutiones Congregationis Anglicanae Ordinis Sancti Benedicti; Formularium E.B.C. Ritualis Compendium E.B.C.*, privately printed, Paris 1784.

[147] BIRT, *Downside*, 134-135.

[148] CLIFTON DIOCESAN ARCHIVES, Bishops' Letter-books, 1800, Acton Burnell, 29 March 1800, Prior Sharrock to Bishop Sharrock.

requesting the permission of Keating, the London publisher, to produce new copies of this music.[149] When the community moved to Downside in April 1814, the Divine Office was continued immediately. Abbot Snow describes how a parlour was converted into a chapel for the purpose:

> the two windows facing the lawn had been blocked up to escape the window tax, and the altar was placed in the exact wall space between the other two windows and on it two plated branch candlesticks and a pair of silver ones; above was a picture of the Resurrection. A carpet covered the predella, common forms for the students filled the body of the room and either side, chairs for the community...a room sixteen by sixteen, a priest clad in unadorned vestment before a makeshift altar, at his heels a thurifer and two acolytes in the only three cassocks, men standing along the sides of the room in double-breasted cut-away coats and profuse neckcloths.[150]

The setting may have been humble and make-shift but the liturgy that was performed there bespoke a strong concern for continuity: "All were called betimes for the Divine Office, and ranged along the sides of an empty room, they stood facing one another and recited the psalms as they had done at Acton Burnell, and as they had done at Douai".[151] A strong concern for continuity was also expressed in the music used in the liturgy, especially in the music of French composer, Faboulier, whose works were sung not only at the priory of St Gregory in Douai, but also in the nearby church of the English Recollects. At Downside an old piano was substituted for an organ and was augmented by "two violoncellos to give fullness of tone". The music

> consisted mainly of Webbe's motets and the chant and motets of Faboulier...his chant was not the tweedledum of Ratisbon, nor the tweedledee of Mechlin, nor the superior touch of Dom Pothier...it was like nothing else, with echoes of boyhood, with reminiscences of Old Douai.[152]

One educated at Downside in the 1830s recalled that

> at night one of the last sounds to reach the ear was that of the Compline Antiphon of Our Lady. Few Downside boys will forget the beautiful melody of Faboulier's *Salve*...from the old choir.[153]

At Broadway in Worcestershire, where the Lambspring community that had been suppressed in 1803 was briefly revived, there was also a concern for continuity. Placid Hall, one of the last surviving members of the

---

[149] BIRT, *Downside*, 134-135.
[150] SNOW, *Sketches of Old Downside*, 7-8.
[151] SNOW, *Sketches*, 5.
[152] SNOW, *Sketches*, 9.
[153] *DR*, 4 (1885) 130.

Broadway community recalled the efforts of the superior, Augustine Birdsall, to continue the Lamspringe liturgical traditions: "The Young men were set to practise plainsong, for in accordance with Lamspringe tradition a good deal of the office was sung, and President Birdsall attached great importance to the worthy rendering of the Divine Office", especially on the major feasts when "it was the Lamspringe custom for the antiphons, capitulum and hymn to be intoned by the community in order".[154]

This concern to preserve earlier traditions is also characteristic of the experience of the nuns in this period. Arriving at Woolton in May 1795, the Cambrai nuns immediately resumed their former timetable and religious practices as far as possible. When they settled at Abbot's Salford, full enclosure was not possible – the nuns set up a wooden grille in front of the sanctuary, the abbey annals reveal, "to console themselves for the loss of the grilles at Cambrai".[155] Most importantly, they carried on the spirituality of the seventeenth-century English Benedictine, Augustine Baker, who had influenced the community so much in its early days. Despite the loss of many of the precious Baker manuscripts at the Revolution, the tradition continued, aided by the fidelity of the remaining Cambrai nuns, such as the Prioress, Dame Mary Benedict Partington who had been professed at Cambrai in 1772. By 1823,

> she was scarcely able to toddle along, still she kept to conventual duties and to the choir, though she could hardly hold or see her breviary, she was to be seen going to choir with it close pressed to her breast.[156]

The annals also record that Abbess Christina Chare "inherited to a remarkable degree the spirit of the Cambrai nuns from whom she had received her religious training and later on as Abbess, she did her utmost to perpetuate the Cambrai tradition".[157] However, it was impossible for the community to preserve the musical tradition of their former home, but after the move to Abbot's Salford, their chaplain, Benedict Wassall "who had a fine voice as well as the knowledge of music, instructed them how to render the Masses popular at that day, for until then there was no singing at any Church service whatever".[158] Dame Magdalen le Clerc, who accompanied Polding to Australia in 1847, was a gifted musician who "began the Stanbrook tradition of regular singing at Mass – her taste being for polyphonic music, especially Mozart".[159]

---

[154] G. DOLAN, "Broadway," 72.
[155] SAA, Annals, 1: 491.
[156] SAA, Annals, 1: 595.
[157] SAA, Annals, 1: 517.
[158] SAA, Annals, 1: 590.
[159] SAA, Annals, 1: 566.

At both Downside and Ampleforth, liturgical developments occurred in the 1840s. The time spent by Benedict Tidmarsh in German monasteries between 1839 and 1841 led to "an immense improvement and advance in liturgical observance at Downside. Processions were introduced and the lanterns, canopy and cross provided for them".[160] At Ampleforth in 1845, Honoratus Garroni, who was professed as a monk at Subiaco, Italy, in 1823, was appointed not only as Professor of Theology but was asked to compile a monastic ceremonial.[161] It was also at this time that Austin Bury and Laurence Shepherd were sent to study in Italy, where Shepherd subsequently was introduced to the writings on the liturgy of Abbot Prosper Guéranger.[162]

In his monastery at St Mary, Sydney, Bede Polding was concerned to introduce customs and traditions of Downside, such as the establishment of a museum, and a monastic brass band.[163] Some of the Downside liturgical customs proved more difficult to transplant in the new monastery. Polding complained:

> I cannot but lament that the opportunity we had of establishing the Downside psalmody, so dear to me, is lost. I must now have chants from Ireland which I detest, from Scotland – modifications of that Gregorian chant which I loved so much in dear Downside.[164]

Yet in 1843, the plainsong *Te Deum* was sung by the monastic choir and many flocked to the cathedral that year, including Protestants "who could not but have been highly edified at the sight of such solemn worship and at the devotional effect of the imposing spectacle and Gregorian chaunt (sic)".[165] Polding was able to provide a solemn High Mass in his cathedral long before such a liturgy was to be a regular feature in an English Benedictine monastery. Liturgical practice in Sydney soon diverged from the English Benedictine Congregation, for in April 1849 the St Mary community ceased to observe the English Benedictine liturgical calendar and began to follow one which Polding himself had drawn up with the approval of Rome. It was a lost link with the English Benedictine Congregation lamented by Edmund Moore, who wrote sadly to a friend at Downside:

> It used to be very pleasant for me to think that we had just said the office and Mass of any Saint's day, which in the space of 9 or 10 hours you in

---

[160] *DR*, 22 (1903) 103-4.
[161] KAVENAGH, "Polding and 19th century Monasticism," 188.
[162] This will be discussed in a later chapter on education, but see E. EDWARDS, "The Influence on the EBC of Dom Guéranger's Revival," *EBHS*, privately printed, 1985, 31-36.
[163] KAVENAGH, "Polding and 19th century Monasticism," 166.
[164] Polding to Heptonstall, BIRT, *Benedictine Pioneers in Australia*, 1: 410.
[165] E. LEA-SCARLETT, "St Mary's Liturgy under Polding," *TJ*, 15 (1978) 107.

> England and at Douay would repeat word for word. I deeply regret the change.[166]

An organ for the new chapel at Downside was purchased from the Brighton Pavilion.[167] This was presumably the organ played by the future Bishop Charles Davis in the 1840s before his departure for Australia. A contemporary remembered how Davis

> played the noble instrument in a style that our best organists would envy. The boys used to say he could knock smoke out of the organ pipes...his playing of the psalms at Vespers was really unsurpassable, and almost unapproachable. Every verse received a different treatment according to its meaning, and the pedal runs were something marvellous.[168]

In contrast, the community at Douai sang their offices unaccompanied until 1832. Thomas Swale, who visited the place earlier that year, noted in his diary for Sunday 29 April: "Attended Vespers – sung - no organ even in the morning".[169] Swale would have been thinking back to his schooldays at Ampleforth, where the organ installed by James Davis in the gallery of the chapel in 1815 presumably accompanied the offices.[170] In the event, at Douai the Council book records that on 17 December 1832, Prior Appleton obtained the Council's permission to install an organ "to strengthen the Divine Office".[171] The nuns were very proud of the organ that was installed in the chapel at Salford Hall in June 1833 with the assistance of public subscription. It replaced a harpsichord and was taken to Stanbrook in 1838.

Finances

All the houses suffered financially as a result of the French Revolution, especially the nuns formerly of Cambrai, who arrived in England in May 1795 "ragged and penniless",[172] dependent on the generosity of a variety of benefactors. All the houses sought compensation for their losses, and in August 1814, no doubt prompted by the terms of the Treaty of Paris, Richard Marsh was directed by General Chapter to go and reclaim English Benedictine property at Dieulouard.[173] By the end of the year, "after a month of disagreeable solicitations", Marsh recovered possession of what remained unsold of the property, namely 70 or 80 acres of woodland, which produced

---

[166] DAB, M 180, 18 April 1849, Moore to Morrall.
[167] SNOW, *Sketches of Old Downside,* 29.
[168] *DR,* 21 (1902) 178.
[169] *Mr Swale's Diary, Rome 1830-1832,* St Laurence Papers, Ampleforth 1995, 60.
[170] CRAMER, *Ampleforth,* 171.
[171] DAA, VII.A.3.b.i.
[172] BENEDICTINES OF STANBROOK, *In a Great Tradition,* 45.
[173] DAA, Parker letters, letter no. 91, 1 August 1814, Marsh to Parker.

a small annual revenue of 300-400 francs.[174] The nuns proved to be much more proactive than the monks, in trying to get political support in England for their claims. The Marquis of Hertford, the Lord Chamberlain, whose country seat was nearby at Ragley Hall, befriended them. Through the Marquis the nuns received visits not only from Lord Castlereagh, the Foreign Secretary, who was the Marquis' nephew, but also the Duke of Clarence, the future King William IV. The nuns believed that it was these visits, which led directly in 1816 to each returned religious being paid an allowance, backdated to 1795, of a guinea per month, by the French government.[175] In 1826 Charles X of France paid a large sum intended to benefit refugee nuns in England, but the nuns did not receive anything from this. The legend at Stanbrook was that the money went to build Buckingham Palace, a variation of the Downside legend on this subject, which held that the money paid to the British government by the French for the benefit of the monks, was actually used to meet the debt incurred by the building of the Brighton Pavilion.[176]

The monks fared rather better, although it was a struggle to make ends meet at Acton Burnell, Downside and Ampleforth. The monks at Downside unashamedly issued what was described as "a begging circular" to their friends and parents in 1817, which sought to "excite the charitable feelings of the opulent and liberal in their regard", to assist them in the building of a new chapel. The appeal was successful and almost £850 was raised as a result.[177] Money was continually needed at Ampleforth for new buildings. President Bede Brewer contributed in 1810 to the extension of the house to provide a large refectory and dormitory wing.[178] Prior Adrian Towers proved to be a disaster at managing accounts, and in 1833 it was found that "the profusion of the expenditure during the four last years had been exorbitant, as funds had been taken up and debts had been incurred to the amount of £5,500".[179] Bede Day, who succeeded Towers as Prior, was forced to make a public appeal for financial assistance as well as to borrow the sum of £3,450.[180] The monks at Douai also struggled to make ends meet. In December 1832, the community annalist recorded that in order to pay off debts totalling £600, "strict economy" was ordered. At dinner (the midday meal) the community was to be served one course of meat, but none at

---

[174] MARSH, *Reminiscences,* 16.
[175] SAA, Annals, 1: 538.
[176] SAA, Annals, 1: 539; *DR,* 8 (1889) 54-55.
[177] BIRT, *Downside,* 176-180.
[178] *AB,* 305; CRAMER, *Ampleforth,* 57.
[179] *AB,* 381.
[180] H. WILSON, "Ampleforth obituaries," <http:www.monlib.org.uk/obits/willson/willson2.htm> [accessed 8 January 2005].

supper.[181] Later, the prior of the time, Francis Appleton credited himself with the improvement of the house finances:

> When I became Prior in May 1833 the Community had a debt of £1200…I left the debt nearly paid off…I got the French government to sell some of our old property in France and have from a revenue of £30 per annum obtained an income from it of £175.[182]

In a later chapter, it will be seen that monks serving on the Benedictine mission were entitled to their own allowance, or *peculium,* and after their death, the residue of their money was divided between the missionary province and the monastery of their profession. However, as will be shown later, monastic superiors sometimes attempted to claim all of a missioner's money for their priories.

Monks, their Benefactors and the desire for monastic independence from lay control

Although the monks of St Gregory's came to regard Sir Edward Smythe and his wife, Catherine Maria "as among the principal benefactors of their house",[183] the early decades of the nineteenth century marked a gradual shift away from the monks' dependence on lay patronage.

Inevitably there were tensions during the twenty-year sojourn at Acton Burnell between the monks and their hosts. Some of the community complained about "inconveniences suffered under Sir Edward's government, for he only allows those he likes to reside at Acton Burnell." Prior Peter Kendal complained that "Sir Edward frequently encroached on the prior's authority".[184] Following the death of Sir Edward in 1811, the monks were asked to vacate Acton Burnell Hall to make room for the new squire and his family. Although some of the monks viewed this as "a favourable circumstance," Prior Kendal fulminated that the monks' departure from the Hall "was not a free act and deed of their own…", but "only in conformity to the wishes of the family" whom Kendal contended had "sufficiently made known to us that they leave it not as our option to remain".[185] This bitter pill was no doubt sweetened by the generosity of the Smythe family in contributing £400 of the £1070 donated towards the cost of establishing the community at Downside in 1814. Yet it is interesting that the family name

---

[181] DAA, VII.A.2¹, "Materials for the annals of St Edmund's," 29 December 1832.
[182] *AB*, 387.
[183] *DR*, 33 (1914) 20
[184] DAB, C 112, 9 September 1804, Pembridge to Lorymer; DAB C 481, 3 July 1809, Kendal to Lorymer.
[185] 3 October 1813, Kendal to Lorymer, quoted in L. GRAHAM, "Benefactors of Early Downside," *DR*, 182 (1942) 171-172.

does not appear on the principal list of subscribers towards the cost of building the new chapel at Downside five years later. The Dowager Lady Smythe is acknowledged as having made a donation on the opening of the chapel on 11 July, 1823, but neither she, nor her son, the sixth baronet, attended this important event. Although the list of subscribers for the chapel is an impressive one, peppered as it is with the names of old Catholic families such as the Arundells of Wardour, the Welds of Lulworth and the Throckmortons of Coughton, less than half of the total donations for the chapel came from the Catholic Gentry. Significantly, the largest donation to the building of the Downside chapel came not from a lay benefactor, but from a monk of the house, Ambrose Naylor, who had been missioner at Bidlestone in Northumberland for over fifty years. At his death in 1821, Naylor left a sizable *peculium* of £1270 to the house of his profession, without which, according to Prior Barber of Downside "the building would have been left incomplete". [186] The opening of the chapel aroused a great deal of interest, both locally and nationally, for "persons came from far and near" to view it.[187] The chapel must have made an imposing sight on the Somerset countryside. From the Fosse Way which passed close by, travellers could not fail to notice a building that was clearly identifiable as a church. The papal coat-of-arms on its façade clearly proclaimed the monks' desire for independence from lay control.

By 1850, the conventuals in the monasteries of the English Benedictine Congregation could look back with some satisfaction on all that had been achieved in a remarkably short period of half a century: new buildings, expanding communities and new apostolates were the fruits of courage and perseverance in difficult times. Despite the changes forced on them by the French Revolution, it is striking to what extent continuity rather than change characterised English Benedictine monasticism in these years, as evidenced by the sterling efforts made to reproduce, albeit in simpler form, many of their monastic customs from their former houses on the continent. But with the restoration of the English Catholic hierarchy in 1850, and the winds of monastic reform beginning to blow across the Channel from continental Europe, the Congregation could not resist change for very much longer. Having explored the externals of early-nineteenth-century English Benedictine monasticism; it is now time to consider the spirituality which underpinned them.

---

[186] 25 February, 1822, Barber to Jenkins, quoted in GRAHAM, "Early Benefactors of Downside," 186.
[187] Prior Barber quoted in BIRT, *Downside*, 184.

CHAPTER 3

Prayer and Devotion

The author has no great taste for fanciful devotions, which he would rather repress than encourage at any time.[1]

A recurring feature of English Benedictine life since its revival in the seventeenth century has been the struggle between action and contemplation, yet in the years that followed the repatriation of English monks and nuns on their native soil, the struggle was a more fundamental one, namely the struggle to survive. Although action rather than reflection was the order of the day between 1795 and 1850, prayer and devotion were not entirely neglected. This chapter will consider the devotional life of the English Benedictines in their monasteries as well as on their missions, together with their writings on the subject, and the influences that shaped them.

Although the keynote in this period was continuity, rather than change, there were hints, both of a revival of traditional forms of prayer, and of development of newer devotions that were gradually gaining popularity. In assessing the nature and development of English Benedictine spirituality in this period, several different types of evidence may be drawn upon; firstly the books they read and contemporary writings which provide evidence of their personal piety; secondly, their writings, whether in manuscript or published form; and thirdly, material which indicates their reaction and response to new ideas and devotions coming from the continent. To begin with, however, consideration will be given to one particular theme that was to colour English Benedictine spirituality for half a century.

Millenarianism

During the 1790s, the French Revolution stimulated among churchmen of differing allegiances an interest in biblical prophecy. Among Anglican divines, the mouths and pens of Samuel Horsley, William Jones of Nayland and Stanley Faber were all engaged in drawing contemporary lessons from texts of scripture in the light of events in France, in which these divines believed, man had descended to unprecedented depths of depravity and wickedness.[2] Yet, even before the French Revolution, the English

---

[1] E.B. GLOVER, *An Explanation of the Prayers and Ceremonies of the Holy Sacrifice of the Mass in familiar discourses addressed to a congregation,* Ambrose Cuddon, London 1825, iii-iv.
[2] S. HORSLEY, *Critical Disquisitions on the Eighteenth Chapter of Isaiah,* J. Nichols, J. Robson, London 1799; W. JONES, *The Man of Sin,* Rivington, London 1796; G.S. FABER,

Benedictines already had a spiritual theme that enabled them to face the challenges of their new situation, and make some sense of it. This outlook was heavily influenced by the biblical scholarship and scientific outlook of the English Benedictine mathematician and bishop, Charles Walmesley. In 1770, Walmesley had published, under his *nom de plume* Pastorini, *The General History of the Christian Church*, in which he used the prophecies contained in the Book of Revelation to give stark warnings of what dark forces may be unleashed when reason was preferred to religion.[3] Walmesley was not the first to use this form of writing, with its view of historical stages separated by apocalyptic events, but his book was notable for three main reasons: firstly, it was penned by a Catholic. Secondly he anticipated by a quarter of a century the later "chorus of apocalyptic voices", in the form of biblical commentators who, provoked by the crisis of the French Revolution claimed to interpret the signs of the times through the use of Revelation.[4] Finally, Walmesley's work was significant because it continued to be published until 1851. Subsequent generations utilised the book as a useful apologetical weapon in a number of different circumstances. These ranged from the defence of the church against Napoleon, aspirations of English Catholic emancipation against Protestant objections, and justification for frontier Catholicism in the United States.

The coming of the French Revolution appeared to vindicate Walmesley's pessimistic outlook on the state of society, and his book provided the English Benedictines with a perspective from which to reflect upon their fortunes. Thus it was the Congregation which promoted and financed the book's second publication in 1799, through the energy of Walmesley's confrère, Benedict Pembridge. Early in 1799, Walmesley's successor as Vicar Apostolic of the Western District, Bishop Gregory

---

Two Sermons Preached Before the University of Oxford Feb.10 1799, Oxford, University Press 1799.

[3] SIGNOR PASTORINI (Bishop Charles Walmesley), *The General History of the Christian Church,* privately published, London 1771, J.P. Coghlan, London 1798, privately published, Wigan 1782, Dublin, 1790, 1797, 1800, Fitzpatrick, Dublin 1805, 1812, Belfast, 1816, Cork, 1820, 1821, Hopkins & Seymour, New York 1807, 1834, 1846, 1858, Boston, 1851; see also G. SCOTT, '"The Times are fast approaching," Bishop Charles Walmesley OSB (1722-1797) as prophet,' *JEH,* 36 (1985) 590-604. Walmesley's scientific career is explored in G. SCOTT, "The Early Career of Bishop Charles Walmesley," *DR,* 115 (1997) 249ff.

[4] SCOTT, "The Times are fast approaching," 596. For surveys of such literature at the end of the eighteenth century, see J.C. HARRISON, *The Second Coming: Popular Millenarianism 1780-1850,* Routledge, Kegan & Paul, London 1979; W.H. OLIVER, *Prophets and Millenialists,* Auckland University Press, Auckland 1979; See also J.A. ODDY, unpublished Ph.D. thesis, *Eschatological prophecy in the English theological tradition, 1700-1840,* University of London 1982, 46-54. For the European apocalyptic movement, see T.A. KSELMAN, *Miracles and Prophecies in Nineteenth-Century France,* 81-83.

Sharrock wrote to his brother at Acton Burnell: "Mr. Pembridge should be alert about reprinting Pastorini, lest somebody should get the start of him, as the book is actually in great request".[5] For Walmesley, the age of Revolution not only called for an age of atonement, but for an age of reparation. In 1796, in one of his last letters to the faithful in his District, Walmesley clearly enunciated what he considered to be the appropriate response to events both at home and abroad:

> We must endeavour to appease the anger of God and conciliate his favour. This is to be done by addressing our supplications to him in the spirit of true humility, to weep for our own sins and those of the people, and to offer him the agreeable sacrifice of Fasting and Mortification…The Divine Scourge striking France with such dreadful calamities calls upon the exiles of that country to humble and prostrate themselves before an angry God and with Compunction of heart and flowing tears to acknowledge his justice…we powerfully exhort them to endeavour by means of fasting and fervent prayer to deprecate the Wrath of the Almighty, to prevail on him to call his eyes of mercy on their unhappy country, and restore it to his favour.[6]

Here again, Walmesley was notable for anticipating later more famous voices, such as Comte Joseph de Maistre who, just before his death in 1821, published his critique of Enlightenment thought, in which he asserted that there had been ample warning of the Revolution: "There are never any worldly events that have not been predicted in some fashion…You have a recent example in the French Revolution, predicted on all sides and in an incontestable way".[7] Maistre, like Walmesley, invoked the need for public and private prayer and seasoned his call for repentance with apocalyptic warnings: "We must be prepared for an immense event in the Divine order, toward which we march with an accelerated speed which must strike every observer…Fearsome oracles announce everywhere that *the time has come*".[8]

Already, in 1798, members of the English Benedictine Congregation were taking up Walmesley's apocalyptic theme and using it to reflect on the fragile state of the Congregation. At the General Chapter of the Congregation held in that year, Benedict Pembridge prophesied the end of the Congregation itself, describing it as "our ancient and tottering mother…a venerable vessel that is nearly sinking, splitting, going to wreck".[9]

---

[5] DAB, B 147, 9 January 1798, Bishop Sharrock to Prior J Sharrock.
[6] *Charles, Bishop of Rama, Vicar Apostolic, to all the faithful, clergy and laity, in the Western District,* 1796, cited in F. BLOM, J. BLOM, F. KORSTEN AND G. SCOTT, *English Catholic Books, 1701-1800,* Scolar Press, Aldershot 1996, 307.
[7] J. DE MAISTRE, *Les soirées de Saint-Petersburg,* Librairie Grecque Latine et Française, Paris 1821, 323.
[8] DE MAISTRE, *Les soirées de Saint-Petersburg,* 320
[9] DAB, B 170, 12 July 1798, Pembridge to General Chapter.

John Turner, one of the few surviving monks of the monastery of St Edmund in Paris also jumped on the millenarian bandwagon, greatly affected by his own personal experience of the Revolution. Caught up in the confusion of the events in Paris, he had detached himself from his community in 1792 and demonstrated his sympathy for the Revolution by joining the National Guard. France's declaration of war on Britain in 1793 led to all British religious being suspected of being enemy agents, even those who, like Turner, had taken oaths in favour of the Revolution. He was imprisoned for 18 months before briefly returning to his community which for a time was restored to its monastery. From 1796, Turner taught at a public college, and tutored private pupils, living in an apartment in Paris. During this period he continued to build up an extensive collection of books and pamphlets relating to the French Revolution. One of the volumes contains a number of fashionable prophecies predicting war and the persecution of the church.[10] Apocalyptic imagery also coloured the writings of Liverpool English Benedictine missioner Archibald Benedict Macdonald. In a sermon published in 1801 under the title *Select Discourses on the Gospels*, he reflected upon the Last Judgement:

> There are few articles of Christian belief more capable of exciting a salutary fear than this tremendous period, for which reason no doubt, the church at this time reminds us of this terrible scene. The race of men...will clearly perceive that the world is tending to ruin...they will feel the earth quake, behold their cities fall and the general conflagration begin to kindle around them.[11]

Referring explicitly to the prophecies contained in the book of Revelation, Macdonald continued: "many prophecies remain to be fulfilled...some of the rising generation may experience a part of the forerunning calamities which will be sufficiently severe".[12]

English Benedictine millenarianism continued after the revolutionary wars, with its colourful imagery being applied to a number of different issues, both in England and abroad. A preoccupation for many members of the Congregation in the period after Waterloo was the question of whether it was possible to return to France, and therefore keen interest was shown in

---

[10] Turner's collection is now on permanent loan to the Reading University Library: "The Turner Collection of French Revolution pamphlets",<http://www.library.rdg.ac.uk/colls/special/turner.html> [accessed 5 May 2003]. The volume referred to here is volume 189. For Turner himself, see G. SCOTT, "English Benedictines and the Revolution: The Case of Dom John Turner, Guardsman and Grammarian," in BELLENGER (ed.), *The Great Return*, 38-43.

[11] A.B. M (MACDONALD), *Select Discourses on the Gospels for all the Sundays and Holydays throughout the Year*, J. McCreery, Liverpool, 1801 2-3.

[12] A.B.M (MACDONALD), *Select Discourses*, 346-348.

both political and religious events there, especially in any slight occurrence that may indicate the possibility of such a return. During 1816 and 1817 a series of letters passed between Prior Augustine Lawson at Acton Burnell and Prior Henry Parker in Paris concerning the possible return of the community of St Gregory to its former monastery at Douai, and in the middle of one such letter in 1816, Lawson enquired:

> What is the curious report about the Archangel Raphael having appeared to a peasant in the department de Versailles? Is it credited as fact? Les spirits forts will ridicule, but such visions have happened before this present time. If the Almighty choose to grant such an extraordinary manifestation to attain his end and to accomplish his mercifulness towards France, let them smile and sneer, as long as France is spared and saved, that is all we wish.[13]

At this time, a French peasant, Thomas Martin, reported a series of apparitions of the Archangel Raphael which began just after the Restoration of King Louis XVIII, and reports of apparitions of the Virgin Mary and the saints were not uncommon in early nineteenth-century France.[14] It is noteworthy that such visions came to be interpreted as signs of divine approval of English Benedictine aspirations.

As the likelihood of the monks of St Gregory returning to France receded, and with the revival of the community of St Edmund in the Gregorian buildings at Douai, the transplanted communities in England began to settle down in their new centres. When Catholic emancipation became a reality in 1829, English Benedictines made less use of apocalyptic imagery to bewail their own uncertainties about their future, and seemed content to apply such imagery to describe the state of society in general. "Babylon", the term which non-Catholic writers seized upon to describe the Catholic Church, gained a more general usage as a term to describe London or other European cities, or the world in general. In 1824, in a conference to her community at Abbot's Salford, Abbess Christina Chare remarked: "How much we are indebted to God for our vocation, and what could induce Him to cast so favourable an eye upon us, as to select us from the Babylon of this world and shelter us in the harbour of religion, in which he places his favourite spouses".[15]

By the 1840s, apocalyptic imagery had returned with a new focus, and had found new English Benedictine voices such as William Bernard Ullathorne, who was appointed Vicar Apostolic of the Western District in 1846. In his 1848 Lenten indult he wrote: "Let your eye behold God's dealings, for they are very visible...all things proclaim that God is visiting

---

[13] DAA, Parker letters, 21 May 1816, Lawson to Parker.
[14] R. GIBSON, *A Social History of French Catholicism, 1789-1914*, Routledge, London 1989, 139.
[15] SAA, Box 6: 19/3.

the earth...his fan is in his hand to purge the wheat of the elect from the chaff that is destined to be consumed by fire".[16] This colourful imagery was applied to the recent Irish famine, as well as what Ullathorne perceived as a famine in society of a desire for God: "we see famine even unto death, and pestilence consuming what famine has left...the priests are stricken down from the altars, the chief shepherds are taken from their flocks, and of all famines, the worst has befallen us, a famine of the word of God".[17] Ullathorne continued this theme in his pastoral letter for the same year:

> We live in calamitous times...the crimes of mankind have reached a fearful height, and insult the face of heaven...need we wonder that the cataracts of the deep have burst upwards - that the passions of men, made wild by the shocks of crime, in the going and returning of their sensualities, have shaken loose the bonds of society in many nations...few alas are those who read aright what God intends by the troubles of their weary life.[18]

Ullathorne's solution to the evils of the day echoed the call of Walmesley fifty years before, the call to reparation: "when all our life is change and commotion, how can our souls be rooted in God? Let us consider our last end. Let us fast, let us weep and let us pray".[19] In 1828, Abbess Christina Chare reminded her nuns that "by the fervour of our prayers and the ardour of our love, we strive to make some reparation for the increasing wickedness of the world".[20]

Personal piety

As was emphasised in the previous chapter, the tone of English Benedictinism in the early nineteenth century was active, rather than contemplative. Yet, from the 1840s, it is possible to detect a slow revival of interest in the English mystical tradition favoured by earlier generations. This revival needs to be seen in a wider context, and especially within the Romantic Movement that originated in Germany which was "characterised by a new introspection, a preoccupation with the self's deepest aspirations and experience," together with a new emphasis on human imagination (in contrast to the emphasis on human reason in the previous century.) This in turn led to a commitment to the pursuit of beauty and meaning, which in turn evoked new interest in the spiritual life. The granting of Catholic

---

[16] *The Lenten indult of William Bernard OSB, Bishop of Hetalonia and Vicar Apostolic of the Western District, for the year 1848*, H.C. Evans, Bristol 1848, 4.
[17] *The Lenten indult*, 5
[18] *A Pastoral Letter addressed to the faithful of the Western District by W.B. Ullathorne, DD, OSB, Bishop of Hetalonia and Vicar Apostolic of the Western District*, H.C. Evans, Bristol 1848, 2.
[19] *A Pastoral Letter*, 7.
[20] SAA, Box 6, 19/18, Advent 1828.

Emancipation in 1829, and the restoration of the hierarchy in 1850 encouraged English Catholics in particular to develop their own literary culture, especially the publication of works of hagiography and new translations of the English spiritual classics such as *The Cloud of Unknowing* and the *Shewings* of Julian of Norwich. However in the early decades of the nineteenth century, English Catholic spirituality was still heavily influenced by practical concerns. The spiritual works of the Counter Reformation continued to dominate and were favoured because of their activist dynamic, works like Alfonso Rodriguez' *Practice of Religious Perfection*, and Lorenzo Scupoli's *Spiritual Combat*. Editions of these works continued to be published after 1800 and were to be found in the libraries of Benedictine monks and nuns.[21] Moreover, such works were also standard textbooks for early nineteenth-century English Benedictine novices such as the future bishop, Bernard Ullathorne, who in his autobiography recalled reading both Rodriguez and Scupoli, as well as Gobinet's *Instruction of Youth*.[22] At Ampleforth, another Christian classic, Thomas à Kempis' *The Following of Christ*, was favoured by President Bede Brewer.[23] Also at Ampleforth are preserved several collections of books belonging to early nineteenth-century Benedictine missioners in which the works already mentioned are well represented, together with other well-known Counter Reformation authors such as St Francis de Sales, whose pastoral guidance was evidently drawn upon by generations of nineteenth-century Benedictine missioners.[24]

Other favoured authors were the English secular priests John Gother and Richard Challoner, whose works were characterised by an individualistic and meditative approach to piety, as opposed to one that was

---

[21] A. RODRIGUEZ, *The Practice of Christian and Religious Perfection*, 3 volumes, J. Reynolds, Kilkenny 1806, R. Coyne, Dublin 1840-43; L. SCUPOLI, *The Spiritual Combat*, F. Needham, London 1742, T. Holliwell, Birmingham 1769, Keating & Brown, London 1816, 1828.

[22] *The Devil is a Jackass*, 39-45; C. GOBINET, *Instruction of Youth in Christian Piety*, F. Needham, London 1741, Newcastle-upon-Tyne 1783, R. Coyne, Dublin 1824.

[23] T. À KEMPIS, *The Imitation or Following of Jesus Christ*, Thomas Meighan, London 1744, J. P. Coghlan, London 1779, R. Cross, Dublin 1786, L.B. Seeley, London 1826, 1829. This work was Brewer's 'constant companion', see *AB*, 306.

[24] C. GOBINET, *The Instruction of Youth in Christian Piety* for instance, is featured in the collections of a number of missioners, notably John Fisher and John Turner. Another favourite work is *The Spiritual Entertainments of St Francis de Sales…translated from the original French by William Henry Coombes*, I. Norris, Taunton 1814. I am grateful to Father Anselm Cramer, the archivist at Ampleforth, for bringing these collections to my attention. For the influence of de Sales see SR. M.X. COMPTON, "Saint Francis de Sales and John Bede Polding OSB," *TJ*, 7 (1974) 9-18. Later in the nineteenth century at the purpose-built English Benedictine monastery and house of studies at Belmont near Hereford, the spirituality of the saint was actively promoted by the future bishop, Cuthbert Hedley. See SCOTT, "The English Benedictine Mission and missions," 314.

communal and monastic. Both Gother and Challoner's works stand in the tradition of the Counter Reformation, in that they favoured neither a retreat from the world, nor a gloomy or melancholy temper of mind. Thus Challoner's *Garden of the Soul*, first published in 1740, was pastoral and activist in its orientation, as can be gleaned from its alternative title: *A Manual of Spiritual Exercises and Instructions for Christians, who (living in the world) aspire to Devotion.* Its practical spirituality probably ensured its continued popularity with English Benedictine missioners in the period after 1795, and the work, in its various editions, finds a place in most of the book collections of individual missioners now preserved at Ampleforth.[25] One of the most unusual editions of this work is that by Placid Metcalfe, onetime monk of Ampleforth, who produced an edition of it in Welsh in 1837, perhaps for the use of his congregation at the mission of Newport in Monmouthshire.[26]

Indications of personal spirituality in other Benedictine houses can be gleaned from specific sources. At Douai, where the community of St Edmund settled in 1818, it took several decades to build up the library, but the auctioneer's catalogue of the volumes left there after the expulsion of the community in 1903 reveals an eclectic collection of spiritual texts.[27] Alongside the works of the early Christian Fathers are listed those of Rodriguez, Challoner, à Kempis, Francis de Sales, and the English Cisalpinists Charles Butler and John Fletcher. As may have been expected, the provenance and character of St Edmund's as an English *petit seminaire* in France also led to a large collection of French spiritual works, among which were titles by Fénelon, Gobinet, and devotional manuals designed for French seminarians, such as those compiled by Monsignor Émery of St Sulpice in Paris. An inventory drawn up by the nuns at Abbot's Salford in 1825 lists among the "books of piety" not only 'Father Baker's works' but Rodriguez' *Treatise on Christian Perfection* and the works of Butler, Benedict Macdonald and St Francis de Sales.[28]

---

[25] *The Garden of the Soul: or, A Manual of Spiritual Exercises, and Instructions, for Christians, by…Dr Richard Challoner,* Catherine Finn, Kilkenny 1779, J.P. Coghlan, London 1781, 1800 , J. Smart, Wolverhampton 1801, Rockcliff & Duckworth, Liverpool 1832, Thomas Bolland, York 1839, Rockcliff, & Ellis, Liverpool 1840.
[26] *Llyfr Gweddi y Catholig; Nou Ymarfrion Bywd Cristionogol, yn ol Arthawiaethau Gwir Eglwys Jesu Crist, ac yn ol Egwyddorion ac Yspryd Ei Efengyl Ef,* Edward Metcalfe, Lle'rpwll 1837; J. GILLOW, *A Biographical Dictionary of the English Catholics,* 4: 570.
[27] *Catalogue de la Bibliothèque des Pères Bénédictins Anglais de Douai,* privately printed, Douai 1904.
[28] SAA, Box 4, 18 bis.

Contemplative Prayer

The 1784 Constitutions of the English Benedictine Congregation, which continued to be re-published intermittently during the nineteenth century until the new constitutions of 1889, repeated the traditional obligation for monks, whether conventual or missioner, to spend half an hour a day in mental (contemplative) prayer. There was no mention of the prayer of affections, desolations and consolations that had been included in the 1661 Constitutions, no doubt as a result of the influence of the English Benedictine writer, Father Augustine Baker (1575-1641).[29] Given that the late eighteenth century favoured a more utilitarian spirituality, this is hardly surprising. In the eyes of several early nineteenth-century commentators, such as Charles Butler, it was not the Enlightenment, but the effects of the earlier Quietist controversy that "had brought devotion itself into discredit, and thrown ridicule on the holiness of an interior life".[30]

Signs of a re-discovery of the importance of the interior life among English Benedictine monks can be detected within the first few decades of their return to England in the 1790s. Thus President Bede Brewer, who had had a distinguished academic career at the Sorbonne in the 1770s, in his last years at Ampleforth "appeared to give up all his literary pursuits' and confine 'his reading to a few works on Spirituality...Prayer and Meditation may be said to be his constant occupation". Moreover, "in the exhortations he made to the Community, he frequently attempted to impress upon their minds that Priests ought to be men of prayer and what he preached to others he faithfully practised himself".[31]

Father Augustine Baker

During the eighteenth century, a distinctive feature of English Benedictine spirituality had been the practice of contemplative prayer in the tradition of the English late medieval mystical writers such as Julian of Norwich (c1342-1413) and Richard Rolle (c1300-49). A leading figure of this renaissance had been Father Augustine Baker who fostered this form of prayer particularly the English Benedictine nuns at Cambrai.[32] Although the spiritual formation of the earliest monks of St Gregory's, Douai, was firmly centred on Baker's teaching, through his disciples Peter Salvin and Serenus Cressy, Baker's influence had long been in decline in that community by the time of its migration to England. Bakerism had not lost its appeal for the nuns, despite the fact that the community founded in Cambrai lost most of their precious

---

[29] On Baker's teaching see D. LUNN, *The English Benedictines 1540-1688*, 213-217.
[30] CHINNICI, *The English Catholic Enlightenment*, 183.
[31] *AB*, 306.
[32] SCOTT, *Gothic Rage Undone*, 127-128.

Baker holographs and books at the French Revolution. The spirit of Baker continued to be passed on through the new post-revolution generation of nuns. The English nuns of the community of Our Lady of Good Hope (which settled at Colwich in 1834) succeeded, in spite of the Revolution, in maintaining their strong spiritual tradition of Bakerism. Many Baker manuscripts were still in the community's possession when it settled in England, and interest in Baker's teaching endured due to the determination of Mother Teresa Catherine Macdonald.[33] The Colwich nuns were responsible for passing on the Baker tradition to their chaplain, Benedict Dullard, who, according to Bishop Ullathorne, had the spirit of Father Baker.[34] Dullard had been professed at Douai for the revived Lamspringe community at Broadway, and he and two other monks from this community can be said to have preserved the Baker tradition that was active at Lamspringe right through until the mid-nineteenth century. Wilfrid Price made a copy of Baker's manuscript edition of the Rule of St Benedict in 1838. This copy is now at Stanbrook, where Anselm Kenyon, the last surviving monk professed at Lamspringe, ended his days. Among his papers after his death in 1850 were discovered some fragments of spiritual verse belonging to Dunstan Hutchinson, onetime novice master and prior at Lamspringe, who had been a Baker disciple and had made a copy of Baker's edition of the Benedictine rule.[35]

Geoffrey Scott contends that although interest in Baker declined in the monasteries at Douai, Dieulouard and Paris, "many Bakerite missioners carried their strain of Bakerism into Catholic households where it was discreetly refashioned to suit a lay audience".[36] Whilst this may have been the case in the late seventeenth century, there is no direct evidence that subsequent generations of missioners and laity were Baker disciples.

Evidence of a slow revival of Baker can be detected in the communities of St Gregory and St Laurence. In 1823 Prior Bernard Barber of Downside wrote to a confrere to request a copy of Baker's *Sancta Sophia*.[37] Barber was venerated by Bernard Ullathorne, who recalled that his superior's

---

[33] Teresa Catherine McDonald, "Some reflections on the Holy Rule of our most Holy Father, the glorious St Benedict," in C. BOWDEN & L.LUX- STERRIX (eds), *English Convents in Exile, 1600-1800*, Pickering & Chatto, London 2012, 2: 237; B. ROWELL, "Baker's influence on Benedictine nuns," in M. WOODWARD (ed.), *That Mysterious Man: Essays on Augustine Baker*, Three Peaks Press, Abergavenny 2001, 87-88.

[34] B. ROWELL, "Absent Brethren: The Monastery of Our Lady of Good Hope and the English Benedictine Congregation," unpublished paper given to the English Benedictine History Symposium, April 2000.

[35] See J. CLARK (ed.), Fr. *Augustine Baker OSB, St Benedict's Rule*, Institut für Anglistik und Amerikanistik, Salzburg 2005, iii; M. TRURAN, "Spirituality: Fr Baker's Legacy," in CRAMER, (ed.), *Lamspringe*, 95.

[36] G. SCOTT, "The Image of Augustine Baker," in Woodward (ed.), *That Mysterious Man*, 92-122.

[37] DAB, F 32, 14 April 1823, Barber to Lorymer.

greatest gift "was his direction of souls...he encouraged them to denude their imagination and transcend above the suggestions of the inferior soul...taught them the real tendency of their soul amidst aridity and darkness; and inspired them with patience and with courage".[38] Barber was probably responsible for encouraging Ullathorne to read Baker. The bishop noted that when visiting Australia in 1840, among the "valuable ascetic writings" he took with him, was Father Baker's *Sancta Sophia*.[39] Barber, later President of the English Benedictines, ended his days as chaplain to the nuns at Stanbrook. There a copy of Cressy's *Life* of Baker has been preserved, which is inscribed with the name of Barber, and the date of 1824.[40] The community of St Laurence, to which Baker himself had belonged, had kept a copy of *Sancta Sophia* on the open shelves in the library at Dieulouard, but "judging from the number of copies which have survived" at Ampleforth, "it was quite, but not very, widely read".[41] It was only in the 1830s that a revival of interest in Baker in the community at Ampleforth came through Anselm Cockshoot, who made a copy of a 1678 Baker manuscript in 1837.[42] As Prior at Ampleforth, Cockshoot actively worked to improve the quality of monastic observance and in 1845 he sent Austin Bury and Laurence Shepherd for studies to Parma in Italy. But it is also likely that he was responsible for introducing the young Shepherd to Baker when, on his return from Italy, Shepherd was appointed novice master at Ampleforth. He recalled:

> When I was entrusted with my first real set of five promising young novices, I began in all good earnest to train them. I took every book I could lay hands on. One of the elders warned me against Father Baker: but I took him from the Library, and became enamoured by his style...I epitomised Sancta Sophia and passed it thus to my novices.[43]

Shepherd believed that Baker "was the holiest man that ever belonged to our Congregation",[44] and when he was appointed novice master at the newly established house of studies at Belmont near Hereford in 1859, Shepherd was well placed to impart Baker's teaching to all the novices of the Congregation.

---

[38] E.C. BUTLER, "Record of the century," *DR*, 33 (1914) 30.
[39] *The Devil is a Jackass*, 205.
[40] *Memorials of Father Augustine Baker and Other Documents, CRS (R)*, 33 (1933) 274-293; SAA, Baker MS 12.
[41] CRAMER, *Ampleforth*, 196.
[42] *Memorials*, 275.
[43] SAA, B. ANSTEY, MS *Life of the Rev. Dom L. Shepherd* (1897) 18.
[44] ANSTEY, MS *Life*, 30.

Although the full flowering of this Baker revival properly belongs to a later period, nonetheless important seeds were sown in the years before 1850.[45]

Bishop Bernard Ullathorne is representative of the new generation of English Benedictines, trained in England, who recognised the need for a more contemplative spirituality. In 1842, in his *Sermons with Prefaces* Ullathorne perceived that contemporary believers yearned for "the mysterious and supernatural" and were "grateful for whatever may exalt them above their trials and restore hope to their future". What was needed was a religion not of the head, but of the heart, for "there is an appetite for profound emotion in the human soul…" Ullathorne continued: "every soul…yearns for a mysterious and divine emotion". He contended that the contemporary method of preaching, based on the countering of objections to faith, did not satisfy the hearers, for "man wants divine influence to fill the soul with a divine light and move her with spiritual emotion". Ullathorne countered the view that "the English mind is too calm and rational to draw profit" from the writings of the Fathers, or the great medieval English mystical writers.[46] He commended the Fathers to his readers, pointing out that many of their writings were now "accessible to most of us" through new editions being produced by the 1830s.[47] For Ullathorne, the value of the Fathers was "their profound and intimate conviction, arising out of their constant union with God. Their inward life was one of faith, of love of prayer", and, Ullathorne believed, they provided an "irresistible attraction" to "the sacred scriptures themselves".[48] He went on to sing the virtues of the medieval English mystical writers, asserting that "the admirable treatises of that profound contemplative, Father Baker…the Scale of Perfection, written by that eminent contemplative, Father Walter Hilton…and the Cloud of Unknowing" were deemed "worthy to be placed on the same shelf as St Teresa and St Francis of Sales, all of which with many others are now made accessible in our own language".[49]

---

[45] See the ground-breaking article on this subject by G. SCOTT, "Something of the Struggle for Belmont's Soul," in A. BERRY (ed.), *Belmont Abbey Celebrating 150 Years*, Gracewing, Leominster 2012, 72-109.

[46] W. ULLATHORNE, DD OSB, *Sermons with Prefaces,* T. Jones, London 1842, 7-10.

[47] The Oxford Movement in England was responsible, for instance for the publication of *The Library of the Fathers,* beginning with *A Library of the Fathers of the Holy Catholic Church edited by the Rev. E.B. Pusey…the Rev. J.H. Newman,* John Henry Parker, London 1838.

[48] ULLATHORNE, *Sermons and Prefaces,* 17, 26.

[49] ULLATHORNE, *Sermons and Prefaces,* 29, 36. In 1833 Ullathorne assembled a collection of "a thousand volumes of Theology, Fathers, Canon Law", to be taken to Australia. See *The Devil is a Jackass,* 60 n.1. For a more detailed description of the collection see J. FLETCHER, "The Library of St Patrick's College, Manly," *The Book Collector,* 29 (1980) 179-200.

Benedictine writing

Already during the eighteenth century, a number of monks, notably Anselm Mannock, had begun writing and disseminating catechetical works. These were based on two forms already in existence: Benedictine manuscript compilations and those based on traditional English works already in print, such as the Manual, Primer and Douai Catechism. Both forms are evident in the work of Mannock, whose works became popular because of their practical directions, so much so that one of his works, *The Poor Man's Controversy* continued to be published long after his death in 1764.[50] In a similar vein were works such as *The Whole Duty of a Christian,* and *A Manual of Daily Prayers* from the pen of Bath missioner Benedict Pembridge,[51] whilst another important eighteenth-century English Benedictine work, Bishop Charles Walmesley's *Catechism for First Communicants,* was re-published in 1829, the first edition having appeared in 1781.

From the late eighteenth century, catechisms became a more important feature of English Catholic life, particularly in the new town chapels in areas such as Bath and Liverpool. Here missioners recognised that the liturgy needed to be made more accessible to the laity, through works that took two forms: firstly those which contained explicit catechesis on the liturgy; secondly, those which were designed to enhance personal devotion and participation in the liturgy itself. In 1823, Benedict Glover, missioner at Little Crosby near Liverpool published *Explanation of the Prayers and Ceremonies of the Holy Sacrifice of the Mass,* the preface of which explained that the author "ever since he has been charged with the care of souls, has observed with grief that many derived not that advantage from the sacred mysteries which he thought they might", and that therefore the motive "which first induced him to compose these instructions, was to furnish poor uneducated people with a plain and simple explanation of the Mass, because he found nothing exactly like them in the English language".[52] The work fulfils its title, as a step-by-step commentary on the Mass, written in a simple, intelligible style. Dr George Oliver later commented that Glover's was "a most useful work, full of unction, wisdom and moderation".[53] Glover included some directions on how the laity should

---

[50] J.A. MANNOCK, *The Poor Man's Controversy,* published by his friends, London 1769, R. Cross, Dublin 1794, B. Dormin, J. Robinson, Baltimore 1815, J. Booker, Liverpool 1843. For Mannock and Pembridge, see SCOTT, *Gothic Rage Undone,* 138-141. Account books for the South Province of the English Benedictines show that it was responsible for financing the re-publication of Mannock's catechism right up to 1843. See DA, IV.B (iv) MS 165.
[51] M.P(EMBRIDGE)., *A Manual of Prayers and Duties of a Christian, with Historical Lessons from the Old and New Testaments, very useful for Children,* C. Pugh, Hereford 1777.
[52] GLOVER, *An Explanation of the Prayers and Ceremonies of the Holy Sacrifice of the Mass,* iii.
[53] OLIVER, *Collections,* 517.

hear Mass, recommending that they should "join the priest in saying the same prayers as he says", for "the Church has permitted the sacred ritual to be translated, and the laity have their missals as well as the clergy".[54] Although he commended the laity to use missals, Glover recognised that the prayers of the Mass were "so profound and sublime...that their meaning cannot be comprehended but by persons who have considerable information on these subjects".[55] He contended that "...a missal to a child is a sealed up fountain from which he can draw no streams of devotion".[56] Glover appears to be ahead of his time in discouraging the practice of private devotions during Mass, for he criticised those who "employ[ed] the time of Mass in private devotions", for he believed they showed "a great want of judgment in withdrawing their attention from the most important of objects".[57]

The second tradition in the development of the Benedictine catechism, namely as a tool for personal devotion and participation, needs to be seen in a wider context. The growth in urban congregations at the end of the eighteenth century helped to foster a movement to introduce the vernacular into collective worship, especially in devotional services. It was development that was keenly advocated by many English Cisalpinists. Among these were some prominent English Benedictines, notably Cuthbert Wilks and Gregory Gregson, the Benedictine chaplain to the Throckmorton family. Gregson had already incurred the displeasure of the Benedictine bishop, Charles Walmesley, by publishing, in 1791, a prayer book called *Devout Miscellany* which Walmesley condemned because of its use of Protestant versions of the Bible and translation of parts of the Ritual from Latin into English.[58]

As early as 1778, the Liverpool Benedictine missioner, Benedict Macdonald published his *Layman's Afternoon Devotion*, in the preface of which he advocated the need to encourage greater lay participation in the liturgy, regretting the fact that "Evening Prayers are seldom, if ever, frequented by the bulk of the people".[59] Macdonald's work was largely based on Challoner's evening devotions in the *Garden of the Soul* and consisted of the Litany of Saints and a number of prayers and responses from the liturgical offices of Vespers and Compline. Macdonald however was prevented by English Benedictine censors from editing the unintelligible sections of the psalms. The work proved to be so popular that it was republished in 1793, and again in 1820, with the addition to its title, *as used at Brownedge, Ormskirk and Warrington Catholic chapels*, all of which were

---

[54] GLOVER, *An Explanation*, 165-166.
[55] GLOVER, *An Explanation*, 166.
[56] GLOVER, *An Explanation*, 168.
[57] GLOVER, *An Explanation*, 169-70.
[58] SCOTT, *Gothic Rage Undone*, 141.
[59] (A.B MACDONALD), *The Layman's Afternoon Devotion*, Walker & Kay, Preston 1778, 1793, 1820, v.

Benedictine. A later example of such a work can be seen in the collection of prayers published in 1816, by James Calderbank, the Benedictine missioner at Bath.[60] In contrast to Macdonald's work, Calderbank's is a much shorter publication, and unlike Macdonald, he includes the original Latin alongside the English translations of the psalms, hymns and prayers of Sunday Vespers, an indication that Calderbank did not favour the introduction of the vernacular in the liturgy. This view was shared by Glover who in 1823 in the work mentioned above defended the preservation of Latin in the liturgy, asserting that "great would be the inconveniences of using for public worship any language which is always changing or growing obsolete".[61]

Another English Benedictine author in this period was Augustine Birdsall, President of the Congregation from 1826 until his death in 1837. Whilst missioner at Cheltenham, Birdsall published translations of two French devotional works, no doubt for the edification of French aristocratic Catholic émigrés who were attracted to the spa town. First to appear was his translation of the 1714 work of Étienne-François Vernage, *Christian Reflections for Every Day in the Month*.[62] This was followed in 1834 by Birdsall's translation of an unknown French author's work, *Christian Reflections on the Advantages of Poverty; intended principally for People in Humble Life*. The theme of the work was an encouragement to the poor to accept their lot, and was followed by an appendix containing various prayers and admonitions.[63] This second work was perhaps published by Birdsall for another, less distinguished group in his congregation, namely the Irish labourers who had begun to arrive in the town to find work on the new railways.

In the north of England, at Holme-on-Spalding in the East Riding of Yorkshire, where he was chaplain to the Stourton family, John Turner, who was mentioned at the beginning of this chapter, found a new interest away from his collection of revolutionary pamphlets, writing a large collection of sermons and "afternoon lectures" in his clear copperplate hand. These manuscripts reveal an active concern to educate the congregation, not merely in the essentials of Christian doctrine and the sacraments, but also in the practice of prayer, to which Turner devoted over eighty pages.[64] Turner encouraged his listeners to practise not only vocal prayer but also the prayer

---

[60] *Bath Chapel Prayers*, privately printed, Bath 1816. On Calderbank see D.A. BELLENGER, "Calderbank, James (1770–1821)," *ODNB*, <http://www.oxforddnb.com/view/article/4371> [accessed 9 May 2013].
[61] GLOVER, *An Explanation*, 191.
[62] J. BIRDSALL, *Christian Reflections for Every Day in the Month*, G.A. Williams, Cheltenham 1822.
[63] J. BIRDSALL, *Christian Reflections on the Advantages of Poverty*, W.E. Andrews, London 1834.
[64] AA, MC147, 6U68, J. TURNER, *Sermons for Sundays and Feasts; Sermons for the different Sundays and Principal Feasts of the Year*, 2 volumes; *Sunday Afternoon Lectures*, or *Instructions on the Christian Doctrine*, 3 volumes.

called <u>mental prayer</u> because ye tongue has no share in it…both ye one and ye other are necessary: for how can a person exercise himself in continually acquiring yet virtues of Jesus Christ? The only means of stopping the progress of ye disorders which reign in the world, is ye frequent use of mental prayer and meditation on the truths of salvation.[65]

This passage, and others in Turner's catechesis on prayer, reflect his own experience of having been both inspired by and disillusioned with the French Revolution. Its idealism of social equality had underpinned the importance for him of Christian fraternity and equality and in particular the role of the church as a "holy place, where ye rich join with ye poor, ye just with ye guilty", a place in which is offered "a holy violence to God and engage him to grant us what we ask for".[66] On the other hand, Turner came to reject the utilitarian enlightenment spirituality in which he had been formed, believing that in essence, prayer sprang not from the intellect, but from the heart. He told his listeners: "it is yr heart that prays…it is your heart alone which [God] pays attention to…whenever prayer is ye expression of ye heart, it is always fervent".[67]

Continental influences

As has been demonstrated in the previous chapter, the English Benedictines were slow to respond to the monastic revival taking place on the continent. However, important foundations were laid in the period before 1850, when a number of English Benedictines were beginning to be influenced by the French abbot, Prosper Guéranger and his two principal published works, the *Institutions liturgiques* (1840-1851), and *L'Année liturgique* published in five volumes between 1841 and 1846. Mention has already been made of Laurence Shepherd, who found in Guéranger's work the ideal texts to inspire a revival of liturgical and spiritual life at Ampleforth, and later, at Stanbrook. Much later in the century Shepherd found himself unwittingly at the centre of a major debate within the English Congregation, where Guéranger's ideas were used as ammunition by those monks who wished to see a greater monastic observance in the houses of the Congregation.[68]

Shepherd however was not the first English Benedictine to encounter the French monastic reformer. Bernard Ullathorne recalled meeting the celebrated abbot in 1837 when both men were en route to Rome.[69] Ten years

---

[65] J. TURNER, *Sunday Afternoon Lectures*, 1: 374.
[66] TURNER, *Sunday Afternoon Lectures*, 1:387.
[67] TURNER, *Sunday Afternoon Lectures* 1: 375.
[68] M. TRURAN,"Dom James Laurence Shepherd's Vision of the EBC," *EBHS*, privately printed, 1985, 1-6.
[69] *The Devil is a Jackass*, 142.

later, Brother Edmund Moore, a monk from Downside set out on the long voyage to Australia with his confrère, Bede Polding, who had recently been appointed the first Archbishop of Sydney. Moore noted in his diary that on the voyage Polding gave him a review of *L'Année liturgique* to read.[70] Furthermore, it is clear that the French monastic reformer was already being read at Douai in the 1840s, for among its large collection of French theological books are listed a number of Guéranger's earlier works. Nevertheless it was Shepherd who became the principal channel through which Guéranger's reform reached the English Benedictine Congregation. In 1849 Dom Jean-Baptiste-François Pitra, monk of Solesmes, visited both Douai and Stanbrook (of which he was later to become Cardinal Protector) and spoke about the work of Guéranger.[71] The seeds of this revival may only have just begun to be planted by 1850, but they were soon to flower and influence a profound change in the Congregation's perception of itself. The first evidence of this change can be seen in the solemn opening in 1860 of the new purpose-built Gothic monastery of St Michael at Belmont, at which Abbot Guéranger was present.[72]

Some English Benedictines resisted the new devotions being introduced into England after 1840 by the newly founded Italian orders of the Passionists and the Rosminians, devotions that were often in stark contrast to the sober, quiet spirituality represented by Challoner's *Garden of the Soul.* Most English Benedictines in the early nineteenth century had little time for either asceticism or mysticism, and were generally not very receptive to the devotions being introduced into England after 1840. However, the contemporary impact of such devotions on English Catholics needs to be measured with some caution. Mary Heimann has convincingly argued in her monograph, *Catholic Devotion in Victorian England,* that evidence from statistics fails to support the traditionally held view that the introduction of such continental devotions indicated a dramatic change in English Catholic devotional life in this period. Furthermore, it has often been forgotten that many of the devotions commonly believed by later commentators to be "continental", "Italian", or "ultramontane", (such as Benediction and the Rosary) were actually already practised, albeit it in a more sober way, by English Catholics.[73]

The devotional life of many English Benedictines already included devotion to the Sacred Heart, so favoured by the new Italian orders, for the devotion had a long history in the Benedictine order, following the tradition

---

[70] *DR,* 32 (1913) 197.
[71] SAA, Annals, 1, 650.
[72] E. EDWARDS,"The Influence on the EBC of Dom Guéranger's Revival," *EBHS* privately printed, 1975, 1-3; E. EDWARDS & M. TRURAN, "Dom James Laurence Shepherd," *EBHS* (1985) 39-48; G. SCOTT, "Baker's critics" in, G. SCOTT (ed.), *Dom Augustine Baker (1575-1641),* Gracewing, Leominster 2012, 191-192.
[73] HEIMANN, *Catholic Devotion in Victorian England,* 38-69.

of the early medieval Benedictine mystic, St Gertrude, for whom devotion to the Sacred Heart represented a deeper penetration into the mystery of Christ living in His Church through the liturgy. In 1829 Abbess Christina Chare commended the devotion to her nuns at Abbot's Salford, reminding them "you are particularly consecrated to the Sacred Heart by the vows of your Holy Profession...He presents you His Sacred Heart that you may enjoy a close and familiar union with it...by cultivating a true devotion to the Sacred Heart, you will find a model of every virtue".[74]

One English Benedictine mission where the new devotions were introduced with enthusiasm was Coventry, where Bernard Ullathorne, with the help of Margaret Mary Hallahan, who acted as sacristan and teacher, introduced the singing of the Litany of Loreto to the Blessed Virgin Mary, outdoor processions with the statue of Our Lady, and May devotions.[75] Mother Margaret was also instrumental in re-introducing the practice of placing a lamp on the sanctuary near the tabernacle.[76] Ullathorne led the people on a reflection of "the Catholic Antiquities of the city and its old religious customs", and encouraged them to abandon the traditional Lady Godiva procession through the town and take part instead in the solemn ritual that it had supplanted, namely the solemn procession of the Blessed Sacrament. In 1844 Ullathorne appointed the Rosminian, Father Luigi Gentili, to conduct a mission, during which Gentili proclaimed, "You have had your procession of your lady, now we shall have one of Our Lady".[77] Ullathorne at this time was planning the building of a new splendid Gothic church, which will be considered in a later chapter. After becoming a bishop, Ullathorne was active in the promotion of more fervent devotion to the Blessed Virgin Mary, and was the first cleric in England to visit La Salette, the French mountain shrine where the Blessed Virgin was reported to have appeared to peasant children in 1846. The book he wrote on the subject in 1854 was influential in the propagation of the shrine.[78]

Ullathorne's enthusiasm for Gentili and the Rosminians spread north to his Benedictine brethren in Liverpool, where in 1846, Gentili preached a parish mission at the church of St Peter, Seel Street.[79] However, his enthusiasm was not shared by President Bernard Barber, who in 1848 advised Prior Ambrose Prest at Ampleforth not to invite "Fr Dominic Barberi

---

[74] SAA, 4 August 1829, Box 6: 4 August 1829 MS conferences of Abbess Christina Chare.
[75] See *Life of Mother Margaret Mary Hallahan...by Mother Francis Raphael Drane*, Longmans, London 1934, chapter 3; *The Devil is a Jackass*, 270; F.J. CWIEKOWSKI, *The English Bishops and the First Vatican Council*, Universitaires de Louvain, Louvain 1971, 30.
[76] *Life of Mother Margaret Mary Hallahan*, 69-71.
[77] *Life of Mother Margaret Mary Hallahan*, 111-113.
[78] W. ULLATHORNE, *The Holy Mountain of La Salette*, Richardson, London 1854.
[79] LIVERPOOL RECORD OFFICE, 282 PET 3/1, "Seel Street Notice Book, 1845-51."

or Fr Gentili – the latter least of all" to give the community their annual retreat.[80] The English Benedictine attitude to continental devotional practices was coloured above all by practical rather than spiritual concerns. This can be seen in two specific examples, the first involving Peter Augustine Baines, the Ampleforth monk who became Vicar Apostolic of the Western District in 1829, and the second, involving the deliberate promotion of new English Benedictine confraternities. Although, as the next chapter will relate, Baines spent most of his episcopate battling with his former brethren, he retained the seasoned reflexes of a Benedictine missioner he had gained during his years at Bath. These seem to have influenced him in a particular episode which was to bring him into conflict again with the Roman authorities. This concerned his opposition to the introduction of public prayers for the conversion of England composed by Nicholas Wiseman, the future Cardinal Archbishop of Westminster.

Like his fellow Benedictine bishop, Bernard Ullathorne, Baines had encouraged the new Italian orders arriving in England, especially the Rosminians, whose founder Baines had met in Rome in 1827, and invited the Rosminians to teach at the new college he had founded at Prior Park near Bath, where he was happy to allow Luigi Gentili to introduce various devotions, including the Litany of Loreto and the wearing of scapulars and devotional medals. Like Nicholas Wiseman, Rector of the English College in Rome, Baines shared a respect and admiration for these new religious, believing them to hold the key to the Catholic revival in England. Although he was the first English Vicar Apostolic to employ these new religious in his district, Baines came to have great reservations about their methods of introducing their spirituality in a predominantly Protestant country.

The issue came to a head when Baines published a pastoral letter in 1840 forbidding the introduction of public prayers for the conversion of England into his district.[81] These prayers had been drawn up by Wiseman at the instigation of George Ignatius Spencer, a former Anglican clergyman who joined the newly-established Italian congregation of Passionists. Baines was suspicious of Spencer, regarding him as a representative of new converts who were full of their own pride, quick to dictate to their new superiors, and all too eager to take up "dubious" devotions, such as to the Immaculate Heart of Mary. Baines objected to the introduction of public prayers for the conversion of England for two reasons: firstly, he believed that because they were to be offered publicly they would provoke unnecessary Protestant hostility against Catholics; and secondly, he believed the actual cause to be a futile one.[82]

---

[80] AA MS 262, no.106, Stanbrook, 4 February 1848, Barber to Prest.
[81] See E.B. STUART, "Bishop Baines and his 1840 Lenten Pastoral," *DR*, 105 (1987) 40-59.
[82] STUART, "Bishop Baines and his 1840 Lenten Pastoral," 49.

The subsequent publication of Baines' pastoral letter in which he criticised the zeal and extremism of some of the new converts caused a furore, not merely with Wiseman, but with the Roman authorities, to whom Baines was summoned in May 1840 to answer some twenty charges against his pastoral. The dispute brought into clear opposition the different perceptions of Baines on the one hand, and Wiseman and the Roman authorities on the other. The Roman authorities were almost totally ignorant of the religious situation in England, due to poor lines of communication between them and the Vicars Apostolic. Wiseman was based in Rome and had had no direct experience of England since 1818. He was too reliant on the exaggerated and distorted reports of new converts such as Spencer who believed that the conversion of England to Catholicism was imminent. Baines, in contrast, was only too well aware of the English religious situation, having been the Benedictine missioner at Bath. His Western District, which until 1840 included all of Wales, contained very few practising Catholics, unlike the other districts of England where the Catholic population was on the increase. He had direct experience of Protestants, particularly those who, unlike Spencer, did not belong to the High Church tradition, and this experience convinced him of the need to tread a careful, diplomatic path and not take any action that might incite Protestant hostility.[83] Baines gained support for his position from large numbers of English Catholics, among whom many, such as the secular priest-historian, John Lingard were appalled by the new devotions being introduced in England, and suspicious of the motives of the new converts from the Oxford Movement. However it is important to emphasise that Baines' outlook differed from Lingard's. Baines shared with Lingard a sceptical view as to the prospects of the conversion of England but this is as far as the similarities between them stretched. Whilst Lingard was revolted by all foreign devotions, Baines had actually been responsible for introducing some of them, objecting only to those he believed did not have Papal approval. Baines' outlook was a result of his experience as a Benedictine missioner and the environment in which he lived and worked.[84]

Many English Benedictines may well have shared the disapproval of Baines concerning some of the devotions being introduced into England, but they were happy to commend them to the faithful, particularly if doing so furthered their own ends. Promoting certain devotions enabled them to bolster their claims for autonomy on the missions they served in opposition

---

[83] In the 1820s Baines had engaged in debate with the Archdeacon of Bath, so was well versed in the doctrinal issues separating Anglicans and Catholics: P.A. BAINES, *A Letter to Charles Abel Moysey, Archdeacon of Bath...*, H. Gye, Bath 1821; BAINES, *A Defence of the Christian Religion...in a second letter to Charles Abel Moysey...*, H. Gye, Bath 1822; BAINES, *A Remonstrance, in a third letter to Charles Abel Moysey...*, J.A. Robinson, Manchester 1824.

[84] STUART, "Bishop Baines and his 1840 Lenten Pastoral," 53-55.

to the bishops. They were helped in 1838 by Pope Gregory XVI, who issued a decree which once again allowed English Catholics to benefit from indulgences and the membership of spiritual confraternities and other similar associations, which bound its members both collectively and individually to the practice of certain devotions and the wearing of a scapular or medal. During the 1830s and 1840s new devotions designed to assist Catholics in making reparation appeared, and found expression in confraternities, such as the Archconfraternity of Notre Dame des Victoires, which was specifically intended to be an association of prayers for the conversion of sinners. Gradually, especially in France, a network of clerically-controlled confraternities grew up, which were under the direct control of the secular clergy. Thus from the 1840s, English Benedictine missioners enlarged their particular spheres of influence by establishing confraternities which had the loosest of ties with the bishops, such as the "Association of Prayer in honour of the Immaculate Heart of the Blessed Virgin Mary", which was established at St Peter, Seel Street in Liverpool in 1845 and was affiliated to the Archconfraternity of Our Lady of Victories in Paris.[85] Confraternities had been a feature of English Benedictine spirituality in an earlier period as a means of asserting monastic independence from the Vicars Apostolic,[86] and so, as Geoffrey Scott observes, this practice "marked a return to the rivalry in the penal period when missionary clergy competed against each other for pastoral control by promising their own peculiar indulgence and privileges".[87]

Continuity rather than change, therefore, characterised the devotional temper of English Benedictinism in the first half of the nineteenth century. For the most part the practical, sober spirituality of the eighteenth century endured, both through the works of Challoner and the classical writers of the Counter-Reformation period. The adoption of apocalyptic writing was the only significant change within the overall landscape of devotional literature, a genre best suited to a prolonged period of uncertainty and anxiety. Yet the revival of interest in contemplative prayer, and the monastic reform movement, both of which only gained ascendancy later in the century, began to germinate in this early period, when the English Benedictines realised that to guarantee their place in the rapidly developing English Catholic church, they needed to imitate the Gospel virtues of Mary as well as Martha. Yet, for the most part their energies in the early nineteenth century were spent on more practical matters, such as defending their missionary enclaves against interference from the Vicars Apostolic, and it is this issue that will be explored in the following chapter.

---

[85] *Association of Prayer...in honour of the Immaculate Heart of the Blessed Virgin Mary...established...at St Peter's, Seel Street, Liverpool, and affiliated to the Arch-Confraternity of Our Lady of Victories at Paris*, privately printed, Liverpool 1845.
[86] SCOTT, *Gothic Rage Undone*, 133-134.
[87] G. SCOTT, "The English Benedictine Confraternity," *DR*, 105 (1987) 155.

1. Richard Marsh OSB (1762-1843)
Prior of St Laurence's, 1789-1802, 1806-1810
Re-founded St Edmund's, Douai, 1818
President-General, 1822-26, 1837-42

[portrait at Douai Abbey by C. Mayer, 1837]

2. Peter Augustine Baines OSB (1787-1843)
Co-adjutor of the Western District, 1823-1829
Vicar Apostolic of the Western District, 1829-1843

[portrait at Ampleforth Abbey]

3. John Augustine Birdsall OSB (1775-1837)
President-General, 1826-1837

[portrait at Downside Abbey]

4. John Bede Polding OSB (1794-1877)
Vicar Apostolic of New Holland, 1834-1842
First Archbishop of Sydney, 1842-1877

[portrait at Downside Abbey]

5. William Bernard Ullathorne OSB (1806-1889)
Vicar Apostolic of the Western District, 1846-1850
First bishop of Birmingham, 1850-1888

[portrait at Downside by Richard Burchett, 1852]

6. William Bernard Allen Collier OSB (1803-1890)
Prior of St Edmund's, 1826-1833
Procurator in Rome, 1833-1840
Vicar Apostolic of the Mauritius, 1840-1847
Bishop of Port Louis, 1847-1863

[portrait at Douai Abbey]

7. James Laurence Shepherd OSB (1826-1885)
Translator of Abbot Prosper Guéranger's Année Liturgique
Chaplain and Vicar to the nuns at Stanbrook, 1863-1885

[photograph in the archives of Ampleforth Abbey]

8. Water-colour of the buildings at Downside
built to the design of H.E. Goodridge (1797-1864)

9. The old chapel at Ampleforth, c. 1810
Sketched by Dom Maurus Powell OSB

CHAPTER 4

Of Rabbits and Hedgehogs:
Monks, Bishops and the English Mission.

A rabbit had burrowed for herself a very comfortable hole and had long enjoyed it without being molested. One day a hedgehog passed by and spying the rabbit's hole, said to himself, 'that will do very nicely for me, as the storms of winter will soon be here. I will look in and if Mrs Bunny is at home, I will make myself agreeable and ask her to give me shelter'. She very kindly, but not wisely, allowed him to come in. He at first was very careful not to make himself troublesome, or to crush up against so kind a friend. But as the winter came on and the cold increased, the hedgehog pushed further and further in until his spines so hurt the rabbit that she had to complain. 'Oh,' said the hedgehog, 'I am perfectly comfortable and if you find this place too small for both of us, you had better go elsewhere'.

Reflecting in 1904 on the controversy 70 years previously between the English Benedictines and Augustine Baines, the Vicar Apostolic of the Western District, Alphonsus Morrall of Downside remarked that the dispute exemplified the above fable of the rabbit and the hedgehog, with the rabbit symbolizing the generations of Benedictines who had served the mission of Bath, and the hedgehog the Vicar Apostolic of the Western District who did his utmost to eject the monks from their mission.[1] Yet the fable could also fittingly be applied to the whole series of disputes between the English Benedictines and the bishops which were already a century old by the end of the eighteenth century, and which would take almost another century to be resolved.

This chapter will focus on the different facets of the nineteenth-century disputes which concerned ecclesiastical jurisdiction in the English Mission and will examine the entrenched positions adopted by each party. It will argue that, whilst blame can be placed on both sides for the disputes, it was the monks who showed themselves the more entrenched, stubbornly repeating old arguments and defending their corner, rather than responding positively to the new challenges that faced them in a period of English Catholic revival. The chapter will be divided into five parts: the first will set the context by examining the historical background to monastic-episcopal relations in the nineteenth century; the second will consider the disputes of the early years of the century; the third will focus on the controversy between the monks and Bishop Baines in the years 1829-1834; the fourth will examine disputes between the monks and the bishops over territorial jurisdiction, principally in Liverpool, in the years 1836-1843; and the final section will consider the attempts of the English Benedictines to gain episcopal control in

---

[1] DA, VII.A.f, MS 295, 102-103.

the decade leading up to the restoration of the English Catholic hierarchy in 1850.

Monastic-episcopal relations

From 1685 to 1850 the Vicars Apostolic nominally ruled the English Catholic Church. Although called "bishops", Vicars Apostolic had neither a chapter, nor full ordinary jurisdiction and were dependent on Rome, and specifically the Congregation of *Propaganda Fide*, for their authority.[2] In 1688 the Holy See appointed four Vicars Apostolic in England in districts designated London, Midland, Northern and Western, and it was only in 1840 that the number of these districts was increased to eight. In his district, according to canon law, the Vicar Apostolic was regarded as "the true pastor and superior of the clergy and people submitted to him, and... enjoys all those faculties which are necessary for ruling his vicariate".[3] However in practice the Vicars Apostolic encountered problems in asserting their authority, especially over regular clergy working on the English mission who came under the jurisdiction of their provincials. To complicate matters further, the real power in the English Catholic Church in the period up to the late eighteenth century was wielded by the aristocratic or gentry families, who, in Sheridan Gilley's phrase, "paid the piper and so called the tune, hiring and firing their chaplains with scant reference to the bishop".[4]

Successive Vicars Apostolic in England had attempted to subject the regular clergy to their authority, and sought support from Rome to strengthen their position.[5] Two decrees were published in 1695 by the Congregation of *Propaganda Fide* which challenged the independence of regulars on the Mission and ordered them to be subject to the Vicars Apostolic in regard to the missions. These decrees were fiercely resisted by the English Benedictines, who produced two documents in their defence: the *Mandatum* of 1628 and the bull of Pope Urban VIII of 1633 called *Plantata*, which upheld the privileges of the monks on the Mission. These missionary privileges were based on the monks' claim to have inherited the chapter rights of the medieval English monastic cathedrals, and along with these, an ordinary jurisdiction on the Mission. From the time of *Plantata*, the monks had appointed cathedral priors from among their number to further their claims, especially that of exemption from episcopal authority. However, as David Lunn pointed out, whilst the English Benedictine Congregation

---

[2] For the background see B. HEMPHILL, *The Early Vicars Apostolic in England,* Burns & Oates, London 1954. See also N. SCHOFIELD and G. SKINNER, *The English Vicars Apostolic 1688-1850,* Family Publications, Oxford 2009.
[3] E. TAUNTON, *The Law of the Church,* Kegan & Paul, London 1906, 625-626.
[4] S. GILLEY, "The Roman Catholic Church, 1780-1940," in S. GILLEY and W. SHEILS, *A History of Religion in Britain,* 348.
[5] These early disputes are dealt with in SCOTT, *Gothic Rage Undone,* 63-82.

traditionally regarded *Plantata* as "its great charter of liberties...*Plantata* bore no relation to reality, for it assumed that the (pre-reformation) monasteries still existed and were at the Pope's disposal...the bull was an irrelevance".[6] There was little new in the Benedictine armoury, for throughout the eighteenth century "old pretensions based on *Plantata* were again wearily served up to defend the status quo",[7] as can be seen in the monks' revision of the definitive text of *Plantata* in 1748.

Eventually in 1753 the Bull *Apostolicum Ministerium* forced the monks, albeit reluctantly, to recognise the jursdiction of the Vicars Apostolic, who were given full authority to approve, examine and grant faculties to all regular missioners in their districts. Furthermore, by the so-called *sexennium* requirement, every regular missioner was required to return to his monastery on the continent every six years, to live there for three months and to make a fifteen-day retreat. Later, in 1763 Rome, through *Propaganda Fide*, strengthened this requirement by insisting that the faculties of regular missioners could only be renewed, and then only for a year, by taking an oath that the fifteen-day retreat had been made. This was opposed by the English Benedictines, and in the London district Bishop Challoner petitioned Rome to replace the oath with a simple affirmation.[8]

Whilst these various Roman decrees upheld the authority of the Vicars Apostolic, their authority continued to be resisted by some English Benedictines who were still only grudgingly prepared to present themselves before the Vicar Apostolic for faculties, and for whom their procurator or agent in Rome became increasingly important as a mediator between them and the Roman authorities.[9] An example of this is the tendency of monks on the Mission to apply directly to Rome via the procurator for marriage dispensations, rather than going through the Vicars Apostolic.[10] Benedictine resistance to the Vicars Apostolic can also be seen in the way in which the monks asserted their liturgical and constitutional independence. The General Chapter of the English Benedictine Congregation which met in 1753, the year of *Apostolicum Ministerium*, ordered a new liturgical calendar to be produced, which appeared in 1755. This was the first formal calendar for monks working on the Mission, and it deliberately segregated them from their counterparts among the seculars and other regulars who had their own calendars. Furthermore, the Constitutions of the English Benedictine

---

[6] LUNN, *The English Benedictines*, 112.
[7] SCOTT, *Gothic Rage Undone*, 68.
[8] SCOTT, *Gothic Rage Undone*, 76.
[9] SCOTT, *Gothic Rage Undone*, 75-76.
[10] G. SCOTT, '"The Privileges of Trading in that Country": The controversy between the Vicars Apostolic and the Benedictines in the late seventeenth century,' in D.A. BELLENGER (ed.), *Opening the Scrolls: Essays in honour of Godfrey Anstruther*, Downside Abbey, Bath 1987, 84-89.

Congregation, revised in 1784, contained only one reference to bishops, and then only cursorily.[11] The preface to these Constitutions bolstered the monks' role on the mission by claiming that the conversion of England had been primarily the work of monks, sent by Pope St Gregory the Great in the year 597. Monks working on the English Mission had their own constitutions, first drawn up in 1689, the year after the appointment of the first Vicars Apostolic. It is significant that these contained no reference at all to bishops. These constitutions were never revised until late in the nineteenth century, well after the re-establishment of the hierarchy of England and Wales in 1850.

The last decades of the eighteenth century represent a pivotal period in the dispute between the English Benedictines and the bishops due to three main factors: firstly, the increased authority of the English Vicars Apostolic over the regular clergy as a result of the 1753 papal bull *Apostolicum Ministerium*; secondly the gradual shift of focus of the English Benedictines in this period from their houses on the continent to their missions, and new monasteries in England; and thirdly the new mood of religious toleration experienced by English Catholics after the Relief Acts of 1778 and 1791. By the early years of the nineteenth century, the English Benedictines were already responding positively to the demands of the new highly-populated urban areas and new industrial centres of the country, by establishing new missions, and it was their claim of independent possession of them that brought the old dispute with the bishops into sharper focus. There had been little competition for these new missions from other clergy, whether regular or secular, for the Jesuits had been suppressed by Pope Clement XIV in 1773, and the Vicars Apostolic in England generally lacked the financial resources to build new churches and presbyteries, resources which the English Benedictines were able to draw upon.

In 1795, as the prospect of territorial disputes between the monks and the bishops was beginning to form on the horizon, a very different kind of dispute was reaching its climax between two English Benedictines, Bishop Charles Walmesley and Cuthbert Wilks, both members of St Edmund's, Paris. The conflict between them concerned ecclesiology, or the question of the nature of the church, with Wilks representing the interests of an influential group of Catholic clergy who sought to obtain greater toleration for English Catholics from the government, and espoused Cisalpinist views, namely they resisted papal influence over the English Catholic church. The dispute between them and the Vicars Apostolic has been well documented elsewhere and was soon to be resolved.[12] By 1795 the English Benedictines

---

[11] *Constitutiones Congregationis Anglicanae Ordinis Sancti Benedicti*, 4: 204.
[12] SCOTT, *Gothic Rage Undone*, 78-82; G. SCOTT, "Dom Joseph Cuthbert Wilks and the English Benedictine Involvement in the Cisalpine Stirs," *RH*, 23 (1996) 318-340; G. NELSON, unpublished Ph.D. thesis, *Charles Walmesley and the Episcopal Opposition*, University of Tulane, USA 1977.

had other priorities to consider, not least their own survival, threatened by the French Revolution which forced them back to their homeland. Arriving in England, the monks found a country at war with France, becoming increasingly hostile to revolutionary ideas in general and towards the Cisalpinists in particular. It was ironic, as Eamon Duffy observed, that the latter were to find that the very Revolution that had inspired their cause, was ultimately to destroy it.[13] Wilks retired from England, and died in Douai in 1829. The English Cisalpine movement gradually metamorphasised into a new, largely lay association, in which the English Benedictines after 1798 had no direct involvement, but had representation through several of their lay patrons.[14]

Early nineteenth-century relations

The repatriation in 1795 of two of the houses to England seemed initially to generate a new mood of submission among the monks towards the Vicars Apostolic. A meeting held at Vernon Hall, Liverpool, on 2 April 1795 to consider the future of the Congregation resolved that monks returning from the continent "must apply in their own names to the local Vicar Apostolic for faculties...and they must be responsible as well to the Apostolical Vicar in whose district they reside",[15] It was to be a decade before there were any significant conflicts between the parties, and then these were comparatively minor skirmishes compared with some of the later disputes. In May 1807 Bishop John Milner of the Midland District refused to ordain a monk at Acton Burnell because he questioned whether monks of the Congregation were exempt from taking an oath of serving in the district in which they were ordained. Writing to Prior Sharrock at Acton Burnell, Milner smugly remarked that "this difficulty has arisen from Rome's not attending to your ancient privileges when they arranged our faculties".[16] Milner, incidentally, did not enjoy a good reputation among secular clergy, let alone the English Benedictines. Six years afterwards, Paul McPherson, the Roman agent of the English Vicars Apostolic complained to Prior Henry Parker about "that hotheaded goodman, Dr Milner, [who] keeps me in constant and unpleasant occupation".[17] The following year McPherson lamented to Parker that Milner, in Rome "as everywhere else", was "doing much mischief".[18] Later,

---

[13] E. DUFFY, unpublished Ph.D. thesis, *Joseph Berington and the English Catholic Cisalpine movement, 1772-1803*, University of Cambridge 1972, 300.
[14] E. DUFFY, "Ecclesiastical Democracy Detected: III, 1796 – 1803," *RH*, 13 (1975) 138-139.
[15] AR, 2: 289.
[16] AR, 2: 464.
[17] DAA, Parker Papers no.14, 22 November 1813, P. McPherson to Parker.
[18] DAA, Parker Papers, 18 August 1814, McPherson to Parker.

in 1819, Milner and other Vicars Apostolic proved to be obstinate in their refusal to dispense Benedictine missioners from the Roman requirement that they make a retreat in the monastery of their profession. The dispute had been unwittingly provoked by the newly-consecrated Benedictine bishop, Bede Slater, who without reference to his uncle, the English Benedictine president, Bede Brewer, had managed to obtain an exemption from this requirement in Rome.[19]

An important official in the English Benedictine Congregation was the procurator, or agent, in Rome. Until 1808, the monks had benefited from the services of Placid Waters, who was their agent in Rome from 1777. Waters had been of great help to the Congregation, representing their interests in the city, and especially in proposing and promoting Benedictine candidates as bishops in England.[20] Waters was also helpful in correcting false rumours about the reputation of the Congregation at the papal court. For instance, in 1796 he wrote to Gregory Sharrock, whose appointment he had helped to secure as coadjutor to Bishop Charles Walmesley:

> where in the name of goodness could you hear that this court has taken ill the promotion or nomination of Mr Wilks as our vice-president? I doubt this court even know you have held a General Chapter...so much notice was never taken here.[21]

Waters' death in 1808, and the subsequent 25 years it took to replace him with a resident procurator in Rome, (due mainly to the unstable situation in the city in this period) severely affected the Congregation. It is significant that only one English Benedictine, (and this being Augustine Baines, of whom more later) was appointed to head, or be a coadjutor, of an English District in the period 1808-1840. The Western District had traditionally had a Benedictine Vicar Apostolic, but in 1809 a Franciscan, Bernardine Collingridge, was appointed to succeed the Benedictine Gregory Sharrock. Whilst Rome was happy to appoint English monks to new colonial sees in this period, they were reluctant to appoint them as Vicars Apostolic in England. In 1816, the future English Benedictine president, Bernard Barber, gloomily remarked to a confrère: "I hear that Dr Lingard is to be Bishop Collingridge's future coadjutor. The monks may bid adieu to the mitre".[22]

However it was not only the Benedictines among the regulars in England who were disappointed with the Vicars Apostolic. In 1803 Pope

---

[19] AH, 2: 492, 500.
[20] SCOTT, *Gothic Rage Undone*, 75-77.
[21] CDA, Bishops' Letter-books, 1796, no.107, Rome, 25 November 1796, Waters to Sharrock.
[22] DAB, D 489, 30 December 1816, Barber to Lorymer.

Pius VII had given informal permission to the English ex-Jesuits to attach themselves to the Society of Jesus in White Russia, but this was never put in writing, and even when the Pope formally restored the Jesuits throughout the world eleven years later, the Vicars Apostolic in England refused to recognise those officially at Stonyhurst until 1829, largely thanks to the intervention in Rome of Augustine Baines, the Vicar Apostolic of the Western District, who was appointed bishop to the throne by Pope Leo XII and consulted by the Pope on matters relating to the English Catholic Church. According to the English Jesuit provincial, Thomas Glover, Baines had "become acquainted with all the unfair proceedings which had long been practised in Rome against the English Jesuits," and persuaded the Pope to sign a decree on 26 January 1829 which enabled Jesuits in England to enjoy the same spiritual and canonical privileges of religious orders represented there.[23] The Dominicans, too, had battles with the Vicars Apostolic and "had to petition Rome to educate and profess novices".[24] Two reasons have often been given for this: the fear on the part of Rome of re-opening old dissensions between secular and regular clergy; and the fear of the Vicars Apostolic that in officially recognising the Jesuits in particular, the granting of Catholic emancipation might be jeopardised. Francis Edwards suggests other, more practical reasons, namely that among the Vicars Apostolic "there was a feeling that the orders were taking men, or vocations and money, from the bishops…that the orders were drawing off the best, leaving only secondary sources for the bishops".[25]

Not all of the English Vicars Apostolic regarded regulars unfavourably: the Benedictines were fortunate to have the support of Milner's successor in the Midland district, Thomas Walsh, who once declared that his aim was "to obtain zealous labourers in the vineyard, men after God's heart. Those shall always be cherished by me whether they be regular or secular clergy". Soon after his election as English Benedictine President in 1826, Augustine Birdsall, shrewdly summed up the situation when he wrote to a confrère:

> The Vicars Apostolic consider the whole business of the mission to be placed in their hands. They consider that the Regulars are useful and available to assistance but they are only assistants. They have their privileges but these do not exalt them to an independence of the Vicars Apostolic, nor to an equality.[26]

---

[23] Quoted in NORMAN, *The English Catholic Church in the Nineteenth Century*, 89; see also EDWARDS, *The Jesuits in England*, 172.
[24] For the Dominicans, see AR, 3: 94, letter of Provincial Woods to President Birdsall, 16 October 1829.
[25] EDWARDS, *The Jesuits in England*, 175.
[26] AR, 3: 95, 3 November 1829, Walsh to Augustine Lawson

These were fitting words from a person who was later described as being "best suited to wage war with a bishop",[27] and they set the tone for the next phase of the battle to be fought between the monks and their episcopal opponents, namely the controversy with one of their own brethren, the Benedictine Vicar Apostolic, Peter Augustine Baines of the Western District.

The Baines controversy

Before considering the dispute between Baines and the English Benedictines, it is important to set it in context. Until the early nineteenth century it had been the practice for members of the Congregation promoted to the episcopacy to be granted a seat in the General Chapter, and to have active voice in its deliberations. The practice lapsed with the death of the previous Benedictine Vicar Apostolic of the Western District, Gregory Sharrock, for when Bishop Bede Slater applied to be admitted to the Chapter of 1822, strong objections were raised against him because of his unfortunate reputation in Mauritius, and he was refused admittance.[28] The following year, Augustine Baines, the missioner at Bath, was appointed as co-adjutor to Bishop Collingridge of the Western District. Baines' early conflicts with some of his brethren at Ampleforth and his predilection for grand schemes meant that this appointment was not universally welcomed. On learning of it, President Richard Marsh wrote to Collingridge expressing the hope that "Dr Baines will exercise prudence and moderation in his coadjutorship…it is thought he will try to carry things with too high a hand".[29] It turned out to be a prophetic remark; the first glimmers of trouble came soon after his consecration when Baines wrote to the Prior of Downside, asking whether the monks would be willing to put themselves under his authority once he became Vicar Apostolic, so as to enable him to establish his proposed episcopal seminary at Downside. The monks declined this as well as Baines' further proposal that the communities at Downside and Ampleforth should exchange their land, buildings and properties, so that (as Baines thought) his own monastic brethren would be more favourable to him using the buildings at Downside for his new seminary. This was the background to the 1826 General Chapter, when Baines applied for, and was refused admittance. Given the fact that he had been present at Chapter four years earlier when Bishop Slater's request for admission was refused, it surely should not have come as a surprise to Baines when his application suffered a similar fate. But he considered the decision a personal snub and expressed his displeasure by returning the annual salary paid to him by the Congregation in a letter which

---

[27] DA, VII.A.f, MS 295, 9.
[28] On Slater and Mauritius see Chapter 8.
[29] DAB, F 25, 29 March 1823, Marsh to Collingridge.

declared: "I do not wish henceforward to receive any contribution from the body".[30]

It is difficult to overestimate the significance of the subsequent dispute that broke out between Baines and the English Benedictines, for it threatened the very heart of the Congregation's existence.[31] When the Downside monks refused to co-operate with him in the venture, Baines then approached his own community of Ampleforth and persuaded a number of them not only to seek secularisation and transfer their obedience to him, but also to take with them the cream of Ampleforth's pupils and many of its resources for the benefit of the new seminary, which he began to develop at Prior Park on the outskirts of Bath. These sparks of conflict were fanned into a greater conflagration when in 1829 Bishop Collingridge died and Baines succeeded to the District. Angered by what he regarded as the "insolence" of the Downside community, Baines withdrew the missionary faculties of their priests, and also claimed at Rome that the Congregation had been irregularly constituted, and that therefore all English Benedictine vows taken since the repatriation of the monks in England were invalid. Richard Marsh wrote despairingly to Thomas Smith, Vicar Apostolic of the Northern District, lamenting that: "after having survived the Reformation in England, and the Revolution in France", the Congregation might "fall by the hands of one of its own children".[32] Baines also attempted to persuade his fellow Vicars Apostolic to petition Rome to enact a regulation that would subject all regulars in England to their respective bishops, who would then enjoy the same jurisdiction over the monks as over convents of nuns. To Baines' disappointment, none of his episcopal colleagues were willing to support this measure.

The detailed chronology and intricate events of the Baines dispute do not concern us here; it is sufficient for the purposes of this chapter to examine the impact of the conflict on the mission at Bath. The specific dispute over Ampleforth has already been dealt with in a previous chapter. The sheer volume of the documentation produced by both sides is formidable, and many of the key documents were incorporated into the Benedictine annalist, Athanasius Allanson's *History* and *Records* of the Congregation, where the Baines dispute takes up over 500 pages.[33] Attention should also be given to two other documents, both in the archives at Downside: President Birdsall's *Report of the disputes between Bishop Baines and the English Benedictines,* and the *Statement of Facts* produced by Baines for the arbitration that ended the

---

[30] DA, MS I.A 450, 16.
[31] Of all the accounts of the dispute between English Benedictines and Bishop Baines, the best is still WARD, *Sequel to Catholic Emancipation,* 1:15-49. The dispute is also well summarized by NORMAN, *The English Catholic Church in the Nineteenth Century,* 89-96.
[32] AR, 3: 32, Marsh to Bishop Smith (no date).
[33] AH, 3: 49-128, 139-194, 222-271; AR, 3: 31-77, 79-82, 85-87, 91-96, 98-167, 167 bis – 213, 216-444.

dispute.[34] Of these two, the Baines document is the more articulate and illuminating on the case; the Birdsall document is merely a collection of the bulk of the pertinent correspondence, with a limited commentary by the President himself.

It is hard, even almost two centuries after the dispute, to imagine how the bishop's original suggestion to the Downside monks of transferring their obedience and their property to him could have ever been an acceptable or workable proposition, either to Rome, or to the English Benedictine Congregation. Baines' proposal was that Downside "should be nothing more nor less than the seminary of the Western District", and that he should "exercise the same powers over its members within his own District, which are usually exercised by the Benedictine President and the Provincial". Had the monks consented to Baines' proposals, it would have meant that the Vicar Apostolic of the Western District (who might not necessarily always be a Benedictine) would act as the ordinary superior of the Downside community, which would have set up a clash of jurisdictions between the bishop and the English Benedictine President. The proposal would not have been workable from the perspective of the English Benedictine mission, for Baines envisaged that Downside monks should be wholly designated to the Western District, thereby setting up a third missionary province over which neither the English Benedictine President nor the senior officials of the Congregation would have control. Cuthbert Butler has convincingly shown that although there have been instances where a superior of a monastery has also been the bishop of the surrounding district of the monastery, "it is the Abbot that is Bishop, not the Bishop that is Abbot, as Dr Baines wished".[35] Baines' scheme would have been so repugnant to the Benedictines for these reasons that it is difficult then to accept the thesis of John Cashman, who, citing a letter from Baines to Nicholas Wiseman of 17 December 1829, asserted that the monks had already formally expressed their willingness to Baines' predecessor, Collingridge, to depart from the Benedictine body and subject themselves to him.[36] If, however it was true that the monks had expressed a desire to join the Western District, it would demonstrate both the weakness of ties within the English Benedictine Congregation at this time and its lack of direction.

The facet of the dispute which caused the greatest danger to the English Benedictines was Baines' contention that the Congregation had not been properly canonically established in England after the French

---

[34] DA, MS I.A 450 (Birdsall's *Report*) hereafter cited as "DA, Birdsall"; DA, MS 295. VII.A.f (Baines *Statement*, also known as *Dr Baines's Defence*) hereafter cited as "DA, Statement".
[35] See Abbot Cuthbert Butler's convincing arguments of these points in "The Controversy with Bishop Baines," in *DR*, 33 (1914) 93-99.
[36] J. CASHMAN, unpublished M.Litt thesis, *Bishop Baines and the Tensions in the Western District, 1842-43*, University of Bristol 1989, 84.

Revolution. This legal omission, which should have been attended to when the houses of St Gregory and St Laurence were transplanted to England in 1795, was used by Baines to try and bend the monks to his will. To his discredit he used others to pursue this tactic. He wrote to Prior Burgess at Ampleforth in May 1827:

> I should be glad if you would immediately write and inform me whether any authority was obtained from Rome for the establishment of Ampleforth and Downside as Convents and Noviciates and by whom and when – but be cautious about how you make inquiries and say nothing to anyone why you want the information.[37]

The consequence of this legal omission was that it was possible that all the vows made by monks in England since 1795 could be invalid. Abbot Butler commented that this eventuality "could spell nothing less than the dissolution of the English Benedictines as a monastic Congregation, and would make of its priests secular clergy, the subjects of the bishop".[38] The former president, Richard Marsh, and the future bishop, Joseph Brown, were sent to Rome to argue their case against Baines. The monks were able to cite the Rescript of June 1823, obtained by Marsh from the Holy See, which approved the translation of the different monasteries of the Congregation from their former locations on the continent to England, as well as two papal letters, one of 1796 confirming the privileges of the Congregation, and the other of 1814 in which Pius VII expressed his joy that the Congregation had survived the French Revolution. In 1830, Rome issued a *Sanatio*, recognising both the monasteries to be properly erected and the vows valid.

Particularly pertinent for the present chapter is the aspect of the Baines controversy that concerned the mission at Bath. Baines had been a highly successful and industrious missioner there for six years, and he had supervised many improvements to the chapel and had acquired and furnished a new presbytery. He had introduced new ceremonies and music to the chapel which "attracted the notice of all who witnessed it".[39] His preaching drew large crowds, and thus, by the time he became Vicar Apostolic, Baines was well aware that "the mission at Bath had been to the Benedictine body a source of no small emolument" and that there "was no other mission in the western district that could supply a considerable surplus after supporting its clergy".[40] His successor at Bath, Jerome Brindle, decided in 1830 to seek release from his monastic vows at Ampleforth, and transfer his allegiance to Baines and the Western District. The indult for secularisation having been granted, Brindle refused to resign his incumbency at Bath and to

---

[37] Quoted in C. ALMOND, "Ampleforth v. Bishop Baines," *AJ*, 23 (1917) 7.
[38] C. BUTLER, "Prior Park and Bishop Baines," *DR*, 50 (1932) 340.
[39] AH, 3: 37.
[40] AH, 3: 36; DA, "Statement," 73.

hand over the mission to the new Benedictine incumbent, his assistant, Maurus Cooper. Instead, Brindle referred the Benedictines to Baines, his new superior, who contested whether the Bath mission canonically belonged to the Benedictines, arguing: "Monks may be the legal possessors of the Bath property. But are they the Canonical and Equitable possessors to the exclusion of the Bishop? I cannot believe it".[41] Baines considered it his right not only to appoint missioners to Bath but also his duty to "diminish the Benedictine attachment' to the mission"by "reducing its emoluments" as much as he could. He boldly attempted to claim the bench rents in the chapel for himself.

There was a dramatic spectacle at the Bath chapel in November 1831 when Baines chose to preach there on the Sunday when the annual bench rents were due. As the bishop processed into the church, intending to inform the congregation that the rents were to be collected by him in person, Dunstan Scott, the Benedictine Definitor and Procurator of the South Province, began circulating handbills amongst the congregation, giving contrary instructions, informing them that the rents would be collected by the Benedictines at a future date.[42] Undaunted, the bishop then established a second chapel in the town in opposition to the Benedictines, to the consternation of the Pope who objected to "the setting up of altar against altar".[43] It was an extraordinary step to take, and was the second instance of a Vicar Apostolic in England erecting a chapel in a town already served by regulars.[44] The move back-fired because there were not enough Catholics in the town to support a second chapel. Eventually, an inquiry by independent arbitrators appointed by *Propaganda* decided in the monks' favour.[45]

Even a century after the events, the controversy aroused great feeling. A 1931 volume reassessing the legacy of Baines was denounced by Cuthbert Butler as the "white-washing of the hero through the black-washing of other people". Butler believed that the book blackened the Benedictine protagonists of the dispute whom he lauded "among the greatest of Downside's sons".[46] There were faults on both sides. Baines was justly reprimanded by the Holy See for withdrawing the missionary faculties of the Downside monks (which *Propaganda* declared could only be done with the consent of the Holy See) and for setting up a rival mission in Bath. He was not averse to embroiling others in his mischief-making, even to the

---

[41] RSRNC (Anglia, 8), fol. 628.
[42] DA, "Statement,"74, 80.
[43] "Statement," 73.
[44] The first was in Wigan, in 1817. See P. DOYLE, *Mitres and Missions in Lancashire: The Roman Catholic Diocese of Liverpool 1850-2000,* Bluecoat, Liverpool 2005, 33-34.
[45] AR, 4: 103-104.
[46] J.S. ROCHE, *A History of Prior Park College and its Founder Bishop Baines,* Burns & Oates, London 1931; BUTLER, "Prior Park and Bishop Baines,"333-349.

extent of urging them to provide the evidence he needed to support his case.[47]

However, the Benedictines were also at fault: whilst Birdsall as President rightly contested Baines' claims concerning the Congregation's canonical status, he showed himself to be bitter, severe and uncompromising. He refused to meet with the bishop and stubbornly resisted the sound advice given him, both by his fellow monks, and other friendly parties. The following extract is a typical example: "However creditable to the character of a peacemaker", wrote Birdsall to Dr William Coombes, the missioner at Shepton Mallet, and a great friend of the Benedictines, who had preached at the opening of the new Downside chapel in 1823,

> however praiseworthy your endeavours to make peace, be assured the subjects of dissension upon which you now address me, are of a department of adjudication very different from that wherein your kindness would be effective.[48]

Upon receipt of this letter, Coombes wrote disparagingly to Cardinal Weld in Rome, "Dr Birdsall sternly and indignantly rejected the bishop's offer of a meeting. The terms in which he spoke of Dr Baines were violent and disrespectful in the highest degree".[49] Even Birdsall's predecessor as president, Richard Marsh, advised a more moderate approach, observing that "by refusing all sort of communication with Dr Baines we seem to show ill will and a disposition to be unfriendly...civility but firmness would be my motto; no surrender of essentials". Yet Marsh also discredits himself by revealing an anti-episcopal bias, advising Birdsall, "if you have an interview with Dr Baines you should treat him as an equal and appear his equal in every respect", for "a chief of an Order as you are should not even bend the knee to a bishop as others do".[50] Interestingly, of the 24 complaints the English Benedictines made to Rome concerning Baines, shortly before the matter went to arbitration in the summer of 1835, 14 of them were withdrawn (most of them concerning misinterpretations of Baines' actions) in the following letter:

> The Representatives of the English Benedictines beg leave to lay before the Right Reverend and Reverend Arbiters...those portions of their complaints which, now that explanations have taken place, they are willing to abandon, considering it no longer necessary that they may be made matter of further investigation. (Here

---

[47] AR, 3: 44ff.
[48] AR, 3: 354, 3 June 1831, Birdsall to Coombes.
[49] RSRNC (Anglia, 8), fol.705, Shepton Mallet, 15 June 1831, Coombes to Weld.
[50] DA, "Birdsall," 79, 86.

follows the list of the fourteen complaints abandoned)
(Signed) J.A. Birdsall, President-General.

It is probably significant that this letter is not included by Allanson in the vast collection of documentation of the dispute in his *Records* as it represents something of a retreat on the part of the Benedictines.[51] One is left wondering whether much of the controversy could have been resolved earlier with the parties sitting down together, rather than invoking higher authority. Long before the quarrel had reached Rome, in January 1824, shortly after Baines' original approach to Downside, his then friend and ally, Benedict Glover of Ampleforth, commented to Baines: "all these difficulties arise from the stupidity of Prior Barber who refuses to discuss the question...if the affair were to be discussed in chapter, it would be carried to the satisfaction of all the parties".[52] However, Bernard Collier, the new procurator in Rome, believed that the controversy had actually done the English Benedictines no harm in Rome, arguing that "amongst the advantages which we have derived from Bishop Baines' persecution we must count that of being known in Rome" where "the authorities are by no means ill-disposed to us".[53] Yet despite successfully defending themselves against episcopal encroachment, the English Benedictines did not emerge very honourably from the controversy. They had rightly stressed that many of Baines' proposals were unworkable from a Benedictine perspective, but in demonstrating such stubborn resistance to discussion and compromise, to say nothing of expressing anti-episcopal rhetoric, they laid up for themselves unresolved issues which would plague their relations with the bishops in the years to come.

Monastic-episcopal territorial jurisdiction

Between 1836 and 1842 there was a series of skirmishes between the monks and the Vicars Apostolic in the north west. The first incident concerned Aigburth, near Liverpool, where in 1835 the monks were invited to establish a mission by two merchants, Charles and Peter Chaloner. Charles Chaloner promised to pay £50 a year during his lifetime for the support of a priest there, provided it was built within a mile of the brewery he owned.[54] The new mission was envisaged as what the first incumbent, Ambrose Prest, described as "a filiation of Woolton and not an encroachment on episcopal territory...the chapel will be built by the subscriptions of friends alone, without the influence of the bishop's name". Prest expressed the hope that

---

[51] LEEDS DIOCESAN ARCHIVES, Briggs Papers.
[52] CDA, Baines file 2, 17 January 1824, Glover to Baines.
[53] AA, A 268 no.23, Rome, 22 October 1836, Collier to Day.
[54] The controversy concerning the Aigburth mission is covered by Allanson as follows: AH, 2: 272-279, AR, 4: 209-282.

"the bishop would allow even monks" to minister to the people of Aigburth, "rather than the devil who now holds them in his tender keeping".[55] Thomas Penswick, Vicar Apostolic of the Northern District, saw things differently and refused to countenance the project. According to Allanson, Penswick's "zeal for the propagation of Catholic chapels in his district was not equal to his prejudices against Religious Orders having the possession of them". Penswick believed that there were insufficient numbers of Catholics in the area to merit a new church, and that there would be insufficient financial support for its maintenance. An appeal to Penswick's coadjutor, John Briggs, met with similar opposition for, according to Allanson, Briggs' "antipathy to Religious Orders was proverbial".[56] Briggs eventually agreed to allow the mission to be established as long as an income of £90 a year could be guaranteed, and that the monks promised not to undertake any "indiscriminate begging" for its maintenance.

What is striking about this episode is the strength of English Benedictine resentment towards Penswick and Briggs and the almost contemptuous attitude of the monks to the two Vicars Apostolic. From the very first rumour of episcopal disapproval Ambrose Prest was writing to Penswick in sarcastic tones: "I of course as a simple priest", he wrote, "must receive and be content with an unexplained refusal, if it so pleases your Lordship, but there are many who will think themselves entitled to an explanation".[57] President Birdsall, writing to the Provincial of the North, Gregory Robinson, believed Bishop Briggs was treating regular clergy who wished to build churches differently from secular clergy, who, according to Birdsall, were even allowed to incur debts in building. He asserted that the bishops were jealous of regulars and that their "notorious" treatment of them needed to be reported to Rome. Robinson was convinced that Briggs was in collusion with Bishop Baines, and that if the monks "tacitly yielded to the principles of the Bishops' they would then 'give sanction to them".[58] Some blame for the dispute must also be placed at the door of the Chaloner family themselves. They had a long recusant tradition and Peter Chaloner by 1836 was living in Aigburth Hall. In negotiating with Prest and the English Benedictines he was adopting the role of a traditional Catholic gentry patron, offering £50 not for the maintenance of the new mission at Aigburth, but for the personal upkeep of the priest, whom Chaloner clearly intended to be his personal chaplain.[59]

Rome, meanwhile, seemed to be supporting the regulars by a decree in 1838 which allowed them to build public churches and to regard them as

---

[55] AR, 4: 271, Lytham, 10 August 1835, Prest to Provincial Robinson.
[56] AR, 4: 273.
[57] AR, 4: 215, 25 November 1835, Prest to Penswick.
[58] AR, 4: 252, Liverpool, 26 April 1836, Robinson to Brown.
[59] HOLLINSHEAD, "The Return of Papists for the Parish of Childwall…1706," 24. I am grateful to Mr John Davies for information about the Chaloner family.

their own property without any reference to the local bishop. Bishop Baines complained to Thomas Griffiths, Vicar Apostolic of the London District, that "this rescript would form an anomaly in the church...it is repugnant to all canon law".[60] The rescript was eagerly seized upon by the new, ambitious Benedictine Provincial of the North, Anselm Brewer, who was keen to build an ornate church at Edge Hill in Liverpool. Briggs again objected, insisting that, on the contrary, Rome had reversed its previous decree, and that episcopal permission was still required for regulars to build churches. Brewer queried this with Bernard Collier in Rome who confirmed that *Propaganda* had changed their minds without informing the regulars, believing that the decree was "too restrictive of the bishops' rights".[61] Brewer was obliged to seek the permission of Bishop Briggs, which Briggs again refused to give. Eventually the matter was resolved by *Propaganda*, who decreed that the church at Edge Hill could go ahead, provided that an annual payment of twenty percent of the offerings received there was made to the Vicar Apostolic of the Northern District. In the event, this was not paid, prompting some angry correspondence between the Benedictines and Bishop George Brown of the newly created Lancashire District.[62] Relations between the English Benedictines and the Vicars Apostolic in Liverpool throughout the following decade continued to be strained. Early in 1840 Bishop Briggs refused to allow the monks to open a chapel in Leyland near Preston, pointing out that "from time immemorial", Leyland had been connected with the adjacent mission at Euxton. Initially, Bishop George Brown attempted to create better relations with the monks, but he was also determined to diminish their independence; he was persistent in his claims to the tax from the church of St Anne at Edge Hill that had been decreed by *Propaganda*, and he challenged the monks' claim for exemption by forming a new Board in 1844 to administer all funds for all church building projects in the district, including the churches established by regulars.[63]

At about the same time that the church at Edge Hill was being planned, the English Jesuits were also considering a scheme to build a church in the town, and were also encountering episcopal opposition.[64] Despite many similarities between the two cases, the Jesuits approached the issue

---

[60] AAW, III.C. vii, Griffiths papers, Prior Park, 11 November 1838, Baines to Griffiths.
[61] AR, 4: 313.
[62] AR, 4: 317. See 319ff for the continuing dispute.
[63] AR, 4: 339. For details of Brown's abolition of lay committees, see T. BURKE, *Catholic History of Liverpool*, C. Tinling, Liverpool 1910, 79-80. For the Benedictine reaction see AR, 4: 315-318.
[64] N. RYAN SJ, *St Francis Xavier's Church Centenary 1848-1948*, Kilburns, Liverpool 1948; M. WHITEHEAD, "The English Jesuits and Episcopal Authority: The Liverpool Test Case, 1840-43," *RH*, 18 (1986) 97-219.

with greater organisation and more effective support. Not only did they have the benefit of the vision and organisational skills of Father Randal Lythgoe, soon to be Provincial, they also had the backing of a group of local professional and business men, many of whom had been educated by the Jesuits at Stonyhurst. This group rapidly organised itself into a society which to begin with raised funds for the poor school at the Jesuit mission of Gillmoss, and then subsequently formed "the Society of St Francis Xavier," with the purpose of erecting a church for the Jesuits in the centre of the town. This group quickly produced a printed prospectus outlining their aims and objectives, and undertook not only the fund-raising for the project, but also a thorough research of pertinent facts and figures to demonstrate to the bishop and to Rome the viability of the project. It was true that the Benedictines at Aigburth had benefited from the financial support of the Chaloner brothers, and that Peter Chaloner had corresponded with the bishop in support of the project, but the Benedictines lacked the organised professional lay committee from which the Jesuits benefited. Anselm Brewer, the Benedictine Provincial, certainly had imagination and drive, but as will be seen in the next chapter, his schemes were often impractical and ill-conceived, and he lacked the financial acumen and astuteness of the future Jesuit Provincial, Lythgoe.[65]

Although the Benedictines and the Jesuits had attempted to join forces against their common foes, whether it was the government over Catholic emancipation, or the Vicars Apostolic over ecclesiastical jurisdiction, little had come of such negotiations. Some English Benedictines were suspicious of the Jesuits, and not at all convinced that they would make reliable allies in the battle with the bishops. Ambrose Prest, who succeeded Bernard Collier in 1840 as the Benedictine procurator in Rome, wrote to President Barber:

> We should not have the Jesuits to assist us...they do not care to be Parochi...All they desire to have is Liberty to Preach, Instruct Youth and be in the confessional. I believe they would not only yield up all Parochial rights which they now possess in England, but they would gladly see the same taken from us, if thereby they obtained a wider field to pursue the above three objects...The Jesuits will only assist us if they consider that Benedictines being Parish Priests will tend to their advantage.[66]

---

[65] On Lythgoe see M. WHITEHEAD, '"Education and correct conduct": Randal Lythgoe and the work of the Society of Jesus in Early Victorian England and Wales,' in S. GILLEY (ed.), *Victorian Churches and Churchmen*, 75-93.
[66] "A Procurator in Rome," *AJ*, 16 (1911) 149. Rome, St. Calisto, 14 March 1843, Prest to Barber.

In 1836, Prior Joseph Brown had approached the Jesuits suggesting that the two orders might unite together 'for protection against the bishops' but this came to nothing.

Neither the Jesuits nor the Benedictines gained the support of the local secular clergy in Liverpool for their schemes, especially those clergy whose churches were near the projected churches of St Francis Xavier and St Anne. A petition of 12 May 1840 outlining the opinions of the secular clergy was forwarded to Rome, pointing out that *Propaganda*'s decision to allow the church of St Anne, Edge Hill to go ahead, was likely to have "injurious influence... in encouraging the regulars in their projects of establishing themselves more strongly and more powerfully in Liverpool". The petition concluded that "the Bishop should resist more vigorously and more effectively than he has hitherto done the projects and schemes of the regulars...if the bishop is to govern the flock the regulars must be restrained in promoting their own schemes".[67] Secular opposition to the Benedictines was voiced most vociferously when in 1839 it was proposed to divide the English Catholic church into eight districts, and to appoint an English Benedictine as Vicar Apostolic to at least one of these. A conference of Manchester secular clergy sent a petition in February 1840 against such a move to Bishop Briggs, and the missioner at Weld Bank near Chorley, Richard Thompson, also wrote to Briggs contending that "every influence of the clergy should be exerted to obviate such an evil".[68] Another petition, sent to Rome by secular clergy in London complained: "regulars cultivate the favours of the rich and while boasting in Rome of their zeal and labours, they accuse seculars of sloth, whose work is chiefly among the poor and who live on a pittance".[69]

Episcopal control

Once they had heard of the plan to divide the English Catholic church into eight districts, the English Benedictines wasted no time in sending a petition to Rome, asking the Pope "to restore to our Congregation those rights and privileges enjoyed as long as the hierarchy existed, by our Benedictine ancestors".[70] They reminded the Holy Father that in England before the Reformation monks had formed the cathedral chapters in certain dioceses, and had the right of electing bishops. It was another example of the Benedictines restating weary arguments, and as Peter Doyle remarks, the

---

[67] ARCHIVES OF THE ENGLISH COLLEGE, ROME, Wiseman papers, BEN VIII, 73.3.
[68] LDA, Briggs papers, no.662, Manchester, 6 February 1840, Turner to Briggs; no.650, Weld Bank, 2 February 1840, Rev Richard Thompson to Briggs.
[69] AA, MS 262, no.15, 12 May 1840.
[70] This petition is printed in full in WARD, *The Sequel to Catholic Emancipation*, 2: 254-257.

petition is "indicative of a mentality tuned more to the seventeenth or eighteenth century than to the nineteenth".[71] There was nothing new. Bernard Collier at least thought that the Congregation stood a good chance of gaining at least two of the new districts. As the dispute over the building of St Anne, Edge Hill was beginning at this time, Collier advised Provincial Anselm Brewer "to avoid a quarrel at all costs" and to "keep a good understanding" with Bishop Briggs. Collier was anxious that the monks "should not give *Propaganda* the slightest grounds for thinking them quarrelsome".[72] As early as 1838, Collier was telling a confrère in Liverpool about a suggestion in Rome that the monks would be offered a district comprising the counties of Oxford, Warwick, Worcester, Leicester, Stafford and Derby, giving up their missions elsewhere and "taking over all therein to the exclusion of the secular clergy".[73] The Benedictine Vicar Apostolic might even be made the perpetual president of the Congregation. A less attractive proposition was made that the Benedictines be given Wales as their own vicariate, a suggestion which Joseph Brown believed had "come from an enemy" in the shape of Bishop Baines. Brown advised President Marsh that "Collier must not urge our being driven into Wales but set up our claim in equity to two vicariates….Wales will then be united with other and better portions".[74] In the 1840 division of districts that followed, Brown was appointed Vicar Apostolic for Wales, and ironically, before long was proposing the very suggestion he had opposed only a few years before, namely that the Benedictines concentrate their forces into one vicariate, namely Wales.[75]

      Brown's elevation to the episcopate was applauded by many of his Benedictine brethren who hoped that he would "counteract the anti-regular spirit of the bishops" and "defend the monks".[76] In reality, Brown's appointment turned out to be a mixed blessing for them.[77] Although as bishop he initially attempted to bring the regulars and the bishops together, he soon became one of the fiercest critics of his brethren amongst the Vicars Apostolic.[78] In a letter to the Fathers of the Congregation gathered at the 1850

---

[71] P. DOYLE, "Lancashire Benedictines: The Restoration of the Hierarchy," *EBHS*, privately printed, 1983, 4.
[72] AR, 4: 315.
[73] AA, MS 262 no.9, Rome, 1 December 1838, Collier to Fisher.
[74] AR, 4: 302, Bath, 13 December 1838, Brown to Marsh.
[75] AR, 5: 113-118.
[76] DAB, K 381, 30 May 1840, R. Pope to Brown; K 382, 30 May 1840; Cooper to Brown; K 419, 24 August 1840, Cockshoot to Brown.
[77] A. HOOD, "Bishop Thomas Joseph Brown OSB (1798-1880)," in A. BERRY (ed.), *Belmont Abbey: Celebrating 150 Years*, 61-71.
[78] ARCHIVES OF THE SOCIETY OF JESUS, FARM STREET, LONDON, "Letters of Bishops and Cardinals, 1753-1853," no.26, June 1841, Brown to Glover.

General Chapter he warned them that unless they reformed their ways, there would be no place for them in the new Catholic order that would be ushered in by the imminent restoration of the hierarchy. In the new order of things it was highly probable that the secular clergy would dominate, "who will not fail to be aware that it is contrary to the ecclesiastical canons for regulars to have the care of souls". Furthermore, "the special dispensations which regulars will require" would be "liable to dispute and afford no security for the future". It was therefore highly likely not only that "regular clergy will not be allowed to confer parochial sacraments or exercise parochial duties", but also that in the new order, regulars would be excluded from the ranks of the bishops "as is now the case in Ireland".[79]

In the period leading up to the restoration of the English Catholic hierarchy in September 1850, there were rumblings of discontent within the English Benedictine Congregation that their interests were not being sufficiently passed on to the Roman authorities. Athanasius Allanson blamed President Bernard Barber for this.[80] Allanson and others failed to heed the warnings of Brown and wake up to reality. They seemed unaware that Rome was unlikely to give much credence to such claims on the basis of historical fact, or that recent spats with the Vicars Apostolic would support "their claims to a fair portion of the new Sees which would be created".[81] They seemed oblivious to the fact that the Congregation now had to battle against a dominant secular clergy, to say nothing of the new opposition that was presenting itself in the form of new religious congregations, such as the Passionists and Rosminians, whose compliance and willingness to undertake catechetical and missionary work throughout England and Wales endeared them to the bishops. It was significant that *Propaganda* sent the head of one of these new orders to England in 1847 to report on the viability of a permanent hierarchy. In one of his reports, the Rosminian, Luigi Gentili remarked: "in the early days the Benedictines and the Jesuits were real missionaries but now they just run missions and not as well as the seculars... they have the rich missions or the best endowed and they do not obey the bishops".[82]

As we have seen, the traditional contest between monks and bishops continued to rage in England throughout the early decades of the nineteenth century. The only change to occur was that the monks became increasingly more entrenched, failing to offer anything new to meet the requirements of a rapidly changing English Catholic church and preferring to retreat into traditional claims. Despite the vibrancy of their missionary apostolate, the monks were in danger of losing their place on the rapidly changing map of

---

[79] AR, 5: 134-136, Chepstow, 16 July 1850, Brown to General Chapter.
[80] AH, 3: 409.
[81] AH, 3: 409.
[82] See C. CHARLES CP, "The Origins of the Parish Mission in England and the Early Passionist Apostolate, 1840-1850," *JEH*, 15 (1964) 60-75. For Gentili's reports, see RSNRC (Anglia, 12), fol. 63ff.

Catholic England. At the beginning of this chapter it was suggested that the fable of the rabbit and hedgehog was exemplified in the various disputes between monks and bishops. Much as the monks may have perceived themselves to be the rabbits harshly evicted by the sharp quills of the hedgehog bishops, much of the material gathered in this chapter surely suggests that it was the monks, not the bishops who proved to be the hedgehogs. The monks proved to be prickly and defensive about their outdated claims to independence and unwilling to co-operate with the bishops in meeting the new challenges of the Victorian age.

Chapter 5

"The Christian instruction of the English people": Monks and their Missions.

Since the re-establishment of the English Benedictine Congregation in 1619, the majority of its monks had resided not in the monasteries on the continent, but on the English Mission, engaged in what Abbot Cuthbert Butler called "the Christian instruction of the English people".[1] By the 1790s it was not the monasteries, soon to be abandoned because of the French Revolution, but the missions in England, which preserved the Congregation in a period of considerable uncertainty, and would continue to do so until the middle of the nineteenth century. Whilst it took the better part of half a century for the repatriated English monasteries to establish themselves, the Mission underwent a more rapid and more extensive expansion as a result of an ever-increasing Catholic population particularly in new industrial urban areas such as Liverpool. In 1795 the Congregation served 51 missions and chaplaincies and in the period between 1794 and 1850, 105 missions and chaplaincies.[2] In addition the Mission underwent a significant transformation in character, from predominantly a structure of rural chaplaincies under lay patrons to independent urban missions.[3] What follows will demonstrate the vibrancy of the Mission in all its various facets, but first it needs to be considered in the context of early nineteenth-century English Catholicism.

By 1795, involvement in the "Mission", as the English Benedictines have called their pastoral apostolate in England and Wales, had been a predominant feature of English Benedictinism for almost two centuries, and the monks took an oath at profession to undertake pastoral work in England if required. At least until the early nineteenth century, Benedictine missions were mostly all manned singly (except for the larger towns such as Bath), and on the mission the life and work of a missioner belonging to a religious order was not dissimilar to that of his English secular counterpart, except that, in the case of the Benedictines, the missioner worked under two provincials answerable to the President General, whilst the seculars were governed first by Archpriests, and then, from the late seventeenth century, by Vicars Apostolic.

---

[1] Scott, "The English Benedictine Mission and missions," 302.
[2] A full list of these is given in Appendix 2.
[3] The geographical distribution of these missions and chaplaincies is given in *Figure 5*.

Figure 5 - DISTRIBUTION OF PRINCIPAL CHAPLAINCIES AND MISSIONS SERVED BY THE ENGLISH BENEDICTINES, 1795- 1850[4]

---

[4] For the full list of chaplaincies and missions served in this period, see Appendix 2.

KEY TO *Figure 5*

Missions established after 1795 in **bold.**

1.	Aberford, Yorkshire	
2.	Acton Burnell, Salop	
3.	**Aigburth, Lancashire**	**1838**
4.	**Barton, Lincolnshire**	**1848**
5.	Bath	
6.	Biddlestone, Northumberland	until 1839
7.	Birtley, Durham	
8.	Bonham, Wiltshire	
9.	**Brandsby, Yorkshire**	**1805**
10.	Brindle, Lancashire	
11.	**Broadway, Worcestershire**	**1828-50**
12.	Brownedge, Lancashire	
13.	**Bungay, Suffolk**	**1821**
14.	**Cheltenham, Gloucestershire**	**1809**
15.	**Chipping Sodbury, Gloucestershire**	**1838**
16.	**Clayton Green, Lancashire**	**1822**
17.	Coughton, Warwickshire	
18.	**Coventry, Warwickshire**	**1803**
19.	**Cowpen, Northumberland**	**1838**
20.	Crosby Hall, Lancashire	
21.	Easingwold, Yorkshire	
22.	Foxcote, Warwickshire	to 1848
23.	**Goosnargh, Lancashire**	**1833**
24.	**Grassendale, Lancashire**	**1835**
25.	**Great Haywood, Staffordshire**	**1834**
26.	Hindley, Lancashire	
27.	Holme Hall, Yorkshire	
28.	Horsley, Gloucestershire	
29.	**Ince Blundell, Lancashire**	**1826**
30.	**Kemerton, Gloucestershire**	**1841**
31.	**Knaresborough, Yorkshire**	**1797**
32.	**Leyland, Lancashire**	**1845**
33.	**Little Crosby, Lancashire**	**1836**
34.	**Little Malvern, Worcestershire**	**1826**
35.	**Liverpool St Anne**	**1843**
36.	**Liverpool St Augustine**	**1849**
37.	Liverpool St Mary	
38.	Liverpool St Peter	
	*London	to 1832
39.	**Maryport, Cumbria**	**1841**
40.	Middleton Lodge, Yorkshire	

41.	**Monmouth**	**1840**
42.	Morpeth, Northumberland	
43.	Netherton, Lancashire	
44.	Ormskirk, Lancashire	
45.	**Redditch, Worcestershire**	**1834**
46.	**Rixton, Lancashire**	**1831**
47.	**Scarisbrick, Lancashire**	**1824**
48.	**Stockeld Park, Yorkshire**	**1844-46**
49.	Swinburne Castle, Northumberland	
50.	**Wappenbury, Warwickshire**	**1830**
51.	Warrington St Alban	
52.	Warwick Bridge, Cumbria	
53.	**Weobley, Herefordshire**	**1834**
54.	**Westby Hall, Lancashire**	**1821**
55.	Weston Underwood, Buckinghamshire	to 1837
56.	**Weymouth, Dorset**	**c.1823**
57.	Whitehaven, Cumbria	
58.	Woolston, Lancashire	to 1831
59.	Woolton, Lancashire	
60.	**Wootton Wawen, Warwickshire**	**1806**
61.	**Workington, Cumbria**	**1810**
62.	**Wrightington Hall, Lancashire**	**1806**

The ecclesiastical structure of English Catholicism by 1795 was rather *ad hoc* and full of anomalies.[5] As has been noted in the previous chapter, the papal bull *Apostolicum Ministerium,* was issued in 1753 as an attempt to set out the rights and respective obligations of the English clergy and the Vicars Apostolic. By the 1790s its provisions, which had been drawn up for a largely rural, gentry-dominated clergy, did not reflect the contemporary world of urban as well as rural missions that were independent of lay patrons. The Vicars Apostolic had limited powers and financial resources to establish new missions to serve the rising Catholic populations, and it was the religious orders, especially the Benedictines, who stepped in to establish new chapels and presbyteries.

The question of ecclesiastical jurisdiction in these newly established missions was to be a thorny issue throughout the nineteenth century. In 1795, English law prevented the Vicars Apostolic or religious orders from holding property, and whatever property they did administer was considered to be the private property of one or more individuals. In the establishment of new missions in the latter part of the eighteenth century, it was often lay committees who bought sites, built chapels and established powerful congregational committees who could if they wished (and did in Liverpool and Bath) control clerical appointments, fix bench rents and clerical stipends and ward off interference from the Vicars Apostolic.[6] It was not just lay committees or regular clergy who resisted episcopal interference; a similar spirit of independence was found among secular priests such as the historian John Lingard who insisted on clerical rights and opposed the northern Vicar Apostolic gaining control over the seminary at Ushaw. Lingard maintained that seminaries should not be subject to the whim of bishops, but be regarded as the property of the secular clergy as a whole.[7]

English Benedictine missions and the missions of other religious orders

In 1773 the majority of missioners in England had been religious, but by 1830 only 30% were members of religious orders. By far the largest group of the religious in the early part of the nineteenth century were English Benedictines, for although the Jesuits (suppressed by the Pope in 1773) were restored in 1814, it took time for their numbers to increase, and even then in London and in other parts of the country English Jesuits were excluded by unsympathetic Vicars Apostolic. The English Dominican province became

---

[5] For the background see GILLEY, "The Roman Catholic Church in England, 1780-1940," 347-349; AVELING, *The Handle and the Axe,* 307-345; BOSSY, *The English Catholic Community,* 295-322.

[6] For the background to Benedictine involvement in Catholic congregationalism see SCOTT, *Gothic Rage Undone,* 103-107.

[7] PHILLIPS (ed.), *Lingard Remembered: Essays to mark the Sesquicentenary of John Lingard's Death,* 82.

extinct in 1827 and the English Franciscan province in 1841[8]. Two Franciscan missions at Coventry and Goosnargh were taken by the Benedictines, who also succeeded a long line of Jesuits at Scarisbrick in Lancashire and Stockeld Park in Yorkshire, as well as for a time serving the former Jesuit mission of Richmond. However, within two decades, the monks were to face competition from a revitalised Society of Jesus and other, newer religious congregations which also had a missionary apostolate. According to one commentator, after Catholic Emancipation in 1829 "there came a kind of spiritual goldrush; a general staking of claims which could not preclude rivalries" between the religious and secular clergy, and between the religious clergy themselves, "because those involved had the same ends in view, even if those ends were spiritual".[9] However, by 1850, the English Benedictines had little to fear from the parochial aspirations of the other religious orders for a number of reasons.

Firstly the Jesuits gained approval from Rome for the building of new churches, but initially there were restrictions. On 17 April 1842, Propaganda approved the erection of the church of St Francis Xavier in Liverpool under three conditions: Firstly, that the church should not be opened for another six years; secondly, that neither Baptisms, Funerals nor Marriages take place in this church, and finally that the sum of £10 be paid annually to the Bishop. In London, *Propaganda* permitted the erection of a Jesuit Church in Farm Street under similar conditions, except that the Jesuits were to pay rent of £30 per year to the bishop and another £30 to the existing mission in whose jurisdiction the new church lay, as well as undertaking to send a Jesuit priest to a poor part of London if required to do so by the bishop. As it turned out, the building of St Francis Xavier church in Liverpool during the mid-1840s coincided with the Irish Famine and massive Emigration to Liverpool, so the bishop himself petitioned both *Propaganda* and the Jesuit provincial to agree to the new church becoming a parish church in its own right.[10]

Secondly, initially in England and Wales, other religious congregations such as the Passionists, Rosminians and Redemptorists aspired to be itinerant mission preachers rather than parochial clergy, and it was only after 1850 that they were given the parochial care of missions. There were a few exceptions: In 1843 the Redemptorists were given the mission of Falmouth in Cornwall by Bishop Baines, but it soon became clear that parochial work was seen as an unsought-for distraction from what they regarded as their principal work, namely the preaching of missions and

---

[8] AVELING, *The Handle and the Axe*, 319.
[9] F. EDWARDS, *The Jesuits in England from 1580 to the Present Day*, 175.
[10] See N. RYAN, *St Francis Xavier's Church Centenary, Liverpool, 1848-1948*, 22;
R.J. SCHIEFEN, NICHOLAS *Wiseman and the Transformation of English Catholicism*, Patmos Press, Shepherdstown 1984, 178.

retreats.[11] The Passionists, in 1842 took on the existing mission of Aston Hall in Staffordshire which they had been offered in 1840 by Bishop Walsh, Vicar Apostolic of the Central District, but, like the Redemptorists they faced initial opposition both from the secular clergy and local Protestants.[12] Thus, until 1850 the English Benedictines were able to exploit the untidy English Catholic ecclesiastical map, but as we have already seen, their claim to independence led them on a collision course with the bishops that took the greater part of the nineteenth century to resolve.

Management of the Mission

Once a monk had received his theological training,[13] his conventual superior and the President General might consult one another about sending him on the Mission where he would fall under the jurisdiction of one of the two Provincials (of the North or, the South) who were elected by the quadriennial General Chapter. Although issues relating to the Mission were frequently discussed at the General Chapter of the Congregation, the principal forum for such discussions was the Provincial chapter, which met before the General Chapter. The Provincials were required to carry out visitations of their provinces every two years, but they depended on the *Praepositus*, or local superior, for information on the missioners in each area. There seem to have been occasional conflicts between these two officials: until 1818 the *Praepositus* was appointed, but at General Chapter that year it was decreed that the missioners themselves should elect this official. This may well have arisen following a dispute two years earlier between the Provincial of the North and the *Praepositus* of Lancashire concerning the right of the latter to conduct the funeral of one of the brethren.[14]

The period 1795-1850 witnessed a shift on the role of the Provincials from being remote superiors of men in the employ of the gentry to being the real organisers and controllers of considerable manpower in missions actually owned by the Province. With this shift in role came an increase in the power and importance of the office of Provincial, largely due to the expansion of the Mission and the large sums of money administered by the Provincial, much of whose time was spent overseeing the erection of new churches, schools and presbyteries. A contrast can be seen in two Provincials of the North, Michael Lacon and Anselm Brewer. Lacon's 21 years as Provincial, 1785-1806, were uneventful, and he spent the whole of his active ministry in rural Yorkshire. In sharp contrast was Anselm Brewer, appointed

---

[11] See J. SHARP, *Reapers of the Harvest: The Redemptorists in Great Britain and Ireland, 1843-1898*, Veritas, Dublin 1989, 6, 9.
[12] See C.CHARLES, unpublished doctoral thesis, *The Foundation of the Passionists in England, 1840-1851*, Gregorian University, Rome 1961, pt. II, 201-71.
[13] See Chapter 6.
[14] AR, 2: 490.

Provincial of the North in 1837, for whom in the words of Allanson: "the quiet unassuming mode of government adopted by his predecessors was not in accordance with the taste of the new Provincial whose love of show and importance ran through his whole character".[15] In fairness to Brewer, the Provincial system by the mid-nineteenth century was outdated and unsuited to the times, as Provincial and missioners had to grapple with new problems thrown up by social deprivation and urban poverty in ever expanding missions such as those in Liverpool. Provincials also had their work cut out dealing with Vicars Apostolic who, as demonstrated in the previous chapter, were often unsympathetic and even hostile towards the Benedictines. The only similarity between the Provincialships of Lacon and Brewer was their ineptitude in dealing with financial matters: under Lacon the accounts of the Province began to be mismanaged, and whilst Brewer had energy and flair, his lack of financial acumen almost led to the bankruptcy of the Province as a result of his ambitious building projects, the founding of four new missions with large imposing churches, and the building of new churches in three older missions.[16] In 1843, Brewer's confrère, Anselm Cockshoot wrote to President Barber:

> Mr Brewer's projects are as dangerous to Ampleforth as were those of Bishop Baines...His misfortune is that he has a certain impulse within him, which is called by one a love of religion, and by another a craving for distinction.

According to Cockshoot, Brewer's mismanagement highlighted a fundamental weakness in the system: "The rash and dangerous financial schemes of Provincial Brewer", he contended, "can only be checked if there be a real provincial council expressing a real restraint on the acts of the provincial".[17] Provincials were largely responsible for appointments to the specific missions, in consultation with the President, the superiors of the monks to be appointed, and, if there was one, the lay patron. For the most part, this system worked well with few exceptions, such as in 1830 when the Provincial of the South, Benedict Deday, initially refused to allow the appointment of Anselm Cockshoot as missioner at Coventry because he mistakenly perceived him to be an active supporter of Bishop Baines, who, as the previous chapter demonstrated, at that time was doing his utmost to

---

[15] *AB*, 393; see also J.R. RAWCLIFFE, *Birth of a Catholic Mission: St Mary's Brownedge 1690-1918*, privately printed, 2014, 57.

[16] The four new missions were as follows: Cowpen, 1838, Maryport, 1841, St Anne's, Liverpool, 1843 and St Augustine's, Liverpool, 1849. The three new churches built in established missions in the province in this period were at Warwick Bridge, 1841, St Mary's, Liverpool, 1843, and Birtley, 1843. For a full list of missions served by the English Benedictines in this period see Appendix 2.

[17] AA, MS 239 no. 5, 1843, Cockshoot to Barber.

discredit and even destroy the English Benedictines.[18] Provincials in the early nineteenth century tended to live in one of the missions, rather than in separate accommodation, as had been the custom in the previous century.

Mission regulations

Once on the Mission, the monk was bound by a set of missionary regulations, first written in manuscript in 1633, which laid out the respective duties and responsibilities of the Provincial and the missioner. Although these regulations had been revised in 1689, they were substantially unaltered since first being produced in 1633. By 1795 it was clear that a revision of these regulations was required, for as Allanson observed: "many of them had become obsolete, many required modifying and many new rules were called for to meet the existing state of things".[19] In the event it was twenty years before a revision was produced,[20] which some judged to be inadequate, for "while some valuable parts of the old code are omitted…no new regulations are inserted to meet the mighty change of circumstances which had taken place in the English mission during the two preceding centuries".[21] For instance, despite inflation and new expenditures since 1633, the regulations retained the original sums fixed in 1633, which were unrealistic in an age when considerable sums of money had to be found for the building of new churches and presbyteries. Allanson wryly observed that the original figures were retained even though these sums "would then have been worth at least three or four times the value in 1814".[22] Commenting on this, Justin McCann noted:

> The Congregation, whilst practising its fidelity to the traditions of the seventeenth century, was shutting its eyes to the developments of the nineteenth and could not but find itself in difficulties in the very different England of that period.[23]

It was therefore inevitable that both missioners and superiors struggled to adapt to new demands, and although there were no revised editions of the *Regulae Missionis* until 1879, both Provincial and General Chapters in the period up to 1850 did make additions or occasional revisions. Thus in 1822

---

[18] AR, 3, 498; DAB, H143, 25 October 1830, Deday to Birdsall; H145, 29 October 1830, Barber to Deday.
[19] AH, 2: 492.
[20] Two sets were published in fairly close proximity to each other: firstly, *Congregationis Anglo-Benedictinae, in Missione Laborantis Gubernatio,* privately printed, Liverpool 1813, and *Regulae ab omnibus Congregationis Anglo-Benedictinae in Missione Laborantibus Observandae,* privately printed, Liverpool 1817.
[21] AH, 2: 514.
[22] AH, 2: 514.
[23] J. MCCANN, *English Benedictine Missions: A survey,* Alden Press, Oxford 1940, 11.

an additional law was inserted into the *Regulae Missionis* which forbade missioners from erecting new buildings or undertaking extensive repairs on existing ones without the consent of the Provincial Chapter in writing, a decree which almost certainly was enacted in response to situations at both Brindle and Workington, where missioners had not sought permission for such things and as a result had incurred debts.[24] An indication of the extent of external pressures from Rome on the Congregation to reform itself can be seen in the decree of General Chapter in 1846 that missionary residences where two or more monks resided were to be called "priories" and residents where encouraged to wear the monastic habit.[25] At the Northern Provincial Chapter in 1842 the brethren were reminded that they should "say Mass daily and go to Confession weekly". All were also "recommended not to be present at races nor to play for great sums at Cards".[26] Missioners were still required to make a retreat in the monastery of their profession every six years. Yet these changes were superficial and did not significantly change the character of life on the Mission.

Styles of mission

A particular feature of the English Benedictine Mission in this period was the growth of the urban mission. The traditional division of the English Catholic Mission before emancipation into rural chaplaincies and independent, predominantly urban missions is not always helpful, for as Geoffrey Scott has observed,

> some rural chaplaincies lay close to, and often supplied priests to nearby urban centres, and, on the other hand, chaplains serving a family in rural isolation often spent considerable periods in the town houses owned by their patrons.[27]

However, in general, in the early nineteenth century we see the trend continuing from the previous century of the decline of rural chaplaincies and their replacement by large independent missions, principally, but not always, in urban areas. Mission registers of the period witness a growth in these latter, such as Brindle in Lancashire, where the annual number of baptisms rose from 57 in 1795 to 76 in 1815. At Ormskirk, the annual number of baptisms in the last quarter of the eighteenth century averaged 20, but by 1837 the figure had risen to 64.[28] At Coventry, in the first decade of the

---

[24] For Brindle, see *AB*, 273.
[25] AH, 2: 542.
[26] AH, 3: 300.
[27] SCOTT, *Gothic Rage Undone*, 83.
[28] *Lancashire Registers: Brindle and Salmesbury*, CRS (R), 13 (1922) 209-212, 260-61; L. HANLEY, *A History of St. Anne's, Ormskirk*, Causeway Press, Ormskirk 1982, 16.

nineteenth century, in the former Franciscan mission given to the Benedictines in 1803 there were a total of 21 baptisms and 5 marriages. On Easter Day in 1813 there were 59 communicants, and by 1840, 250. The annual number of baptisms rose from two in 1803 to 109 in 1845, in which year were also recorded 100 conversions to Catholicism.[29] Even at rural Coughton in Warwickshire, the annual number of baptisms rose from 12 in 1795 to 33 in 1831.[30] At Bath, where there had been 29 baptisms in 1795, the number had risen to 57 in 1822.[31] Probably the most dramatic growth of all the Benedictine missions in this period occurred in Liverpool, largely due to the influx of Irish immigrants. Twenty years before the potato famine caused thousands to flee their homes in Ireland and sail to Liverpool, Thomas Burke observed that the Benedictine church of St Mary, Edmund Street, "sixty-six feet long and forty-eight broad, was sorely taxed to find room for the thousands who sought to hear Mass therein". In 1795 169 baptisms had been celebrated in the chapel, a figure that was practically doubled in the year 1807. By 1823 there were over 350 baptisms, and by 1845 the annual number of baptisms stood at a staggering 884.[32] The other Benedictine chapel of St Peter, Seel Street, "was utterly unable to cope with the congested Irish population". Such a state of affairs "placed a responsibility upon the shoulders of the Benedictine Fathers, which they were unable to face successfully for nearly twenty years".[33] By 1850, St Mary's church had 6 resident priests, and St Peter's church, three.[34] Not all of the new missions established in this period were in the north. At Kemerton near Tewkesbury a unique foundation was made in 1841, where local Catholic gentry families including the Eystons and the Throckmortons, established and endowed a new mission and then, through a trust deed of 1843 conveyed the property to the Benedictines.[35]

However, there were other Catholic gentry who preferred the traditional role of patron. Although 25 new chaplaincies were established in

---

[29] BIRMINGHAM ARCHDIOCESAN ARCHIVES, P.140/1-4, Coventry Baptismal registers, 1803- 1850; *The Devil is a Jackass*, 271; S. SIMPSON, *A Centenary Memorial of St Osburg's Coventry, 1845-1945*,
<http://www.coventrycatholicdeanery.org.uk/StOsburg/history%20sep%2007.pdf> [accessed 17 October 2013}.
[30] BAA, P.127/1/1.
[31] WILLIAMS, *Post-Reformation Catholicism in Bath*, CRS (R), 66 (1976) 73-174.
[32] LIVERPOOL RECORD OFFICE, 282 HIG 1 / 4-8.
[33] BURKE, *Catholic History of Liverpool*, 37-8; For St Peter, Seel Street, see LRO DAN 1-96, "Materials for a history of St Peter, Seel Street, 1766-1900," this collection is described by J. DAVIES, "The D'Andria Collection, Liverpool Record Office," *NWCH*, 24 (1997) 51-57.
[34] For statistics of resident priests, *The Catholic Directory and Ecclesiastical Register for the Year of Our Lord 1850*, C. Dolman, London 1849, 60.
[35] OLIVER, *Collections,*120; C. COLLINS, *St Benet's Church, Kemerton 150th anniversary: a brief history*, privately printed, 1993, 9.

the early nineteenth century, only nine still had Benedictine chaplains in 1850. The Gregorian, James Higginson served as chaplain to the Riddell family at Swinburne Castle in Northumberland for almost thirty years until 1835, when, following "a battle with the groom in the public street, Mr Riddell...turned away the priest and kept the groom".[36] A more amicable relationship existed between the Laurentian Alexius Pope, and Sir Charles Throckmorton at Coughton in Warwickshire, where Pope served as chaplain from 1823 to 1834. Pope was appreciated by Throckmorton "for his great musical talents which he cultivated with unsparing attention and devotion and his society was much courted at Coughton...being of a lively and jovial disposition". On 13 November 1827, Throckmorton wrote in his diary that "Mr Pope came in the evening and played on the organ". Pope was still entertaining the Throckmortons and their guests seven years later, even after moving to the nearby mission of Redditch. On 5 August 1834 Sir Charles took his guests to visit Pope, who "touched the organ and showed its merits with great success. The ladies were in raptures".[37]

Generally, missioners preferred their independence on missions that had no patron, and not all those who were sent to be chaplains were enamoured of their patrons, such as Ambrose Prest of St Laurence's, formerly Procurator-in-curia in Rome, who was sent to the Middletons at Stockeld Park near Wetherby in 1844. Writing to Alban Molyneux he complained of the squire's interference in pastoral matters:

> The Squire calls from time to time on poor people and induces them to say that they wish to become Catholics...even when the priest is sent for by poor creatures, he is wanted as the Squire's chaplain and not as God's minister.

Prest declared: "I am really glad I get a reduced salary because Mr. Middleton can't in decency complain if I do not do all his biddings". He also clashed with the lady of the house, who complained to Prest that he did not take interest in the family. Humorously reporting the incident to Molyneux, Prest wrote that he would need "six months of lessons from some Prima Donna in Billingsgate" or he would be no match for the Hon. Mrs Middleton. Prest asserted:

> I will tell her to go about her business and be content with her own petticoats and her husband's breeches – she <u>shall not</u> wear the priest's cassock...The family indeed! What are they that I must fall down and adore them? I hope

---

[36] *AB*, 324; DAA, I.A.a.1, no 71, 6 November 1827, Birdsall to Turner.
[37] *AB*, 362, WRO, CR 1998/Drawer 8/9. See also A.Hood, "The Throckmortons Come of Age: Political and Social Alignments," in P. Marshall and G. Scott, *Catholic Gentry in English Society: The Throckmortons of Coughton from Reformation to Emancipation*, Ashgate Publishing, Farnham 2009, 247-268.

at the last day there will be a carriage road up to heaven, for they will never condescend to walk or fly up with the commonality![38]

Prest's letters from Stockeld Park highlight the difficult transition post-emancipation English Catholicism had to make from a lay-dominated church to a new clerically-dominated institution, where gentry Catholic families, new, socially diverse mission congregations, and the clergy did not always sit easily alongside one another.

Some English Benedictines in this period preferred to be chaplains of a different type, such as to the convents of Benedictine nuns at Princethorpe near Rugby, Cannington in Somerset (later to move to Colwich in Staffordshire) and the English Benedictine nuns at Abbot's Salford near Evesham and then at Stanbrook Hall near Worcester. The chaplain often combined the pastoral care of the nuns with that of the congregations that often attached themselves to the convent chapels.[39]

By the 1840s, a vision of a different type of English Benedictine mission was forming in the mind of the future bishop, Bernard Ullathorne, who in 1842 became missioner at the former Franciscan mission of Coventry. His experience in Australia, where he gained an insight into the struggles of monk missioners living in isolation, and his awareness that new religious orders such as the Passionists and Rosminians were establishing themselves in England and demonstrating that it was possible for religious to live in community whilst exercising pastoral ministry inspired Ullathorne with the idea of the missionary priory. He later recalled in a letter to President Placid Burchall:

> …If, on the mission, and especially in important towns, we could only live in community, and with as much community life as the circumstances of a mission would allow of, we should not only ourselves have the kind of life which is natural and proper to us, but that the spirit of our Holy Order would become understood, and fit and generous minds would be drawn towards us and towards our state of life, and our parent monasteries would thus become supplied with a proportionate supply of men and means.[40]

The idea was already crystallising in Ullathorne's mind, as can be seen from a letter of 1843 to the Prior of Downside, outlining his hopes for the mission

---

[38] AA, MS 243, no.18, Stockeld Park, 14 March 1845; no. 18a, Stockeld Park, 26 May 1845, Prest to Molyneux.

[39] When the nuns moved from Woolton to Abbot's Salford in 1806, Mrs Stanford, the owner of the house into which the nuns moved, undertook to pay the chaplain 25 guineas, whether the nuns brought their own or not, or continued the services of Père Louvel, an émigré priest who "lives in a corner of the house, and takes care of the congregation". In the event the nuns' chaplain from Woolton, Maurus Shaw moved with them and Père Louvel was retained to look after the congregation. [SAA].

[40] AA, 246/46, 20 July 1874, Ullathorne to Burchall.

at Coventry, "...which is planned with a view to a priory attached...Thus may we return to our Holy Apostolate even on the mission, and what a force would it not give us". Ullathorne dreamed of "a full choir of *habited* missionary monks".[41] In a letter to Bishop Thomas Brown he declared:

> What ample work would there be for a small community of say, six monks, priests and choir monks, or let them be lay brothers...I shall require a person for music, then two schoolmasters...it would take very little more than our present resources to do all this with the right spirit. Why seek for Brothers of Christian Doctrine, or pay schoolmasters when we could have monks to keep choir, observe discipline and do all this much better?[42]

Although there was already a Benedictine presence in the other large towns of Liverpool and Bath, where no doubt Ullathorne hoped missionary priories would be established, he was a man before his time, and it was left to others in the following century to make Ullathorne's dream a reality.

The Apostolic Life

Missioners in this period continued to be engaged in the traditional employments of celebrating Mass and the Sacraments, and catechising their people. The apostolic work of Prior Peter Kendal at Acton Burnell was highly regarded by Bishop Milner who "held him up as an example to his clergy". Kendal's manuscript instructions on the Douai catechism written both for the college students and the local children are extant at Downside Abbey. At Cheltenham, Augustine Birdsall was regarded not only as "a model of missionaries" but also as "a first class catechist".[43] At Ampleforth are preserved several manuscript volumes of John Turner's "Afternoon lectures" composed for his congregation at Holme-on-Spalding Moor.[44] Elsewhere the personal spirituality of monk missioners, such as Francis Davis of Downside.

Richard Francis Davis was born in Usk, Monmouthshire and was clothed as a monk of St Gregory's, Downside in 1824, where both his brothers, Henry Charles Davis (1815-1854), the future Bishop of Maitland in New South Wales, and Edwin Oswald Davis (1819-1880) and his cousin, George Joseph Davis (1828-1900) followed him. Davis served for 55 years as missioner at Coughton, Warwickshire, from 1834 until his death in 1889. One who knew him described his "long and holy life" being one of monastic stability, similar to "the lives of the fathers of the desert, and of those strange old hermit saints," those "who took up their abode in the hollow of an oak

---

[41] DA, L 230, 15 February 1843, Ullathorne to Prior Wilson.
[42] AA, 30 January 1844, Ullathorne to Brown.
[43] DAB, H 272, 17 January 1839, Walsh to Brown; *The Devil is a Jackass,* 47; GRAHAM, "Prior Kendal and Downside," *DR,* 61 (1943) 61-62.
[44] AA, MC 147, 6U68.

tree in the middle of a wood, and who seldom, or never, strayed beyond the shadow of its branches." He continued:

> Two of the leading characteristics of Father Francis' life were its evenness and its sameness…He rose at half-past four, and paid a visit to the Blessed Sacrament as soon as he came down stairs; then he sat in the vestry saying his prayers, making his meditation, &c, always allowing an hour's preparation for Mass, which he never failed to say. Immediately after midday he recited his vespers and compline, and at two o'clock precisely he begin his matins and lauds for the following day…He dined at either one o'clock, or three, and always preceded it by a visit to the Blessed Sacrament. He gave a certain portion of time to study each day.

So regulated was his life, that "it required no slight matter to oblige him to break through his routine". It was recalled that:

> On one occasion some friends were taking him down the Thames to Greenwich, and on looking round for him to direct his attention to some special beauty of the scenery, or other object of attraction, he could not be seen. One of his friends, who knew his regularity, on looking at his watch, exclaimed, 'Depend upon it he is saying his matins,' and on descending to the cabin there found him immersed in his breviary…when at home…he always had the servants in for night prayers at eight.

It is unsurprising then to learn that "in his personal and household expenditure he was most frugal, but without being in the last parsimonious." Davis died in 1889 and was buried near the church of Saints Peter and Paul in Coughton, where he is commemorated by an inscription in the sanctuary.[45]

Other Benedictine missioners were not so well regarded. James Ambrose Duck was born at Thornborough, Yorkshire on 9th August 1797. Educated at Acton Burnell, he was clothed at Downside on 21 November, 1815. Soon after ordination he was sent on the mission, and after unsuccessful postings at Standish, Cheltenham and Weobley, was appointed missioner in 1840 at Bungay, maybe because he was difficult to place elsewhere. The laity wrote a letter of complaint to the Provincial, who arranged a visitation by the future bishop, William Bernard Ullathorne. Ullathorne recommended Duck be removed, for "the congregation has been falling away …the people do not look up to their pastor: he has no command over them". Furthermore, Duck, "owing to a want of mental vigour and coherence" was "incompetent to the sole charge of a congregation".[46] He was

---

[45] J.A. MORRALL, "The Davis Memorial," *DR*, 10 (1891) 124.126.
[46] DA, Coventry, January 1845, Ullathorne to Barber. See also E. CROUZET, *Slender Thread: Origins and History of the Benedictine Mission in Bungay, 1657-2007*, Downside Abbey, Bath 2007, 57-59.

then moved to Chipping Sodbury, where he stayed a few months before being sent back to Downside. He died in Bristol in 1848.

Another monk who proved difficult to place was Basil Bretherton. Born in Lancashire in 1796 and educated at Ushaw, Bretherton was clothed at Ampleforth in 1818 and ordained priest in 1824. Allanson records that after his ordination, Bretherton "was not found to be of much use" and was appointed to Coventry, where "his instability of mind and great irregularity of habits totally disqualified him for missionary life" and he was recalled to Ampleforth. In 1828 he was appointed missioner at Knaresborough, where "once again his want of prudence and judgement compelled his Provincial to give notice to the President that he was unfit for the Mission" and he was sent back to Ampleforth. Eventually Bretherton was "pensioned off" to France, from where he wrote dejectedly in 1836 to President Birdsall: "I think I am expelled as much as a man can be. I cannot enter the house of my Profession, nor have a shilling when starving."[47]

In contrast, the future bishop, Augustine Baines was sent to Bath in 1817, and his diary of his life there provides a picture not only of life in early-nineteenth century Bath and the development of its mission, but also the energy and drive of Baines himself. His diary reveals that his life as missioner was busy and varied, ranging from preaching, baptising, catechising, as well as administration.[48] Within a few months he acquired a new residence and no effort or expense was spared in furnishing and equipping it. On September 13, 1817 he noted: "went to look at furniture…bought a dining Pembroke table".[49] Two days later Baines acquired "10 chairs at a guinea and 2 Grecian couches for 11 guinea, screens, fire-irons".[50] His experience at Ampleforth in attracting the sons of the gentry to the College evidently stood Baines in good stead, for the names of several notable Bath Catholic gentry families feature often in his diary: Lady Mount Earl, Lady Stourton and Lady Butler to mention but a few, all of whom Baines visited and with whom he dined regularly. But those of humbler rank was not forgotten: on 24 September he "saw 2 poor men at Walcot poor house" and on 3 October he "attended several calls from the poor".[51] On 4 October he heard confessions in private houses, and in the chapel, for 90 minutes each. Administration was a dominant feature; soon after his arrival Baines re-arranged the chapel seats and published new regulations about letting them. Whole days were spent receiving rents, either for benches in the chapel, or from the various tenants in church property.

Baines is a good example of a new breed of cleric that was emerging in English ecclesiastical circles in the early nineteenth century. John Bossy

---

[47] *AB*, 337-338.
[48] WILLIAMS, *Post-Reformation Catholicism in Bath*, 200-239.
[49] *Post-Reformation Catholicism in Bath*, 203.
[50] *Post-Reformation Catholicism in Bath*, 204.
[51] *Post-Reformation Catholicism in Bath*, 204.

has argued that English Catholic clergy also shared in the revival of strength and self-confidence that has been detected in other churchmen in this period, a self-confidence that was gained both through seizing the opportunities for leadership that came their way "by demographic growth, migration and social transformation and by the freedom from external restraint" secured by the Catholic Relief Act of 1791. "A growing separation from and independence of the laity through the widening range of social functions which fell to them in the age of improvement" accompanied this revival in self-confidence.[52] Despite his concern for the gentry, Baines soon proved that he would brook no opposition from them, silencing voices of opposition when he announced that there would be improvements to the chapel, and disbanding the school management committee and replacing it with one appointed by himself.[53]

Baines could however appear philanthropic when it suited him. He used his respected position in the local community to pen a letter to the press to criticise the Bath police for their lack of discrimination in dealing with the poor.[54] To other English Benedictine missioners, philanthropy took a more active form, such as at Whitehaven, where Gregory Holden gained prominence and respect from all social ranks. In 1831 he devoted himself to the welfare of his flock during the cholera epidemic of that year, and "when the terror was over, in memory of a charity which never failed", Holden 'could not walk through the streets without people crying aloud to God to remember the blessing he had been to them in their hour of need". But he proved to be of help to the gentry, as well as the poor. Not long afterwards the colliers in the town went on strike demanding higher wages from the owner, Lord Lonsdale. Holden recognised that "the men were injuring their masters as well as themselves", and met with the leader of the strikers to no avail. The following Sunday whilst preaching, Holden saw the leader sitting uncomfortably in church and departed from the text of his sermon to rebuke him by saying "yes, and *you* are the man to whom I am chiefly speaking, you are the man who will be held answerable for the miseries that people have been brought to by following your advice". Following this the miners decided to return to work the following day. Lord Lonsdale was so grateful to the priest that he granted him his wish of a plot of land upon which was built a new church.[55]

English Benedictines in both Leeds and Liverpool made the supreme sacrifice of their lives in the service of their people. Dunstan Tarleton and Vincent Glover, both missioners at Seel Street in Liverpool, were lauded by a monument in the church which recalled that both had died, in June 1816, and August 1840 respectively, "of typhus fever, caught while consoling the

---

[52] BOSSY, *The English Catholic Community*, 355.
[53] WILLIAMS, *Post-Reformation Catholicism*, 65, 230.
[54] *Bath and Cheltenham Gazette*, 17 December 1817, 24.
[55] "Father William Gregory Holden OSB, 1791-1859," *DR*, 53 (1935) 33-39.

sick".[56] In 1847, three English Benedictines, including the former Prior of St Edmund's, Douai, Francis Appleton, were also credited with the title "martyrs of charity" in the great typhus epidemic in the town that year, which spread as a result of massive overcrowding following the arrival of immigrants from Ireland escaping the potato famine. The monument to these men took the form of a new church, dedicated to St Augustine, which was opened in 1849.[57]

Liturgy

Already by the end of the eighteenth century, the town chapels at Bath and Liverpool had begun to develop an elaborate liturgy.[58] In Bath at Christmas 1817, Augustine Baines noted in his diary that at Midnight Mass there had been "a beautiful Mass of Hayden (sic), full band". At Easter, "the music was very fine", under the direction of the director of music at the Theatre Royal. On the Feast of Corpus Christi Baines "preached at High Mass on the Real Presence for an hour and a half".[59] At St Peter, Seel Street, Liverpool, the opening of the new chapel in November 1817 was celebrated with a solemn liturgy in which Baines sang the Preface of the Mass to an organ accompaniment.[60] By 1830, the organist at Bath was paid an annual salary of £20, whilst the 'vocalists' (their number was not specified) received £30 between them.[61] In contrast, in rural Suffolk, at Bungay, in the "small but clean chapel, 40 ft by 20ft", the choir had to disband in January 1845, "because there were only 2 singers of whom one was generally ill".[62]

Both in the towns, and in the rural areas, missioners recognised that the liturgy needed to be made more accessible to the laity, and besides publishing devotional works for this purpose (which have already been discussed in an earlier chapter) it was not unusual for practical instruction to be given during the liturgy. At Bath on Sunday 15 March 1818 Augustine Baines "explained the ceremony of the distribution of the Palms before the blessing" and "requested the people to come one way and to go another at the distribution".[63] Whilst supplying at rural Bonham in Wiltshire in 1823, the future Archbishop of Sydney, Bede Polding not only ensured that the Mass for the children's First Communion "was performed with some little solemnity to produce an impression of its importance not only on the minds

---

[56] DAA Cab IR/A/38, Woolton, 2 July 1816, Brewer to Parker.
[57] "The Fever Year in Liverpool," *DR*, 29 (1910) 178-86; A. Hood, "Fever in Liverpool," *NWCH*, 20 (1993) 12-30.
[58] Scott, *Gothic Rage Undone*, 125-26.
[59] Williams, *Post-Reformation Catholicism*, 65, 225, 231.
[60] *Post-Reformation Catholicism*, 215.
[61] DA, Box marked "Lancashire Benedictines."
[62] DA, Ullathorne to Barber, January 1845.
[63] Williams, *Post-Reformation Catholicism*, 65, 224.

of the children but on the minds of all those present",[64] but also introduced some catechesis within the framework of the Sunday Afternoon Service, a popular devotion for which earlier English Benedictines, such as Archibald Benedict Macdonald had already compiled manuals.[65] At Bonham, Polding reported:

> I have taken the liberty of changing the Afternoon Service. It consisted of Vespers and Complin (sic) with a lesson after which the people departed, the children remaining to say their Catechism. This I have altered-part of the Jesus psalter is said, on the first three Sundays of the month, on the fourth, the Vespers, on the fifth Complin then follow the litanies of Jesus and of the Blessed Virgin. An examination of conscience for the preceding week concludes the prayers. The children then present themselves for Catechism which is explained to them as familiarly as possible, after which I ascend the step of the altar and explain a portion of the Christian doctrine to the whole Congregation...I sometimes interrupted the series to remind the people of different duties they are likely to forget: of the means of sanctifying the day, of rendering their actions acceptable to God and other points of similar bearing.[66]

In the town chapels, especially in Liverpool, the liturgy in Benedictine churches was often far more elaborate than in the monasteries. Arriving in Liverpool in 1845, the future Prior of Ampleforth, Wilfrid Cooper, found himself experiencing something there "which he had never known at Ampleforth...elaborate liturgical music. Vespers was supplanting the afternoon service of Benediction", and for the first time "Cooper heard Vespers sung regularly".[67] At nearby St Peter, Seel Street during Advent 1846 a Solemn High Mass inaugurated the Forty Hours' Devotion of the Blessed Sacrament at 6am, "followed by the chaunting (sic) of the long litanies and solemn benediction on the same evening and for the three days following".[68]

Buildings

It was through its buildings that the English Benedictine Congregation could testify to its growing stature. Like other Catholic churches built soon after the 1791 Relief Act, Benedictine chapels in the early years of the nineteenth century were small and simple in style and similar in appearance to nonconformist chapels. A notable exception was the chapel that was built in 1814 on to the back of Wootton Hall in Warwickshire, funded by the Dowager Lady Smythe. The chapel, which had a Benedictine chaplain, was

---

[64] DAB, F 92, Bonham, 8 September 1823, Polding to Birdsall.
[65] SCOTT, *Gothic Rage Undone,* 141.
[66] DAB, F 92, Bonham, 8 September 1823, Polding to Birdsall.
[67] B. GREEN, "Wilfrid Cooper OSB, Prior 1850-1863," *AJ,* 94 (1989) 6.
[68] LRO, 282 PET 3/1, "Seel Street Notice Book, 1845-51."

80 feet long, 30 feet wide and 32 feet high, a far grander setting than other Benedictine places of worship of the period such as at Horton:

> [Father Augustine Birdsall] said Mass in the upper chamber of a poor cottage; the room was ten feet long by nine, with scarcely head room between him and the thatch...A deal table was used for the altar and the wind blew through the broken panes of the window; about nine or ten persons attended. [69]

When new churches began to be built, the Benedictines, unlike the Jesuits in the first half of the century, did not adopt a uniform design for their churches. Until the 1840s, also unlike the Jesuits, the Benedictines did not tend to favour specific architects, but employed local ones. In the early months of his incumbency at Bath, Augustine Baines' energies were focussed on "changing the situation of the chapel". And in the months that followed he set about making alterations to it, having decided against changing its situation. He consulted a local architect, John Lowder and directed him to enlarge the sanctuary:

> To remove the vestry and confession rooms from the sides where they obstructed the light while the placing of a double row of ionic pillars resting upon their pedestals and supporting a length of entabilature across the whole width of the chapel added to the whole an imposing grandeur. The Altar also with its ornaments, the painting behind it or over it and the flight of steps and the balustrade in front of it assumed a more elegant and improved appearance.[70]

His future opponent and fellow Benedictine, John Augustine Birdsall at Cheltenham supervised the building of a "substantial edifice", the foundation stone of which was laid in December 1809. "As it advanced", wrote Birdsall, "it became evident that some things could be better done and executed cheaper, at that time, than at a subsequent period when it should be finished". Thus: "a Gallery was determined upon, and also a vestry; and a brick-built foundation for the altar was laid and carried up". It was only after the opening of the chapel that "the floor of the Sanctuary was carpeted; the marble credence tables were fixed on each side of the altar, also the ornamental tablets of marble behind the altar". The altar itself "a sarcophagus, a composition in scagliola, was made in London and placed in the Chapel in the latter end of 1813; till that time the body of the altar was of plaster". The chapel was rectangular, 53 feet by 36. Birdsall helpfully provides a list of what was expended on the chapel, which reveals that over

---

[69] OLIVER, *Collections*, 116.
[70] AH, 3, Appendix XV, 507; The oil-painted reredos in the chapel, depicting the pieta, was later taken to Stanbrook, Callow End, by Dom Laurence Shepherd, where it survives today.

£400 was spent enlarging it in 1825-26.[71] Despite other adornments made to the chapel over subsequent years by 1850 it was regarded by Gothic enthusiasts as being "ill-suited for Catholic worship" and 'without a single exception the most unseemly religious structure in Cheltenham'.[72]

By the 1840s, English Benedictine missioners, like their Jesuit and secular counterparts, began to build churches in the Gothic style. Unlike the monasteries, Benedictine missions had Gothic churches and in some cases, a full peal of bells "long before any English abbey enjoyed such a distinction".[73] A contemporary journal included an account of the little Gothic church at Kemerton near Tewkesbury, opened in 1843:

> [The church] is an admirable specimen, at once simple and chaste, of the ecclesiastical architecture of the fourteenth century…the interior of the chancel is fitted up in a truly Catholic style, with an imposing altar, sedilia, sepulchre, etc. In a word, whoever surveys the interior and exterior of this rural Church, will pronounce the architect, Mr Hadfield of Sheffield, to be a gentleman of truly Catholic taste and feeling…architects of greater pretensions, and of more extended reputation, may go to Kemerton and learn.[74]

Hadfield was later given a commission to design a larger Gothic church at Ormskirk, which opened its doors in August 1850. As we saw in a previous chapter, Augustus Welby Northmore Pugin had not been engaged to execute his grand designs for a new monastery at Downside, but he did receive two commissions from the extravagant northern Provincial, Anselm Brewer, to build new Benedictine chapels at Warwick Bridge near Carlisle, and St Mary, Edmund Street, Liverpool, not always to popular approval. A local report of the opening of the church at Warwick Bridge in December 1841 suggested that "the colours about the altar… [are] too garish".[75] Four years later, in August 1845, Pugin's "spacious and splendid edifice" at St Mary in Liverpool was opened, and the new church, according to an observer could not fail "of impressing upon the mind of every individual who enters its portals with a deep religious feeling". During a week of elaborate liturgical ceremonies to mark the completion of the building, there was a "solemn pontifical mass, preceded by a procession around the church" that consisted of 'twenty acolytes and choristers, with cross-bearers robed in surplices and soutanes, followed by seventy priests and five bishops". The chronicler observed:

---

[71] *Journal of the Gloucestershire Catholic History Society*, 30 (1996) 3-16.
[72] LITTLE, *Catholic Churches since 1623*, 60-61.
[73] BELLENGER, "Revolution and Emancipation," 209.
[74] *The Weekly Orthodox Journal*, 29 July 1843, 70-71.
[75] *The Weekly Orthodox Journal*, 18 December 1841, 398. Brewer's architectural fancies are mentioned by Allanson in AH, 3: 310.

> The handsome processional cross, the lights in the hands of the acolytes, the splendid vestments of the priests and bishops, with the gold and silver mitres of the latter, the sublime chanting [were all] so magnificent and impressive, that the *tout ensemble* could not fail of elevating the mind above earthly objects. [76]

Further north, another Gothic church was built in 1842-43 by the Benedictines at Birtley, near Chester-le-Street, to the design of the famous local architect, John Dobson, who had already designed the Catholic Church at Cowpen and some of the finest buildings in Newcastle, including the Central Station.[77]

Brewer was not the only English Benedictine to develop a passion for Gothic architecture. Upon hearing that his brethren at Downside were planning the building of a new monastery, Bernard Ullathorne wrote: "I hope Bloxam's Principles of Pointed Architecture are in operation. Every priest must be an architect now, as in other days"[78] As much as he admired Pugin, Ullathorne regarded his fees as too expensive. Commenting on a forthcoming commission for a church in Australia, he thought "Pugin would be most likely to secure adoption, concerning his reputation, etc. But expense; 2.5 percent on a church and residence would run up".[79] When Ullathorne came to build a new church at Coventry, he turned not to Pugin, but to Charles Hansom, a member of his congregation at Coventry, and Hansom, soon became the favoured architect of the English Benedictines for the next two decades. After designing the church of St Osburg at Coventry he was engaged to design a new church at Edge Hill, Liverpool, which was opened and dedicated in 1846 to St Anne and hailed as "a truly beautiful and appropriate church; much superior to anything hitherto erected" in the area.[80] In a flyer requesting donations for the new church at Coventry, Ullathorne declared that "the proposed church will be built of the most economical materials and in the plainest style consistent with Catholic arrangement and durability".[81]

Hansom's subsequent fame as a Gothic architect owed much to Ullathorne, who noted that when he approached him to build the church at Coventry, Hansom "was more acquainted with the Greek and Palladian styles". Together, Ullathorne and Hansom "made a study of the Gothic,

---

[76] *The Tablet*, 9 August 1845, 502; *The Weekly Orthodox Journal*, 30 August, 1845.
[77] G. SCOTT, "A Brief History of Birtley Catholic Mission and Parish," *Northern Catholic History*, 35 (1994) 44.
[78] H.N. BIRT, "Archbishop Ullathorne on Church Furniture and Decoration," *DR*, 28 (1909) 113.
[79] DAB, L 396, 16 June 1845, Ullathorne to Heptonstall.
[80] CORRESPONDENT, "Church Building in Liverpool and Birkenhead," *Ecclesiologist*, New Series 4, (1847) 217. The original contract for the church of St Osburg is preserved in COVENTRY ARCHIVES, PA/101/153/1.
[81] RSNC (Anglia, 10) 490.

visited and measured the old Catholic churches in several countries and finally fixed on the lancet style of the thirteenth century for the nave", which Ullathorne proposed "should be developed in to the Early Decorated for the chancel and later chapels".[82] The new church, opened in 1845, consisted "of a Nave with clerestory, North and South aisles, Chancel, Lady Chapel, Tower, South Porch and Sacristies". The dimensions are given thus: "The Nave and Aisles form an area of 80 feet long by 50 wide; the Chancel is 35 feet long by 20 wide, thus giving a total length of 115 feet. The Tower at the West end of the South aisle is 17.5 feet square". An impression of the building is given in some detail:

> Entering by the Western door which is deeply moulded and shafted, with sculptured capitals and heads sustaining the arch and label mouldings – the exquisitely proportioned columns-the lofty arches – springing from moulded capitals, the high and graceful open roof, the solemn disposition of light, the deep chancel receding beyond a noble Chancel arch, terminating with the Altar and the richly emblazoned Eastern window, rendered mysterious, but not concealed by the screen and Rood loft, give a solemn and exalting impression, and assist us to comprehend what must have been the effect of our fine old churches before their spoliation.[83]

Like his Benedictine predecessors, Ullathorne proved to be successful in employing the skills of local craftsmen in undertaking work for a fraction of the cost of the better-known professionals. "Our great difficulty" at Coventry, he remembered:

> was to find a sculptor for architectural sculpture, which was, at that time, a lost art that was only beginning to be revived under the celebrated Welby Pugin. However we found a farmer's boy who, though untutored, had a genius for that kind of art, and with the help of casts with which we provided him, he succeeded tolerably well.[84]

Ullathorne was not slow to realise the catechetical potential of his new Gothic church, and later recalled:

> After the church was completed it drew numbers of people of all classes to see it when unoccupied. It was a new thing to see a Catholic church, with all its Catholic appointments, just like old churches as they were furnished in the Middle Ages; and I had a person there to let me know when there were several visitors. I then went in and explained to them both the church and its symbolism, with which the congregation was made thoroughly acquainted.

---

[82] *The Devil is a Jackass*, 267.
[83] SIMPSON, *A Centenary Memorial of St Osburg's*, 21-22.
[84] *The Devil is a Jackass*, 267-8.

This sometimes led to interesting conversations on the Catholic religion, and catechisms were accepted.[85]

However, by the 1840s, not all English Benedictines were able to build such grand buildings for worship. In his first report to Rome as Vicar Apostolic of the Welsh District, the former Prior of Downside, Thomas Joseph Brown lamented the poverty of his district and reported:

> At Abersychan, the only place which can be procured for the congregation is a club room in a public house…at Merthyr Tydfil the best place that can be obtained for Catholic worship is a loft reached by a ladder, ill-ventilated, low, dark, without ceiling, nor secure against wet and wind and running over the public slaughter house of the town, whence issue the confused bellowing, bleating and screaming of pent up butchered oxen, sheep and swine and whence often times ascend through the floors odours exceedingly offensive.[86]

It was to be another decade before Brown was able to build the Gothic cathedral of his dreams at Belmont near Hereford.

Finance

The Provincial Procurators worked under the Provincials to administer the *Commune Depositum*, the central fund, which each Province had, largely financed by the *spolia* of deceased missioners who were obliged to leave at least £50 to the Province before the residue was given to the monastery of their profession. The Procurator, as in earlier times, did not merely oversee the accounts of the Province, but often provided important links with the monasteries, for which they were often responsible for procuring supplies. The correspondence of Anselm Lorymer, Procurator of the South Province, for instance, reveals that he was responsible for obtaining a range of goods from snuff to musical instruments for the gradually expanding school at Acton Burnell.[87] In contrast to earlier times, having his monastery in England rather on the continent was not always a blessing for the Procurator, as inevitably his own monastic observance came under closer scrutiny. In a letter to Lorymer in 1810, Prior Kendal of St Gregory's gently chided the Procurator by saying: "as to the increase of your salary, the Community of Acton Burnell can have nothing more at heart than it should be increased so as to enable you to live comfortably. How much would answer that purpose? Tell us with all confidence".[88]

---

[85] *The Devil is a Jackass*, 270.
[86] RSRNC (Anglia, 9), fol. 1063.
[87] BIRT, *Downside*, 132-133.
[88] 2 September 1810, Kendal to Lorymer, quoted in L. GRAHAM, "Prior Kendal and Downside,"*DR*, 61 (1943) 66.

In discussing how the finances of the Mission were managed, the corporate funds of the provinces and missions will be examined before moving on to look at the personal finances of the monk missioners. However, it should be observed that for the period in question this is an artificial distinction, as it was not until the Second Synod of Westminster in 1855 that any official legislation appeared requiring the finances of the individual missions to be separated from those of the incumbent. Thus in contemporary account books, income and expenditure relating to the specific mission itself were mixed together with the personal income and expenditure of the incumbent. For instance, in the account book belonging to President Augustine Birdsall, expenditure on personal items, such as "1 pair silk stockings 13 shillings" in August 1819 is entered alongside items of expenditure for the chapel, such as "insurance" and "cleaning".[89] Before reforms in the late nineteenth century, the English Benedictine Congregation was a highly centralised body, with executive powers being vested in the General Chapter, when it met, and in the meantime, in the President and the Regimen. By the bull *Plantata* the Congregation was given the power to determine its financial practices, and was considered to be the ultimate "possessor" of whatever moneys were held by any of its provinces, missions or individuals.[90]

Most of the missions relied on income received from the donations of the laity, which mainly took the form of bench rents. At Coventry, a notice in the small red-bricked chapel built by the incumbent, John Dawber stated: "all occupiers of the first front seats who have not contributed £5 towards the erection of the chapel are liable to be displaced on another offering to pay that sum".[91] At Liverpool, in the chapel of St Peter, Seel Street in December 1845 the following notice was read by the incumbent, Francis Appleton:

> The seat holders are requested to have their cushions removed early tomorrow morning and for the sake of uniformity to have them recovered in crimson…it is hoped that all who hold pews in single sittings will see that all arrears of rent are paid up.[92]

However, at Bath and Cheltenham, being spa towns, the congregation consisted principally of temporary visitors, who would "not take benches for the year", and so it was the custom for entrance money to be paid at the door.[93] In 1830 President Augustine Birdsall, missioner at Cheltenham, challenged the view of Bishop Baines that these charges were unnecessary, and that the bench rents were sufficient for the support of the chapel:

---

[89] DA, IV.B (iv) MS 31.
[90] J. McCann, *The Mission Funds*, Ampleforth MS 284 n 15.
[91] BAA, P.140/1/2.
[92] LRO, PET 3/1, "Seel Street Notice Book, 1845-51."
[93] RSRNC (Anglia, 8) fol. 638.

> Besides a part assigned in the chapel to those who cannot or who choose not to pay for using it, there are in the lower chapel 26 benches capable of holding six, or if crowded, 7 persons each. In the gallery there are six benches capable of holding 10 or 11 persons each. In the lower chapel where the resident Catholics principally are, two individuals only pay each 2 guineas per annum. The rest pay various prices, some half a guinea, more pay less than that and many nothing. In the gallery the seats are supposed to be at 2 guineas per annum or one shilling per week for strangers, but some are admitted also for less and some also for nothing.[94]

Both these missions however, did benefit from income from rented property: in 1830 the Bath mission had the old chapel as well as two houses to rent, and income from these and the hire of two schoolrooms, together with the schoolmistress' room, brought in £164 annually.[95] At Cheltenham, Birdsall declared that in the period 1809 to 1836 the mission benefited "from the receipts from boarders and lodgers, which amounted to between £200 and £300 p.a. They often passed £300 and once they passed £400". These boarders and lodgers resided in the third storey of Birdsall's new presbytery, which he had prudently added in order "to have bedrooms to make it a desirable lodging for letting".[96] Chapter six of the *Regulae Missionis* legislates for the *Commune Depositum* "which shall be made up of the voluntary offerings of the brethren themselves of the property which dead brethren leave after them in England...and of moneys given by other benefactors for the same purpose".[97]

In the seventeenth and eighteenth centuries the *Commune Depositum* was used mainly as a relief fund for needy missioners (in the earliest versions of the *Regulae Missionis* special concern was to be given to the needs of brethren in prison). However, by the early nineteenth century, provincial funds came of necessity to be expended upon buildings as independent missions increased. Whilst a great deal of work was done in the second half of the eighteenth century to put the finances of the two provinces on a firm footing,[98] the finances of the North Province began to be mismanaged under the Provincialship of Michael Lacon, a state of affairs that does not seem to have been resolved until after the disastrous Provincialship of Anselm Brewer.[99] Nevertheless, as Geoffrey Scott has pointed out, the practice during

---

[94] RSRNC (Anglia, 8) fol. 639, Cheltenham, 30 October 1830, Birdsall to Baines.
[95] DA, box marked "Lancashire Benedictines."
[96] AR, 3, 497; *Journal of the Gloucestershire Catholic History Society*, 30, 13.
[97] McCann, "The Mission Funds,"30.
[98] Scott, *Gothic Rage Undone*, 46-47.
[99] Allanson remarks: "The Accounts of the North Province had never been kept in regular order since the first quadriennium of Provincial Lacon, ending in 1789...no effectual attempt had been made to require the Provincials of the North to keep their

the eighteenth century of applying mission funds established by the laity to the Province, rather than a specific mission, did provide the Province with sufficient resources to embark on the building projects mentioned above.[100] Yet by the mid-nineteenth century the ambitious schemes of Provincial Brewer nearly bankrupted the North Province. The South Province seems to have fared rather better, under three capable procurators: Anselm Lorymer, Dunstan Scott and Paulinus Heptonstall.[101] A detailed account written in 1822 of the funds of the South Province reveals that there were then 18 funds, three pertaining to the mission at Bath, four relating to the mission at Coughton and the other 11 were sunk into the *Commune Depositum* of the Province.[102] A significant change in the period after the passing of Catholic emancipation in 1829 was the practice of using bank accounts for these provincial funds, rather than the custom in the eighteenth century of moneys being invested by lay friends. The account books relating to the period after 1829 show that the funds of the North Province were banked at the Preston New Bank, whilst the funds of the South Province were banked in London at Wright's.[103] Entries in these account books show that Provincial funds were expended in a variety of ways, from the printing of official directories to items pertaining to individuals, such as on 10 October 1834 "5 shillings Rev T Heptonstall, punch on his feast" and 5 January 1835 "W Scott – 3 stuffed birds and 1 squirrel". Provincial funds were also expended for the personal use of monks on their way to the Australian mission: entries in the ledger for 1834/5 include "£38 clothing for Rev Polding and others…3 prs drawers for Mr Cotham, 7 shillings…journeys Mr Gregory 6 shillings".[104]

As regards personal finances, missioners were entitled to their own *peculium*, an income made up of an annuity from a missioner's family and a salary, paid to the missioner either by his patron if he held a chaplaincy, or from provincial funds, where moneys from particular missions were sunk. Following the suppression of the abbey of Lamspringe, the monks were awarded pensions from the local government, which were certainly of help

---

accounts consecutively in regular books and no remedy had been applied to correct this long standing abuse". (AH, 3: 347).

[100] SCOTT, *Gothic Rage Undone*, 50.

[101] It is significant that today in the Congregational archives at Downside there are more account books for this period relating to the South Province, than the North Province. There is also evidence of meticulous accounting in the South Province accounts, as can be seen in DA, MS 192, the account book covering the period 1810-1854.

[102] DA, IV.B (iv) MS 100.

[103] DA MS 192 reveals that in 1837 "a large cash box marked MR SCOTT" [the South Provincial Procurator, 1826-1842] was to be kept in Messrs Wright's safe room…Three years later it is recorded in December 1840 that "the Province made a loss on the £780 by the failure of Wright's", See also T.G. HOLT, "The Failure of Messrs Wright & co, Bankers, in 1840," *Essex Recusant*, 11 (1969) 66-80.

[104] DA, MS 12, South Province Mission Account Book, 1827-1835.

to monks such as Augustine Birdsall, who went on to serve on the English Mission. Birdsall noted in 1820 that when he went to Cheltenham he had his "own money...between eight & nine hundred pounds arising partly out of the sale of my annuity, which as a suppressed monk in Germany I then enjoyed from the Prussian government".[105] Although the English Benedictine Constitutions declared that "no regular, whether man or woman, may possess or hold as his own...any property of whatever sort or however acquired, whether money or anything else",[106] this regulation does not appear in the *Regulae Missionis,* which, rather than the Constitutions, appears to have governed the life of a monk once he went on the Mission. Rather, chapter seven of the *Regulae* stipulated that the missioner was to give an account to his provincial annually of his receipts, payments and debts and of other things he has for his own use. Should the missioner not have the benefit of a *peculium*, the Province was to fund his needs. If a man entered the monastery with money from his family, the patrimony was invested in the name of three monks. The monk did not benefit from the interest during his years of formation, but was permitted to do so when he went on the Mission. This practice did not always go unchallenged, however, particularly by superiors of the newly repatriated monasteries which were struggling financially. In 1825 the young Athanasius Allanson, then a junior at Ampleforth, was left the sum of one thousand pounds by his grandmother, which according to the custom of the time, would normally be invested and kept available for his use on the Mission. But the Prior of Ampleforth, Laurence Burgess, insisted that it be paid into the funds of the monastery. Allanson challenged the Prior, and successfully petitioned General Chapter for him to benefit from his patrimony.[107] The finances of the missions were endangered when wealthy benefactors promised money to a specific mission, but only as long as a particular missioner stayed there: Charles Chaloner promised a sum of £50 a year during his lifetime if a mission was established at Aigburth near Liverpool. When the founding missioner, Ambrose Prest was removed in 1842, the benefactor announced that the annuity had always been intended as a personal gift to Prest, and not to the mission.[108]

On the Mission, monks were paid a salary, either by the patron, or by funds invested in the Province relating to specific missions. Some missions were better endowed than others: in 1796 the missioner at Ormskirk, Joseph Crook, was paid an annual salary from the Province accounts of £40, whilst the missioner at Birtley, Bernard Slater, only received £19. These figures are somewhat lower than the figure of £60 a year which was believed to be the

---

[105] DAA, MS account of the establishment of the mission at Cheltenham, transcript by R. BARTON, *Journal of the Gloucestershire Catholic History Society,* 30 (1996) 7.
[106] *Constitutionis Congregationis Anglicanae Ordinis S.Benedicti Monachis Observandum,* MS (1689) chapter IX, translation by McCann.
[107] The issue is described by Allanson in detail: AH, 3, Appendix I, 413-422.
[108] AH, 3, Appendix XV, 521.

minimum salary for a missioner in the 1780s.[109] In 1829 the incumbent at Bath, Jerome Brindle, was paid £50 a year in salary, but his allowance was increased by £43 from various other funds relating to the mission.[110] By 1838, Crook's successor at Ormskirk, Oswald Talbot, was paid £44 per year, which was increased to £56 pounds per year in 1843. In 1842 the Provincial Chapter of Canterbury reminded the Fathers that according to the *Regulae Missionis* wealthy missions were required to help the poor ones. One of the stipulations of the Sir Edward Smythe Fund, established for the use of the missioner at Acton Burnell was that "when the missioner of the place lives with the family...the discharge and payment' of the fund was "to be given to some other of the more needy of the brethren".[111] It was the responsibility of the Provincial to ensure that missioners received adequate income. In 1837, Provincial Anselm Brewer used the medium of a printed circular to announce to his missioners that "the Rev. John Turner, of Holme, has, with the magnanimity of mind rarely surpassed, most charitably presented to the Province £200 to be added to the Provincial Fund for the benefit of the poorer missions".[112]

Monks returning to the monastery from the Mission were permitted to retain use of their *peculium*; they were not required to invest their capital in the monastery funds but were expected to contribute to the cost of their maintenance. As in the eighteenth century, anxiety, tension, scandal and envy were evoked when missioners managed to accrue large sums of money. Bede Bennet, Procurator of the South Province for almost forty years left behind the sum of £4,000. A contemporary commented of him in 1799, the year before his death: "I am told by many that Mr Bennet sinks perceptibly under the weight of years, increased by losses and too much fondness of that thing, money".[113] Allanson relates that Francis Cooper, Procurator of the North Province from 1814 to 1842 "was economical in his habits, and as his mission [of Wrightington in Lancashire] was well endowed, he contrived to save a large amount of money which he divided between his Province and the House of his profession".[114] Occasionally monasteries and provinces clashed over the issue of money and property belonging to individual monks: Oswald Talbot, Definitor of the North Province served for 45 years at Ormskirk, where in the words of Allanson: "he contrived to amass a large sum of money...at one of the most lucrative places in the gift of the Benedictines".[115] In 1843 he visited Ampleforth and expressed his intention

---

[109] DA, IV.A. (iv), MS 176, "North Province Funds and Obligations left by Benefactors,"; SCOTT, *Gothic Rage Undone*, 50.
[110] DA, MS 106, South Province Mission Fund Book, 1805-1829.
[111] DA, MS 100.
[112] DA, Box marked "Lancashire Benedictines."
[113] *AB*, 254.
[114] *AB*, 425.
[115] *AB*, 386.

to the Prior of leaving his property (valued at the sum of over £4,000) to the monastery, but before this could be arranged Talbot became seriously ill and at this point the wily Northern Provincial, Anselm Brewer, persuaded Talbot to make a Deed of Transfer of all his property to him on condition of receiving an annuity of £200 per year. Although Talbot's wish to donate most of his money to Ampleforth was to be honoured, the residue was to go to the Province. The Prior, Anselm Cockshoot, insisted that the whole value of Talbot's property should be given to the monastery, as he held that Talbot had been pressured by Brewer to sign the Deed of Transfer. Eventually the Prior appealed to the President who finally judged that Talbot's gift to the Province was valid.[116]

As in earlier times, specific missions benefited from the financial investment of their incumbents from their *peculia*. The presbytery next to the chapel of St Alban in Warrington, was paid for out of the *peculium* of the incumbent, the future President, Alban Molyneux.[117] In 1799, one of his predecessors, Bernard Bradshaw, left £200 to the mission, together with the whole of his household goods and furniture, with the provision that "each incumbent is to leave to his successors the whole of the household goods and furniture in the improved state they were delivered to him".[118] At St Peter, Seel Street in Liverpool, Gregory Robinson initiated a whole series of improvements to the church in 1818, which cost £1,000, a sum, which was borrowed from North Province funds and paid off from Robinson's *peculium* at his death in 1837.[119] At Rixton near Warrington, former President Richard Marsh established a new mission, for which he "took up funds and the rest he paid out of his peculium".[120] There may have been financial disputes and individual discrepancies in mission funding, but in general the English Benedictines had access to greater financial resources than secular clergy and the Vicars Apostolic.

Conclusion

Of all the various facets of English Benedictine life between 1795 and 1850, it was the Mission that underwent the most change, through the transformation in its character that had already begun to take place in the last quarter of the eighteenth century, as well as through new apostolates and challenges that emerged. Yet whilst the setting and the apostolate continued to change throughout the first half of the nineteenth century, English Benedictine assumptions about the role and character of the Mission did not change: we have already noted the absence of new missionary regulations

---

[116] All the documents relating to this incident are to be found in AR, 4: 367-368.
[117] AH, Appendix XV, 531.
[118] DA, IV.A. (iv), MS 424, North Province Record Book 1640-1882, 90.
[119] DA MS 173, North Province Mission Book, 208; AH, Appendix XV, 527-8.
[120] AH, Appendix XV, 532-3.

and the superficial changes made to those that belonged to a bygone age. By 1850, the average Benedictine missioner experienced as never before a measure of independence, both from the laity and from his ecclesiastical superiors. With very few exceptions, missioners still tended to live by themselves. However, there were real achievements in this period, seen not only in the increased number of missions and of their populations, especially in Liverpool, but also in the number of new churches, presbyteries and schools, many of which, as we have seen, were impressive monuments in their own right, many of which had been designed by the leading architects of the day. All of these achievements undoubtedly raised the image, status and the usefulness of the English Benedictine Congregation. Yet by 1850 the Congregation could not afford to be complacent, as a letter written to General Chapter in July 1850 by Bishop Bernard Ullathorne intimated. Ullathorne lamented that "we have not as yet been able to take up in our character of religious men some of those important positions in the English mission, which new orders have come from abroad to take up". These new orders, Ullathorne maintained, were demonstrating "the practicability of a great degree of community life on the mission", and therefore, the survival of the English Benedictine Mission in the future depended on its monks living in community, "especially in important towns". Ullathorne asserted: "with as much community life as the circumstances of a mission would allow, we should not only ourselves have the kind of life which is natural and proper to us", he concluded, "but the spirit of our holy order would become understood and fit and generous minds would be drawn towards us and our state of life".[121] It remained to be seen whether the Congregation would respond to this challenge.

---

[121] DA, Ullathorne Papers, Box 756, St.Chad's, 15 July 1850, Ullathorne to General Chapter.

CHAPTER 6

Monks, Learning and Books

Writing to his counterpart, Prior Richard Marsh, of the St Laurence community in 1795, Prior Jerome Sharrock of St Gregory reflected on the situation which greeted the English Benedictines on their arrival in England and their prospects for the future: "What course of religious studies could we pursue with success in England?" he mused. "What libraries, what Professors for Philosophy, for Divinity, for the scriptures?"[1] It was a very real concern, for after two centuries of relative stability in their houses on the continent, members of the Congregation who had survived the French Revolution were faced with the loss, not only of their homes, but also of their established patterns of everyday life, which included a system of formation and study. Given the problems faced by the Congregation in this period, it is remarkable how capably and creatively its members succeeded in re-establishing systems of study which would lay important foundations for the future. This chapter will be devoted to this theme and will identify the main achievements.

Developments in Philosophy and Theology

By the last decade of the eighteenth century a significant shift in study had taken place away from the reliance on medieval scholastic theology to an emphasis on reason, by which all ancient beliefs and institutions were to be judged. Philosophical and theological thought were influenced by contemporary political thought which was "anti-theocratic, anti-clerical, broadly democratic and at best deistic, though often atheist".[2] Philosophical and theological thought born of medieval Christianity no longer flourished in a climate of "liberty, equality and fraternity". The Dominicans went on producing critical editions of St Thomas' writings but in general, and especially in Rome, ecclesiastics had lost interest in Thomism, which had been the cornerstone of Catholic philosophy for centuries. During the eighteenth century many English monks had availed themselves of theological studies at the continental universities of Douai and Paris, a practice that was broken with the French Revolution and the subsequent repatriation of the monasteries in England.

The English Benedictines had not been unaffected by the shifting trends in theology and philosophy of the eighteenth century.[3] Its scholars

---

[1] AH, 2: 367.
[2] J. HALDANE, "Thomism and the Future of Catholic Philosophy," *New Blackfriars*, 80 (1999) 163.
[3] SCOTT, *Gothic Rage Undone*, 145-171.

were fairly evenly distributed between two divergent schools of thought. There were those like Joseph Cuthbert Wilks who imbibed the ideas of the Enlightenment through their attendance at university in Paris, and those like Bishop Charles Walmesley, who had at first welcomed the Enlightenment but then later rejected it. Both Wilks and John Bede Brewer, the future President of the English Benedictines, were greatly influenced at the Sorbonne by the Irish theologian Luke Joseph Hooke, whose 1752 work *Religionis Naturalis* was later edited by Brewer.[4] Hooke's empiricist approach to theology led him to be regarded as unorthodox and Benedictine students at the Sorbonne were forbidden to attend his lectures.[5]

It was the advent of what were considered to be dangerous Enlightenment ideas that influenced Walmesley in introducing new regulations governing the studies of English Benedictine monks in the 1760s. The "Method of Studies for the Professed" balanced standard theological texts with the writings of contemporary philosophers. Internal dissensions in 1786 caused Walmesley's scheme of studies to fail, thus depriving the Congregation of a well-defined course of theological studies, the like of which it was not to see again until a century later.[6] A "method of studies" was only one part of the attempt to consolidate the unity of the Congregation. In 1778 the priors of Douai and Paris had agreed in principle that there should be one school and one monastic seminary for the Congregation. Dieulouard was to become the monastic seminary, whilst Douai would be a common novitiate and house of studies for philosophy. The scheme was put into operation the following year, but by 1785 it was found to be unworkable due to problems of finance and finding suitable staff for Dieulouard.[7] Consequently, by the end of the eighteenth century each house in the Congregation devised its own course of studies with varying degrees of success, according to the resources at its disposal.

Formal theological studies usually began after the year of novitiate. The novitiate year had no theological component, its principal aim being the training of novices in the basic principles of the monastic life. By 1795 there was a well-established pattern in the Congregation of two years of philosophy and four years of theology, which had been prescribed by the 1617 Constitutions of the Congregation. By the early decades of the nineteenth century, when the three communities settled in their new

---

[4] L.J. HOOKE, *Religionis naturalis et reveletae principia,* Berton, Paris 1774 [ed. J.B.BREWER].
[5] T. O'CONNOR, *Luke Joseph Hooke: An Irish Theologian in Enlightenment France, 1714-96,* Four Courts Press, Dublin 1995.
[6] A copy of this, translated into English, is printed in full in CRAMER, (ed.), *Lamspringe: An English Abbey in Germany,* 240-43.
[7] SCOTT, *Gothic Rage Undone,* 181-82.

monasteries at Downside, Ampleforth and Douai, all experienced problems in providing theological studies: there was a problem with resources, both human and material. Following the devastation inflicted by the French Revolution, there was no longer access to good libraries or continental universities, and there was a dearth of good professors to teach the junior monks in house. Furthermore, pressure from the schools attached to the monasteries meant that the studies of the monks in training often had to take second priority to the work of teaching. Despite these problems, it is striking how successfully the Congregation as a whole managed to provide monastic studies for its members.

Early nineteenth century Catholic Theology and the Revival of Neo-Scholasticism

Throughout the first third of the nineteenth century, the Enlightenment led Catholic theologians throughout Europe to seek an apologetic platform from which to defend the moral and intellectual claims of positive Christianity against rationalism. In France, for example, this generally took one of two forms: "Firstly, the French Traditionalism of Joseph de Maistre (1753-1821) and Louis de Bonald (1754-1840), which advocated a return to the royalism of pre-Revolution France"; or secondly, "the so-called French Liberalism of Félicité de Lamennais (1782-1854), which advocated the ideals of popular sovereignty, individual conscience, and the separation of church and state so that the Church could rely on its own resources rather than civil governments' for its success." In Germany, at Tübingen, the Catholic scholar Johann Sebastian von Drey (1777-1853) and his student Johann Adam Möhler (1796-1838) formulated a historical-cultural apologetic greatly influenced by German Romanticism[8]. The development of the Tübingen school coincided with the development of natural science which undermined the biblical view of the world, and the discovery of biblical manuscripts and records of other ancient civilizations challenged traditional notions of biblical inspiration and revelation.

Protestant theology, especially in Germany in the nineteenth century, is a history of response to the challenge of Enlightenment rationalism and the new historiography. In the first half of the nineteenth century there were tentative attempts by Catholics (like the members of the Catholic Tübingen school) to incorporate emerging biblical scholarship and to dialogue with its proponents.[9] However, as Scott Seay has emphasised: "early nineteenth-

---

[8] W.L. FEHR, *Birth of the Catholic Tübingen School: Dogmatics of Johann Sebastian Drey*, Scholars Press, Chico, California 1982.
[9] J.R. DONAHUE, "Biblical Scholarship 50 Years after *Divino Afflante Spiritu*," *America: The National Catholic Review*, 18 September 1993,
http://americamagazine.org/issue/100/biblical-scholarship-50-years-after-divino-afflante-spiritu> [accessed 24 October 2013].

century Catholic thinkers, though unified by their desire to develop a defence of positive Christianity against Enlightenment rationalism, lacked any unified method for formulating that defense".[10] They were to find such a method in Neo-Scholastic Thomism, which was already being rediscovered among Catholic philosophers and theologians, particularly in Germany and Italy, as early as the 1820s. What these scholars rediscovered in Scholastic theology was a coherent and orthodox theological method that could defend positive Christianity against the critiques of Enlightenment rationalism. As Seay remarks: "Neo-Scholastics wrote treatises, published journals, instructed clergy, and debated with the proponents of emerging modernism, and thus gained increasing prominence in Catholic intellectual circles throughout Europe by the middle of the Nineteenth century."[11]

Theological formation within the monasteries

By 1795 the community of St Gregory, newly settled at Acton Burnell, was blessed by the presence of three émigré French professors who taught the junior monks. Martin Joseph Leveaux was a Maurist monk who transferred his stability to the English Congregation and took on the roles of professor of theology and novice master at Acton Burnell. Hilaire le Wengue of St Vaast's had been professor of philosophy at the University of Douai. The Abbé François Elloi de Malancourt, formerly of the Sorbonne, also taught the juniors.[12] The presence of French émigré priests elsewhere in the country helped to improve the delivery of theological education for future priests, notably at Crook Hall near Durham, where, in 1797 they assisted in the examinations (known as "defensions") of students' philosophical and theological theses.[13]

At Acton Burnell, the system of philosophy was scholastic, though attention was paid to English philosophers such as Hobbes and Berkeley but not, apparently, Hume. Moral theology was that of St Alphonsus and Billuart. Jansenist textbooks were used and church history was taught from a Gallican standpoint, indicating the pre-revolutionary influence of the university at Douai and the Maurist background of the Frenchmen who lived and taught in the Acton Burnell community. The teaching of Leveaux and Elloi was to have a great influence on Joseph Brown, the future prior and bishop, who began teaching theology at Downside in the 1820s and in whose teaching could be found "traces of the great traditions of the Congregation of

---

[10] S.D. SEAY, "For the Defense and Beauty of the Catholic Faith: The Rise of Neo-Scholasticism among European Catholic Intellectuals, 1824-1879," *Logos: A Journal of Catholic Thought and Culture*, 5:3 (2002) 131-2.
[11] SEAY, "For the Defense," 132.
[12] A. BELLENGER, "The Exiled Clergy and Religious of the French Revolution and the English Benedictines," *EBHS*, privately printed, 1985, 19-21.
[13] D. MILBURN, *History of Ushaw College*, Ushaw College, Durham 1964, 62.

St Maur".[14] Brown was also remembered for his "strong Gallican leanings".[15] Gallican theology textbooks were also used, such as the theological compendium written by Louis Bailly, whose work was later condemned and placed on the Index by the Holy Office. Bailly's work was also used at Douai and in Archbishop Bede Polding's seminary in Sydney, Australia.[16]

In the late eighteenth century, the anti-papal premises of Gallicanism influenced the English Cisalpinist movement, and inspired a number of English Benedictines, notably Cuthbert Wilks. He spearheaded the Cisalpinist movement in England in this period in direct opposition to the English Vicars Apostolic. Both Wilks and Bede Brewer, as stated earlier, were educated at the Sorbonne. It is likely that Brewer's Gallican leanings influenced the first generation of Ampleforth monks, notably the future bishop, Augustine Baines, who wrote in 1821: "Some divines, chiefly Italians, have believed the pope infallible when proposing *ex cathedra* an article of faith. But in England or Ireland I do not believe that any Catholic maintains the infallibility of the pope".[17] Bernard Ullathorne, who was taught by Joseph Brown at Downside, admitted that "the influence of Gallican teaching lingered upon me for a certain time".[18]

It is thanks to Ullathorne that a detailed description has survived of the theological studies at Downside in the 1820s, and of the teaching of Brown and Polding. Of Brown, Ullathorne recalled that:

> He was a teacher who really taught systematically, and not only with method, but with considerable preparation and from an accumulation of knowledge...a teacher who spoke from the digested stores of his mind. [19]

Another formative influence on Ullathorne was Bede Polding:

---

[14] C. BUTLER, "The Record of the Century," 38. The Maurist monks were well-known for their literary achievements. See the recent work by P. Lenain which emphasizes these contributions to the literature and scholarship of the seventeenth and eighteenth centuries, P.LENAIN, *Historie Littéraire des Bénédictins de Saint -Maur,* Brepols Turnhout, 4 volumes, 2006-2014 and specifically for the work of Levaux, LENAIN, *Historie Littéraire des Bénédictins de Saint –Maur,* 4: 487-489.

[15] C. BUTLER, *Life and Times of Bishop Ullathorne, 1806-1889,*Burns & Oates, London 1926, 2: 48.

[16] L. BAILLY, *Theologia dogmatica et moralis.* Lugdini, Lyon 1789, 1804; DAB, G 173, 28 January 1828, Morgan to Brown; K.T. LIVINGSTON, *The Emergence of An Australian Catholic Priesthood,* Manly, Catholic Theological Faculty of Sydney 1977, 21. On Gallicanism see H.C. SHELDON, *Sacerdotalism in the Nineteenth Century: A Critical History,* Eaton & Maines, Jennings & Graham, Cincinnati and New York 1909, 55-6.

[17] P.A. BAINES, *A Letter to Charles Abel Moysey, Archdeacon of Bath,* H. Gye, Bath 1821, 230.

[18] BUTLER, *Life and Times of Bishop Ullathorne,* 2: 48.

[19] BUTLER, *Life and Times of Bishop Ullathorne,* 1: 21-22.

As junior professed, we remained under his paternal care. Under him we studied rhetoric, logic, and mental Philosophy. During the year of rhetoric our textbooks were Cicero, and a manuscript by Eustace, who was first a student and then professor of the priory at Douai,[20] Quintilian and parts of Longinus, whilst for private reading we had Blair, Rollin on *Sacred Eloquence*, and Campbell's *Philosophy of Rhetoric*... from rhetoric we passed to logic. Our textbooks were Watts and the *Port Royal Logic*, after which we took up the scholastic logic in another manuscript treatise by Eustace...Fr Polding was not himself a very deep or persistent thinker, but with the use of his books he made the study attractive. We were grounded upon the Scotch philosophy of that day, using Reid as our principal Class book...after thus interesting us in philosophic thought especially in the beautiful style of Reid and Beattie, Fr Polding passed us on to the Catholic philosophy. All the chief systems were analysed excepting those of Germany, which at that time were scarcely known in England. We were then set to analyse Hume, Berkeley, Locke, Hartley, and to write essays upon them. Then we were introduced to Natural religion, which brought me into contact with the *Pensées de Pascal*, Paley and the large works of Bergier and Bishop Butler.[21] The studies were not confined to philosophy, however. The scriptures were also studied as part of the regime, and Ullathorne expressed gratitude to his old teacher for 'the long continued study of St Paul's epistles and the diligent committing them to memory'.[22]

At Ampleforth, Bede Brewer, who became President of the Congregation in 1799, expressed his concern that the house give particular emphasis to ecclesiastical studies. In 1801, the year before the move of the community to Yorkshire, he declared: "I would not admit to Ampleforth any other boys than such, if the parents are willing, if they have a vocation, to take to the Church".[23] Unfortunately no records survive of the content of theological studies at Ampleforth in this period, but occasional references give the impression that it lacked the talented faculty of teachers possessed by Downside, and the few it did have were taken by Bishop Baines for his new seminary at Prior Park. The studies appear to have reached their nadir in the 1830s, when two junior Ampleforth monks petitioned General Chapter in 1834, complaining of being neglected in their theological studies. In 1846 Prior Ambrose Prest complained that "the theology and philosophy breed has long been defunct in this house". For several years Ampleforth had to

---

[20] T. Chetwode Eustace, was not only a student and professor at St Gregory's, Douai, but was also a novice there for a time. He became Professor of Rhetoric at Maynooth and died at Naples on 1 August 1815. "He left to his Benedictine friends such books as they might wish to select out of his library; and thus many of his books repose on the shelves at Downside". BIRT, *Downside,* 149.
[21] BUTLER, *Life and Times,* 1: 19-20.
[22] BIRT, *Benedictine Pioneers in Australia,* 2: 384-388.
[23] J. MCCANN and C. CARY-ELWES, (eds), *Ampleforth and its Origins,* Burns, Oates & Washbourne, London 1952, 213.

import professors from elsewhere, such as the Italian monk, Honorato Garroni, and then, an Irish priest called Dr Donovan who was engaged to teach philosophy, theology and elocution, and who later applied to join the Ampleforth community. Garroni returned to Rome in 1845 with the arrival of Basil Thomas, who taught dogmatic theology until 1850.[24]

Augustine Baines continued to take an interest in the life of Ampleforth after his departure for Bath in 1817, and his experience of a busy mission led him to reflect on the sort of training that should be given to future missioners. He wrote to Prior Burgess in 1819:

> I hope you will begin to think seriously about making all the religious good preachers – for this purpose I would strongly recommend the frequent public recitation of pieces of prose and poetry learnt by heart and studied with great care…written discourses delivered in the chapel at stated times composed with care and attention will be of great use to chasten the language of your young orators.

No record survives from this period to demonstrate whether or not Baines' advice was followed, or his further recommendation that "amongst your other studies you could make all your young divines perfect masters of the history of the reformation in general and of the change of religion in this country in particular".[25] Baines was soon to prove that he was an accomplished apologist, and it is interesting that even as early as 1819 he was making recommendations in the light of his own experience on the mission, where his advice to newly ordained priests was apparently: "be pious, be learned, be gentlemanlike and not less than any of these be quiet, plain-dealing, honest upright fellows".[26] Later, as Vicar Apostolic of the Western District, he outlined a comprehensive programme of studies for future clergy at Prior Park and employed the Rosminian, Luigi Gentili as professor and examiner in theology. In 1837, Prior Joseph Brown informed a confrère that "a new system of theological studies is now forced upon us by Dr Baines. Dr Gentili is the examiner in moral theology".[27]

Throughout the late eighteenth century, the abbey of Lamspringe in Germany developed an impressive course of studies under the talented Placid Harsnep. A pamphlet of 1795 shows that studies within the monastery covered a wide range of subjects, including meteorology and zoology.

---

[24] Garroni was a professed monk of Subiaco, who went to Sydney in 1842 where he caused trouble and led Archbishop Polding to describe him as "impudique habitué." For details of Garroni's career see T. KAVENAGH, "Polding and 19th century monasticism," 171.
[25] AA, B 267 no.5, 5 July 1819, Baines to Burgess.
[26] P. CORNWELL, *Prior Park College: The Phoenix,* Halsgrove, Tiverton 2005, 17.
[27] P.A. BAINES, *The course of studies in the colleges of Ss Peter and Paul, Prior Park,* privately printed, Prior Park, Bath 1838 ; AA, MS 243 no. 6, Downside, 27 February 1837, Brown to Philips.

Harsnep introduced his students to the leading thinkers and scientists of the day, and even, as Scott observes, "showed some interest in the first dawnings of romanticism by debating Rousseau's writings in relation to the supposed corruption of nature by human society".[28]

In contrast, at Douai in France, where Richard Marsh re-established the community of St Edmund in 1818, the studies were initially limited in scope. Marsh took with him from Ampleforth Charles Fairclough to help him in this undertaking and the work began with six students. Fairclough "gathered the boys around him and started them in their studies. For some time he was everything to them - professor, prefect and cook".[29] Initially, Marsh had to send the first two church students to the local seminary at Cambrai and one to St Sulpice in Paris but by 1824 there were fifteen church students in the house. A letter from one of the first novices to be clothed for the monastery of St Edmund at Douai, Francis Appleton (later to be its Prior) to Brother Stephen Morgan is very illuminating about the nature of the studies pursued:

> We three that were last professed...began our course of theology on the 17 November (1827.) After we had finished the prolegomena we began the treatise De Deo. The plan which Mr Collier has adopted in teaching us is to make us learn the author by heart and afterward follow our lessons with our seniors by making an analysis of them...As for my private studies I am obliged to lay all these aside. There are many things I should like to apply to but time will not permit. However to perfect myself in English I generally continue to write a short sermon every month and if I have any time remaining I employ it either in reading ecclesiastical history or in learning by heart a portion of the old Scripture. [30]

Marsh's success at laying good foundations at Douai is shown by the high proportion of vocations he nurtured; of the 33 students admitted by Marsh, 5 became secular priests and 12 became monks. Of the 35 boys in the school in 1832 after Bernard Collier succeeded Marsh as prior, 14 became monks and 9 secular priests.[31]

Development of ecclesiastical studies in the English seminaries

In many respects the development of ecclesiastical studies in the English Benedictine houses mirrored the developments in the secular seminaries, which had also had to transplant in England after the French Revolution. The northern college of Ushaw, for instance, like the monks, benefited from the

---

[28] G. SCOTT, "Library and Publications," in CRAMER (ed.), *Lamspringe*, 59.
[29] DOYLE (ed.), *Tercentenary of St. Edmund's Monastery*, 45.
[30] DAB, G 173, 25 January 1828, Morgan to Brown, quoting a letter to him from Francis Appleton.
[31] MARSH, *Reminiscences*, 26.

assistance of Sir Edward Smythe, who owned property at Ushaw near Durham, and sold it to Thomas Eyre for the new seminary, which was established at Ushaw in 1818.[32] After the Revolution a northern seminary was housed at Crook Hall, where Thomas Eyre endeavoured to follow as far as possible the system of studies at the English College, Douai which had the tradition of "dictates", defenses of theological and philosophical propositions which had been taken down during the second half of the eighteenth century. The historian of Ushaw, David Milburn, notes that these "dictates became more necessary than ever because of the small number of books available in the college library. In the very early days there appear to have been no more than a hundred volumes".[33] Copies of theses (known as "defensions") that were defended at Crook Hall and in the early days of Ushaw reveal the inadequacy of the course, being very limited in their scope.[34]

Academic standards at Ushaw, as at Downside, dramatically improved in the 1820s. The important figures were Charles Newsham and Robert Tate. Newsham, appointed professor of philosophy in 1819, was sent to study at Edinburgh University in 1821 which enabled him to re-invigorate the philosophical studies and thus enable the seminary to "flourish in…those branches in which Ushaw was nearly a century behind".[35] The 1820s also saw Ushaw create a separate chair of scripture, a significant innovation. The high standard of the Ushaw studies at this time is shown by the success its students achieved in the international examinations held at the Gregorian University in Rome. In 1821, five Ushaw men gained "first" medals in the examination. No college in Rome had ever achieved this. Given this it is unsurprising to find occasional references in English Benedictine correspondence in this period of monks being dispatched to Ushaw to find out more about studies there.[36]

Ecclesiastical studies in the Society of Jesus

A comparison can also be made with the academic experiences and achievements of the Jesuits. Although the Society of Jesus had been

---

[32] MILBURN, *History of Ushaw*, 73.
[33] MILBURN, *History of Ushaw*, 60.
[34] See for instance: *Theses theologicae de septem ecclesiae sacramentis, quas…tueri conabuntur in coll. Cath (vulgo Crook Hall) in comitau Dunelmensi. Dom. Thos Penswick…Ric Thompson…Tho Gillow…Car. Saul,* Ushaw, Durham 1795; *Theses theologicae de Deo, revelatione, ecclesia, &c…praeside rev.dno Thoma Eyre…prius tueri conabuntur Thomas Cock…Thomas Dawson…Joannes Bradley…Thomas Lupton…Josephus Swinburn…Joannes Rickaby,* privately printed, Newcastle 1798.
[35] ARCHIVES OF USHAW COLLEGE, DURHAM, Wiseman correspondence, 14, 13 May 1822, Errington to Wiseman.
[36] DAB, D 361, 12 June 1815, Slater to Jenkins; D 452, 25 August 1816, Slater to Jenkins.

suppressed by Pope Clement XIV, in practice the English ex-Jesuits of the former English province continued their work as teachers and missionaries. In continental Europe, they were obliged to transfer their college from Saint-Omer first to Bruges and then to Liège, where they were protected by the prince bishop of that city in their work of educating boys. In 1794, as a result of the French Revolution, the college was re-established in England at Stonyhurst in Lancashire, where, unlike the English Benedictines, the ex-Jesuits immediately found themselves at odds with the Vicars Apostolic, a situation which severely hampered the training of future Jesuit priests.[37] The issue concerned their claim that at Stonyhurst they had the same rights and privileges that they had enjoyed at Liège as a missionary society with the special object of educating priests for any part of the English mission once served by the Jesuits, and without restriction. This claim was challenged by Bishop William Gibson of the Northern District who asserted that all priests ordained at Stonyhurst were subject solely to him and could only serve in his district. The dispute lasted until 1829, and led to those destined for ordination as Jesuit priests being sent to Rome for theological studies and ordination. It was 1828 before a purpose-built seminary was able to be built at Stonyhurst, and 1830 before it was ready to educate Jesuits studying theology and philosophy.

By 1839 Stonyhurst offered a wide range of education on one site, and became "everything, for a time, from preparatory school to University",[38] that was envied by the English Benedictines. On 7 October 1839, Dr George Oliver wrote excitedly to the Prior of Downside to announce that "there are now 170 students at Stonyhurst, 12 divines, 13 novices, 6 priests and 2 tertians. Would that Downside had as many".[39] Yet common to the English Benedictine houses, the English secular seminaries, and the Jesuit seminary at Stonyhurst in the early part of the nineteenth century was the concern to provide teachers of philosophy and theology. The monastery of St Gregory was fortunate in having the services of trained teachers such as Dom Leveaux, and the Abbé Elloi, but this was unusual. Professors of divinity at Downside and at Ushaw were not specially trained for their work, but had just graduated through the system. Such a system worked well when men of outstanding ability emerged, such as Joseph Brown, but this was by accident rather than design. The added pressure of needing to provide priests for the Mission affected the length and quality of monastic studies. Prior Bernard Barber complained in 1821 to a confrère about the effect this had on the spirit of study in the house: "nothing can be done,' he wrote, "if our best men are withdrawn to the mission".[40] By 1836 complaints were being expressed about the lack of theological formation of English Benedictine missioners.

---

[37] M. WHITEHEAD, '"In the sincerest intentions of studying," *RH*, 26 (2002) 169-189.
[38] EDWARDS, *The Jesuits in England from 1580 to the present day*, 186.
[39] DAB, K 272, 7 October 1839, Oliver to Brown.
[40] DAB, E 303, 5 February 1821, Barber to Lorymer.

The Provincial of the North, Gregory Robinson, lamented to Dr. Brown that Bishop Penswick of the Northern District had "complained that our young men do not know their theology".[41] The situation needed to be remedied.

New educational experiments

A university education for Catholic clerics in early nineteenth-century England was not possible because English Catholic students were prevented from obtaining degrees at the ancient universities of Oxford and Cambridge. In 1803 the English bishops petitioned Rome to grant the new seminaries of Ushaw and Ware the power of conferring the degree of doctor of divinity on worthy students. Recognising the inability of students to travel to continental colleges because of the political instability of Europe, Rome granted the faculty in 1813, but at Ushaw the degree was never conferred.[42] A similar faculty was granted to the President General of the English Benedictines in 1823. The refounding of the English College in Rome in 1818 enabled English students for the secular priesthood to again have access to a Roman education at the Gregorian University. Although such an education was not yet open to the English Benedictines, it seems this may not have been the disadvantage it first appeared. The weaknesses of the Roman system were only too apparent to the new Rector of the English College, Robert Gradwell who believed the Roman philosophy and theology courses to be "too scholastic and too limited" for those destined for the English Mission. He favoured a system whereby the students were taught within the English College so that there was "no reducing of all scholars to one uniform standard and pace". Instead, he declared: "each student is under the necessity of learning every question in his treatises well. The dull are helped forward and the clever are not retarded".[43]

Gradwell expressed these views to the Secretary of State, Cardinal Consalvi, but to no avail. The students of the English College were, without exception, to attend the Roman College and adapt themselves to the method of study of the university. Gradwell's successor as Rector, Nicholas Wiseman who was appointed in 1828 succeeded in modelling the priestly training at the College on the pattern of the Roman education he himself had received. Wiseman had no complaint with the Roman system of priestly training. He considered the city the ideal place for the formation of the clergy, considering that the student there, through his studies felt "himself entirely under the direct tuition of the Holy See; however pure and sparkling the rills at which others drank, he put his lips to the very rock which a divine word had struck, and he sucked in its waters as they gushed forth living".[44] Such an

---

[41] DAB, J 166, 14 June 1836, Robinson to Brown.
[42] MILBURN, *History of Ushaw*, 143.
[43] M. WILLIAMS, *The Venerable English College, Rome*, 86-87.
[44] M. WILLIAMS, *The Venerable English College, Rome*, 100-101.

ultramontanist, centralised system of training was a far cry from the Gallican-centred theology taught by Joseph Brown at Downside in the same period. Despite Brown's later delation of John Henry Newman to Rome in 1859, it seems likely that Brown would have agreed with the future Cardinal that Rome was not a suitable environment for the pursuit of theological study, and with the view of Robert Gradwell that "the life of an English missioner requires a peculiar mode of education, more extensive and more active than the education of those who aspire to study alone".[45]

However, in 1835 an opportunity came for monks to have access to an English university education when the House of Commons urged King William IV to confer upon the newly-founded London University College a charter of incorporation by which it would be possible to grant degrees to its students in all the faculties except divinity and medicine. Later that year the Chancellor of the Exchequer, Thomas Spring Rice declared: "it should always be kept in mind that what is sought is equality in all respects with the ancient Universities, freed from those exclusions and religious distinctions which abridge the usefulness of Oxford and Cambridge".[46] English Catholics therefore now "could take degrees without violating their consciences".[47] The especially attractive feature of the new university was that its teaching was to be undertaken in affiliated institutions, which put degrees in reach of Catholic colleges all over the country. Alan McClelland states that Downside was the first Catholic college to apply for affiliation[48], but a letter in the Downside archives suggests this to be incorrect. In 1840 Dr George Oliver informed Prior Brown that the Catholic colleges of Oscott, Ushaw and Stonyhurst had just affiliated themselves to the new University and questioned why did Downside not avail itself also of this new facility?[49] Brown saw immediately that "here was afforded an opportunity of supplying in some degree the long-felt want of a university course".[50] In February 1841 Downside received a warrant of affiliation to the University of London, only for its first students to fail the University examinations that year, in contrast to the students from Ushaw who passed. It was 1844 before a Downside monk, Benedict Blount was awarded the new external London University Bachelor of Arts, but a tradition was established which was kept up until the foundation of Benet House, Downside's House of Studies at Cambridge in 1896.

---

[45] M. WILLIAMS, *The Venerable English College, Rome*, 86.
[46] *University of London: Historical Record (1836-1912)*, University of London Press, London 1912, 9.
[47] MILBURN, History *of Ushaw*, 168.
[48] V.A. MCCLELLAND, *English Roman Catholics and Higher Education, 1830-1903*, Oxford University Press, Oxford 1973, 26.
[49] DAB, K 347, 8 March 1840, Dr Oliver to Dr Brown.
[50] BIRT, *Downside*, 215.

However, the London B.A. still did not resolve the problem of obtaining degrees in philosophy and theology, for which study in a continental university was still the only option. It took the vision of two superiors, Joseph Brown of Downside, and Anselm Cockshoot of Ampleforth, for this to take place. In 1839, Brown sent Brother Benedict Tidmarsh to Augsburg in Germany for studies. At the outset the aim of doing so seems to have been to acquire fluency in German, which Brown hoped to introduce into the curriculum at Downside, but Tidmarsh was also to study theology. His diaries of his two years at Augsburg can be found in the Downside archives, but sadly contain little information about his studies. To one of his contemporaries at Downside, Tidmarsh wrote:

> St Stephen's is chiefly an Institute for the education of Youth. At present there is no keeping choir, no public meditations or other duty of that kind, no enclosure, no reading in the Refectory at meals, no meeting in the calefactory after meals, no fixed hours for getting up, or going to bed, no summum silentium, and no fixed hours for studies, scarcely any rule at all...We have no Divinity schools...the theological students are obliged to be sent elsewhere.[51]

To his Prior, Tidmarsh wrote in rather more restrained tones: "you wish to know the discipline observed here...it is not quite so monastic as I first understood". He continued: "there are no young religious here as they leave as soon as they are professed, to study theology. Their novices I understand are kept strict, but I do not think so strict as with us".[52]

A more successful experiment was directed by Prior Anselm Cockshoot at Ampleforth, in sending Brothers Austin Bury and Laurence Shepherd to Parma in Italy in 1845. Cockshoot "was anxious to see the monastic life assuring higher theological and religious training to be supplied to the young men of his monastery".[53] Bury was to receive a thorough training in philosophy and theology from the learned Abbot Oduardo Bianchi. Shepherd was sent "for the sake of learning everything that could enable [him] to be of service to [his] own monastery in what concerned the Divine Office".[54] Cockshoot's judgement in sending the two monks to Parma was questioned by Bishop Brown, who, no doubt following the experience of Tidmarsh at Augsburg, had fears about standards of discipline.[55] Abbot Bianchi's reputation as a teacher was well founded. Shepherd described him as "a perfect Thomist...an extremely clever person"

---

[51] DAB, K 324, 15 January 1840, Tidmarsh to Hodgson.
[52] DAB, K 421, August 1840, Tidmarsh to Brown.
[53] SAA, B. ANSTEY, MS *Life of the Rev Dom James Laurence Shepherd* (1897) 16.
[54] SAA, LAURENCE SHEPHERD, MS "My personal souvenirs of the Abbot of Solesmes," 1.
[55] AA, MS 240 no. 24, Chepstow, 2 August 1845, Bishop Brown to Prior Prest.

who introduced the two English monks "to authors which are not to be found elsewhere",[56] such as Joseph Kleutgen, a German Jesuit, who identified the weaknesses in Catholic intellectual responses to modern thought. He argued that only Aristotelian metaphysics could provide a sure foundation for Catholic theology and expounded his own version of Neo-aristotelianism. Such works represented a revival of Neo-Scholasticism mentioned earlier which was openly supported by Pope Pius IX.[57]

Brother Austin Bury was well placed in Parma to drink deeply of this new Thomist revival, which he was later to transmit to his students at Ampleforth. One of these was the future Bishop Hedley, who later wrote:

> Before Fr. Bury's return from Parma, metaphysical theology at Ampleforth had been represented by such writers as Locke, Watts, Reid and Stewart, as at other Colleges in England. Whilst studying in Italy, Fr Bury had put into his hands a MS course of Logic and Metaphysics by Padre Sordi, S.J. This he brought to Ampleforth...Members of the community were set to multiply copies of this...these copies our class had to use...They were not laid aside until 1858 or 1859, when the teaching of Philosophy was transferred to St Michael's, Hereford.

Of Bury's qualities as a teacher, Hedley wrote:

> He knew St Thomas perfectly. Moreover he possessed that keen, analytical mind which distinguishes between term and term, which fixes the scientific value of patristic phrases...from him one certainly learned to be accurate in theological expression, and to appreciate the connection of dogma with dogma. One also learned, by the example of his powerful analysis, how much more there may be in a theological formula than appears to the superficial observer...[58]

Whilst Bury's legacy to future generations of English Benedictines was an appreciation of the importance of Thomism, Laurence Shepherd's studies at Parma benefited the Congregation in a different way. Alongside his philosophical and theological studies, Shepherd came in to contact with the liturgical writings of Abbot Prosper Guéranger of Solesmes, which he was later to transmit to novices at Ampleforth, Belmont and to the nuns at Stanbrook, where Shepherd spent the rest of his life as chaplain. His was a rich inheritance to the English Benedictines in the second half of the century, for he enabled the Congregation to have a renewed appreciation of its monastic heritage, which was to provoke a crisis of identity within the Congregation later in the century.

---

[56] AA, MS 240 no. 24.
[57] HALDANE, "Thomism and the future of Catholic Philosophy,"; 163; SEAY, "For the Defense," 131-132.
[58] *AJ*, 10 (1904) 298.

Libraries

Alongside the content of monastic studies and the personnel who directed them, some consideration needs to be given to the resources available to English Benedictine students following the dissolution of their monasteries abroad, and their extensive libraries there. The monastic library of St Laurence, Dieulouard had been destroyed by fire in 1717, but by the eve of the French Revolution had grown to contain some 2,429 books, of which theology and patristics numbered 887 volumes. The philosophy section, although relatively small (215 volumes) "corresponded exactly to the state of the philosophical teaching that was prevalent in the Congregation at the end of the century".[59] According to Marsh, some 3,000 books were lost at the Revolution. At Ampleforth after 1802 the community "quite quickly set about collecting a substantial library…some 400 volumes survive from this time".[60]

A document drawn up by Henry Parker, the last Prior of St Edmund, Paris in 1790 shows that the monastery possessed "a library of 5,000 valuable and useful books".[61] The auctioneer's catalogue of the library that remained at Douai after the expulsion of the community in 1903 reveals a variety of early nineteenth-century theological works, including books by Bossuet, the French Ultramontane writer Joseph de Maistre, the Scots Protestant theologian Thomas Chalmers as well as a large collection of patrology published by Migne in the 1840s.[62] The collection also includes a number of volumes penned by the second Prior of St Edmund, Douai, Bernard Collier.[63]

At Lamspringe there was a fine library which at one time contained a number of precious manuscripts, including the famous St Albans Psalter, as well as a number of manuscripts by the seventeenth-century English Benedictine, Augustine Baker. After the monastery was suppressed in 1803, the library remained there until 1821 when the last monk professed at Lamspringe, Adrian Towers, attempted to remove some 1100 volumes, only for them to be intercepted by the Hanoverian customs.[64] The collection was thus scattered, the majority remaining in the Hildesheim area (where they

---

[59] AVELING, "The Education of Eighteenth-Century English Monks," 151-152.
[60] A. CRAMER, "The Librarie of this Howse: Augustine Baker's community and their books," in J. HOGG (ed.), *Stand up to Godwards: Essays in Mystical and Monastic Theology in honour of the Rev John Clark on his 65th birthday*, Institut für Anglistik und Amerikanistik, Universität Salzburg, Salzburg 2002,104, 107; CRAMER, *Ampleforth*, 64.
[61] DOYLE (ed.), *Tercentenary of St Edmund's monastery*, 26.
[62] DAA, *Catalogue de la Bibliothèque des Pères Bénédictins Anglais de Douai*.
[63] *A Philosophiae seu morali*, 3 volumes, privately printed, Douai 1822.
[64] *AB*, 380.

were later auctioned) and some eventually brought to England, where they now survive in a variety of English Benedictine monastic libraries.[65]

Another prestigious library in the Congregation was that belonging to the monastery of St Gregory at Douai, which by the time of the French Revolution numbered some 80,000 volumes. Such an extensive library may well have been shared by the Vedastine monks who also lived in the monastery at Douai. By 1793, these collections had been scattered. Some of the books from the St Gregory's library had been torn up for war-time cartridges. Others had been claimed as national property, and had been transferred to the public library of the town, where many of them are still to be seen, bearing the old stamp of the monastery.[66]

The re-settled community therefore had to build up its library again from scratch, and were dependent upon benefactions from friends "to promote the learning of which many were themselves splendid ornaments". One such benefactor was the late Bishop, Charles Walmesley, whose "bequest formed the nucleus of the collection at Acton Burnell".[67] The collection belonging to his successor as bishop, Jerome Sharrock, also found a home in the library at Acton Burnell, a collection mainly of liturgical works. But the most significant additions to the library came after the removal to Downside in 1814, with substantial legacies from Sir Henry Lawson of a set of the *Acta Sanctorum* of the Bollandists, and the library of Chetwode Eustace, already mentioned. Records show that by 1826, a more ambitious policy was being followed to purchase books: "no money was frittered away in fancy purchases; the books bought were proper to form the foundation of a good ecclesiastical library". It was soon discovered that theological books could be obtained more cheaply in France, where the presence of Brother Stephen Morgan in 1827 assisted the acquisition of important theological texts.[68] The receipt for these purchases is to be found in the Downside archives and the following were acquired: 'two copies of the eighteen volumes of Labbe's *Councils*, the works of Francis de Sales, Bossuet and Gaventus'.[69]

A number of English Benedictine missioners also accumulated libraries. Maurus Cooper was missioner at Chipping Sodbury for over twenty years, where he built up an impressive collection of books, 60 of which are now in the Douai Abbey library. They include works by the

---

[65] SCOTT, "Library and Publications," 49-55; CRAMER, "The Suppression," in CRAMER, (ed.), *Lamspringe*, 159-161.
[66] *DR*, 5 (1886) 257.
[67] *DR*, 5 (1886) 258.
[68] Stephen Morgan had been professed at Downside in 1816 but later obtained permission to go to join Fr. Marsh at Douai. He later went to Rome for studies, where he encountered Bishop Baines, who, without consulting Morgan's monastic superior, enlisted him for his Western District. Allanson describes him as a "wayward character," *AB*, 444-445.
[69] DAB, G 63, 1 April 1827, Morgan to Scott.

English Cisalpinist, Peter Gandolphy, Pascal, Bossuet, and a set of Charles Dodd's volumes of *The Church History of England*. Ampleforth houses the substantial library of Alban Molyneux, President of the English Benedictines from 1850 to 1854, which numbers some 450 volumes of theology, apologetics, patrology and church history. In addition, there are a number of titles on contemporary science as well as a selection of works by Anglican divines and apologists.[70] In Australia, the Douai Benedictine, Ambrose Cotham built up an extensive library. His collection included a number of books by St Alphonsus Liguori and Richard Challoner as well as a substantial collection of reprints of spiritual classics by Richardson and Sons of Derby. These ranged from devotional treatises to pamphlets devoted to the immorality of drunkenness.[71] Mention has already been made in an earlier chapter of the library of 1,000 volumes purchased by Bernard Ullathorne in London and Dublin and shipped with him to Australia. The collection, which included volumes of patrology, church history and even 19 volumes of tracts by Martin Luther was later merged with the collection built up by Bede Polding, which by the 1860s grew to 6,000 volumes, thanks to Polding's many benefactors, who included Mrs Sarah Neve of Cheltenham, who also donated a substantial number of books to Maurus Cooper at Chipping Sodbury.[72]

Given the paucity of resources and the limited scope of theological studies in this period, it is hardly surprising that the early nineteenth century was not a particularly productive time for theological scholarship within the English Benedictine Congregation. In the early years of the nineteenth century the only English Benedictine who seems to have taken an active interest in continental trends in theology was Cuthbert Wilks, who was in contact with the German rationalist, Heinrich Paulus, professor of exegetical theology at Jena.[73] It was only from the mid-nineteenth century that English monks began to respond to newer continental trends, such as the revival of Neo-Scholasticism.

Conclusion

By 1847 preparations were well in hand for the restoration of the Catholic hierarchy in England. The potential of the English Benedictines to provide a more centralised system of formation for its members was recognised by the

---

[70] CRAMER, *Ampleforth,* 195.
[71] W.T. SOUTHERWOOD, "A Benedictine Pioneer in Van Diemen's Land (Tasmania)," *Australasian Catholic Record,* 54 (1977) 59.
[72] J. FLETCHER, "The Library of St Patrick's College, Manly," *The Book Collector,* 29 (1980) 179-182; G. SCOTT, "English Benedictine Missions in Seventeenth and Eighteenth Century Gloucestershire," *Worcestershire Recusant,* 50 (1987) 10.
[73] SCOTT, "Dom Joseph Cuthbert Wilks (1748-1829) and English Benedictine Involvement in the Cisalpine stirs," 335.

Rosminian Luigi Gentili, who had been sent to England to compile a series of reports for the Holy See. Gentili observed that

> many of the young Benedictines would like to see their order flourish once more and if Mgr Ullathorne and Bishop Thomas Brown, both Benedictines, had authority, they could soon build up the order with a fine Abbey and novitiate, which could become the seminary of Apostles of Great Britain, as in the days of St Augustine...[74]

Gentili had rightly identified Brown as a key influence in improving the formation of the English Benedictines in the future, for it was Brown who was the principal advocate of the establishment in his diocese, of a common novitiate and house of studies for the English Benedictines. Interestingly, one of those entrusted with drawing up a report for the viability of such a project and for supervising the building operations was Anselm Cockshoot, who as Prior of Ampleforth had been responsible for sending Bury and Shepherd to Parma.

The establishment of the common novitiate and house of studies at Belmont in 1859 and its later importance for the English Benedictine Congregation belongs to a later period, outside the scope of this present work. Suffice it to say that by the time the English Catholic hierarchy was restored in 1850, firm foundations had been laid for the provision of a more satisfactory theological training for the monks of the English Benedictine Congregation. The pessimistic outlook of Prior Jerome Sharrock in 1795 concerning the prospects for English Benedictine studies in nineteenth-century England had proved to be misplaced. Although the standards of studies in each of the houses of the Congregation in these early years on English soil varied in quality, one is struck by the foresight and grit of determined superiors such as Marsh, Brown and Cockshoot which enabled the Congregation to lay solid academic foundations for the future. Their vision, and the newly-acquired wisdom and experience of individuals such as Austin Bury and Laurence Shepherd enabled the English Benedictines to face the uncertainties of their future place in the Church of the second half of the century with new confidence in their educational preparation and achievement.

---

[74] C. LEETHAM, *Luigi Gentili: Sower for the Second Spring,* Burns & Oates, London 1965, 290-291.

CHAPTER 7

"Schools for the Lord's Service":
English Benedictine Education

Therefore we intend to establish a school for the Lord's service[1].

Throughout the eighteenth century, the education of the young had been a principal apostolate for many exiled religious communities on the continent, and this continued after the communities arrived in England in the 1790s. The English Benedictine schools on the continent had often been called "seminaries" because their primary purpose was to educate recruits for the monasteries, and although this tradition continued in England after 1795, gradually a broader policy was adopted of educating lay students alongside those destined for the monasteries. Before examining the continuities and changes in English Benedictine education in the early nineteenth century, its context needs to be established, with regard both to the general theme of education in this period, and in the overall tradition of English Benedictine education.

The education landscape by 1795

English secondary education was at low ebb in the eighteenth century.[2] There were the grammar schools, which taught a narrowly classical curriculum and were bound by foundation statutes and tied to the established church. There were also academies, notably nonconformist academies, which had a wider range of studies and prepared students for a variety of professions. Once restrictions upon dissenters keeping schools were removed in 1779, the need for the older academies disappeared. Their place was taken by a large number of private schools opened in London and the large industrial centres and modelled upon the older academies. There was an important development at this time of schools offering a commercial curriculum, one of such being Sedgley Park, near Wolverhampton, founded in 1763. This was an important school because it was the only one in the late eighteenth century that provided a complete education for Catholic boys from the middle classes. Bishop Talbot, Vicar Apostolic of the London District, in a letter of

---

[1] *RB 1980 : The Rule of St Benedict in English,* ed. T. Fry, Liturgical Press, Collegeville, Minnesota 1982, 18.
[2] See W.H.G. ARMYTAGE, *Four Hundred Years of English Education,* Cambridge University Press, Cambridge 1970; A.S. BARNES, The Catholic Schools of England, Williams & Norgate, London 1926; A.C.F. BEALES, "The Struggle for Schools," in G.A. BECK (ed.), *The English Catholics 1850-1950,* Burns & Oates, London 1950, 365-409;

1787 believed the school to be "ye best of ye kind since ye Reformation".[3] Finally, there were the public schools, such as Eton, Winchester and Rugby, which by the late eighteenth century were beset by indiscipline and rebellion, and offered only a narrow classical curriculum.

Greater toleration towards Catholics in England throughout the eighteenth century led to a small number of Catholic schools being established. At first these were small institutions providing an elementary education such as Dame Alice's school at Fernyhalgh in Lancashire, from the early eighteenth century until 1795.[4] Another such institution was the school at Wootton Wawen in Warwickshire, the regulations for which reveal that children were admitted from the ages of four to seven:

> Children negligent in attending the school are to be deprived of the benefit of it…children subject to any infectious distemper are not to be admitted until cured. Children dirty and filthy are to be dismissed until their parents send them clean and decent. Children subject to the vice of cursing and swearing are to be dismissed if after three months correction and admonitions they remain incorrigible.[5]

Peter Kendal, who was appointed Benedictine missioner at Acton Burnell, established a Dame school in the village in the late 1790s where boys and girls could be educated together. [6] Other mission schools were established as feeder schools for the Catholic continental schools. In the 1760s Placid Naylor founded such an establishment at Brindle in Lancashire to feed the Benedictine school at Dieulouard.

However, throughout the latter part of the century there was continual concern about the quality of educational provision for English Catholics. In 1793, two years before the return of the exiled English Benedictines, plans began to be made to establish a school "for the Catholic laity of this kingdom". Representatives of the leading "old Catholic" families attended a meeting of the Cisalpine Club, where it was decided to set up a public school for Catholic boys. United by their continuing distrust and dislike of the English Vicars Apostolic, it is hardly surprising that not one of these bishops was invited to such a momentous meeting nor consulted, nor that the projected school was to be free of episcopal influence; the governors were to consist only of priests and Catholic nobility.[7]

---

[3] F. ROBERTS, *A History of Sedgley Park and Cotton College*, T. Snape, Preston, no date, 35. Sedgley Park was an important feeder school for some of the English Benedictine schools on the continent. The English Benedictine, John Turner, was educated at Sedgley Park from 1774-1776.
[4] J.A. HILTON, *Catholic Lancashire*, Phillimore, Chichester 1994, 68.
[5] DAB, B 146, 8 January 1798.
[6] L. GRAHAM, "Prior Kendal and Downside," 64.
[7] See WARD, *The Dawn of the Catholic Revival*, 2: 54-56.

At the same time, the Vicars Apostolic were laying their own plans for establishing an English successor to the English College at Douai in the wake of the French Revolution. The English Benedictine bishop, Charles Walmesley got wind of the plans of the Cisalpines and declared that the Vicars Apostolic should not give their approval to its establishment.[8] Weeks before the arrival of the English Benedictines in England, the future Vicar Apostolic of the Midland District, John Milner, warned that the interests of the secular clergy would be threatened by the involvement in education of "ex-Jesuits, monks and Benedictines", and stressed that the bishops "ought to have a good classical school, with masters of first rate talents; and head superiors who are not only capable of conducting but also forming a college".[9] In fact, the year before, the bishops had opened a school catering for both clerical and lay students at Oscott, near Birmingham. Bishop Thomas Talbot of the Midland District cleverly appointed Dr John Bew as the school's first head; Bew was known to be sympathetic to the Cisalpinist cause and had been selected by the Cisalpinists to lead their projected school. Oscott opened its doors in May 1794. Stonyhurst closely followed it in August of that year and then Ushaw in October (although in fact there had been boys at Crook Hall and Tudhoe before Ushaw). It has been asserted that the school at Old Hall Green, near Ware in Hertfordshire was the first, for it claims to have been formally established as a successor to the English College at Douai as early as November 1793.[10]

Catholic educational provision, therefore, enlarged considerably in the last decade of the eighteenth century. Oscott was to be a formidable competitor for the schools set up by the Jesuits and Benedictines at Stonyhurst, Acton Burnell, Downside and Ampleforth. Moreover, there was also the competition created by the two other educational centres descended from the English College at Douai, at Old Hall Green near Ware, and Ushaw near Durham. But it was Oscott that became the main rival of the Jesuit and Benedictine schools, largely because of the breadth of its curriculum and its success during the first half of the nineteenth century in attracting the sons of the Catholic nobility.[11] However, as will be shown, it would not be long before the English Benedictine schools began to be serious competitors for this sector of the Catholic population.

---

[8] WARD, *The Dawn of the Catholic Revival in England*, 2: .56.
[9] Milner to Douglass, 3 March 1795, WARD, *Dawn* 2: 106.
[10] BARNES, *The Catholic Schools of England*, 142.
[11] For the background to this see V.A. MCCLELLAND, '"School or Cloister?" An English Educational Dilemma, 1794-1889,' *Pedagogica Historica*, 20 (1980) 108-128.

The English Benedictine Schools in 1795

During the eighteenth century, there were five English Benedictine schools on the continent. Douai was the largest of these educational establishments in the eighteenth century, and at its height in 1700 numbered up to 50 students, principally the sons of the English Catholic gentry. The school at Dieulouard near Nancy was a much smaller institution with no more than a dozen pupils at any one time, whilst the English Benedictine nuns at Cambrai ran a small school of no more than twenty girls. In Germany, at Lamspringe, there was another small school, again of no more than 20 pupils. Due to falling numbers in the schools at Douai and Dieulouard there was an attempt in the 1770s to adopt a Congregational scheme of education, whereby Douai became a novitiate house and Dieulouard a school at which aspirants for the monastic life might be educated. However the scheme proved to be unsuccessful due to financial difficulties and the fact that both monasteries were too interested in educating their own students. In any event, both establishments were forced to close at the Revolution when the communities of St Gregory and St Laurence were repatriated to England. Douai had certainly begun to decline in the 1770s after reports of rioting by the boys, and of educational standards falling. The English Catholic gentry from this time favoured the college run by the Jesuits in Liège and this led to the school at Douai being filled up from the 1770s with French and other pupils. [12] The English Benedictine school at Lamspringe was not included in the scheme, but it too declined considerably at the end of the century, despite its innovative curriculum referred to in the previous chapter. Being outside France, it escaped the fate suffered by the schools in France at the Revolution, but in 1803, the monastery was suppressed by the King of Prussia, its remaining pupils being transferred to Ampleforth. Due to lack of space at St Edmund's, Paris, it had proved impossible to establish a recognisable school there and thus boys destined to be monks were educated at La Celle-sur-Morin near Meaux. By the mid-eighteenth century the school there numbered a dozen pupils.[13]

It was thanks to the far-sighted English Benedictine provincials of the 1770s that by the time of the Revolution, the Congregation already had educational establishments in England. Both Anselm Bolas, Provincial of the North, and Bernard Warmoll, Provincial of the South, were quick to realise that circumstances would force the Congregation to consider seriously founding a school in England. As a result, General Chapter of 1781 appointed Bede Brewer, the Benedictine missioner at Woolton, near Liverpool, to open a

---

[12] Some interesting details about life in the school at St. Gregory's, Douai in the last quarter of the eighteenth century are provided in H.N. BIRT, "An Old Douai Account Book," *DR*, 18 (1899) 18-35, 140-146.
[13] G. SCOTT, "Paris 1677-1818," in G.SCOTT, (ed.), *Douai 1903-Woolhampton 2003: A Centenary History*, 53, 59.

school there.[14] This was to be a small feeder school, of no more than 12 pupils, whose aim was to prepare students for the monastic school at Dieulouard. The school flourished, and by April 1792 there were 35 pupils.[15] Brewer's success encouraged other Benedictine schools in the area, notably Vernon Hall, where in 1794, President Gregory Cowley established a private college,[16] and Scholes, near Prescot, under the direction of Richard Marsh. These schools combined at Vernon Hall in 1797, and in 1802 this united school moved to Parbold before becoming established at Ampleforth. The school at Vernon Hall will be considered in a further section.

Meanwhile in the South Province, Bernard Warmoll envisaged a college on a rather grander scale, in the style of the monastic colleges on the continent, which he believed would soon be closed because of the unsettled political situation in France.[17] He planned a large lay school, rather than a seminary, which had been the English Benedictine style of establishment, but Warmoll was a man ahead of his time, and in the 1780s the Congregation was more interested in consolidating its educational apostolate on the continent, which was under pressure due to falling numbers and hostile political forces.

The English Benedictine schools after 1795

It was against this background that the English Benedictines arrived in England in 1795, desirous of establishing not only new monasteries, but also schools attached to them. Some consideration should be given to the new Benedictine educational establishments. Like the Jesuits, the monks of St Gregory were fortunate in being given a new home immediately on abandoning their house in France. But whilst the Jesuits had the benefit of a large mansion at Stonyhurst which soon housed 50 students and 170 within eight years, the school that the monks of St Gregory opened at Acton Burnell was on a much smaller scale. The school at Douai, by the time of the Revolution had dwindled to 9 English boys and 3 years after arriving at Acton Burnell the number had fallen to 6, rising to 17 by 1803. 15 pupils moved with the community to Downside near Bath in 1814, and the number rose to 60 by 1829.

---

[14] J.E. HOLLINSHEAD, "John Bede Brewer: Priest and Property," *RH*, 28:2 (October, 2006) 276-277.
[15] Brewer had competition from other schools in the area, see M. WHITEHEAD, '"Not inferior to any in this part of our Kingdom": Woolton Academy and the English Career of the Reverend Bartholomew Booth, Schoolmaster,' *Transactions of the Historic Society of Lancashire and Cheshire,* 142 (1993) 28-39; S. M. LEWIS, 'Bishop Eton – a post script,' *Woolton Annual,* (1986) 8-10.
[16] M.J. MOORE-RINVOLUCRI, "The Catholic Contribution to Liverpool Education in the Eighteenth Century," *Dublin Review,* 228 (1954) 284-285.
[17] For details see SCOTT, *Gothic Rage Undone,* 177-183.

Unlike the Gregorian monks, the community of St Laurence did not have the benefit of a generous benefactor, and spent the seven years after 1795 leading a nomadic existence. It was 1802 before the monks settled at Ampleforth and were able to devote their energies to a single educational establishment. In 1796, the former prior of Dieulouard, Richard Marsh, opened a school at Scholes, near St Helens in Lancashire. Its prospectus of June 1796 declares it to be dedicated to "the education of young gentlemen from seven to fourteen years of age", where the pupils were to be "taught the principles of Religion and Morality, Reading, Writing, Grammar" as well as "French, Latin, Greek, Mathematics, Geography, Algebra".[18] The following year it merged with President Cowley's school at Vernon Hall, Liverpool. Cowley's school, according to an advertisement in the *Laity's Directory* of 1795 admitted boys between the ages of eight and fourteen and the curriculum included reading, writing, English, French, Latin and Greek, elocution, book-keeping, arithmetic and mathematics as well as "a daily lecture on morality from the New Testament" and "weekly lectures on history either sacred and profane and on geography."[19] Writing about the merger of the two schools of Scholes and Vernon Hall, Marsh recorded:

> Mr Cowley, the President, not finding his establishment of Vernon Hall to go on as he wished, partly from a want of a sufficient number of masters to attend to the management of the house and of the scholars who were of the most respectable number and family connections, wished to resign it reserving only to himself a living in the house, and thus giving to the establishment the countenance of his name, which was considerable.[20]

The united school employed the services of a French émigré priest, Jean-Baptiste Gérardot, who was to minister to the Catholics of Liverpool until his death in 1825. In 1797 he published a textbook, *Elements of French Grammar as taught at Vernon Hall, Liverpool*.[21] From Vernon Hall, Marsh moved his school to Parbold near Wigan. Not long afterwards, in 1802, the community settled at Ampleforth, where it was decided that a school for vocations should be established, and that the secular school at Parbold should continue. The following year, the monastery and school at Lamspringe were suppressed, and President Brewer immediately saw an opportunity to transfer its pupils to the new school being established at Ampleforth. Undoubtedly, the closure

---

[18] CDA, Bishops' Letter books, 1796-1797, no.52.
[19] CDA, 1796, IV; MOORE-RINVOLUCRI, "The Catholic Contribution to Liverpool Education," 284.
[20] MARSH, *Reminiscences*, 4.
[21] *Elements of French Grammar as taught at Vernon Hall, Liverpool*, J. McCreery, Liverpool 1797. On Gérardot see A. BELLENGER, " A Tale of Two Churches: The French Revolution and the English and French Catholic Communities: Some Reflections," in J.A. HILTON, (ed.), *The Loveable West: Essays presented to Dr M.J. Moore-Rinvolucri*, North West Catholic History Society, Wigan 1990, 25

of Lamspringe proved to be the saving of Ampleforth College, which immediately gained not just twelve new pupils, but also an infusion of energy and ideas which were to assure its later development and expansion.[22] A notable figure in relation to this later expansion is the former Lamspringe pupil, Peter, later Bishop, and Augustine, Baines. In the early years, however, neither Ampleforth nor Parbold flourished. In 1804 Dr Marsh complained that the progress of the Parbold school was being hampered by the failure of the parents paying the fees, and declared:

> At Ampleforth they have overburdened themselves with taking the young people and boys from Lamspringe, whom however it was thought a pity to abandon as they were desirous of taking to the church, appeared promising subjects for it, and had already made some progress in their studies.[23]

It was clear that the situation could not last. In November, the Benedictine Bishop, Gregory Sharrock wrote to President Brewer:

> It gives me pain to see two men of abilities, Mr. Marsh and Mr. Cooper, detained at Parbold on a service which everybody seems to think not worth such a sacrifice. Would it not be better to break up the school or to put it upon the footing you conceive would render it valuable? [24]

In 1805, notice was given to parents that the Parbold school would close, and that their sons would be transferred to Ampleforth. By 1830, the number of pupils at Ampleforth had risen to 80, but in the ensuing years the fortunes of the school suffered from the ambitious educational schemes of one of its own monks, Augustine Baines, who plundered Ampleforth's capital and resources to found his own school at Prior Park near Bath.[25]

From their foundation at Cambrai in 1625, the Benedictine nuns of Our Lady of Consolation had run a small school of no more than 20 girls. Girls formally entered the enclosure of the monastery for an education, which was seen as possible preparation for admittance to the novitiate. As both the postulants and the young women who came to be educated were known as "scollers", it is difficult to distinguish between the two. On their arrival in England after the Revolution, the nuns settled first at Woolton where they took over the running of the school set up by Bede Brewer, which by 1795 was being run as a girls' school under a Miss McDonald.[26] 11 pupils were enrolled by the time of the nuns' arrival, and 17 by the time the nuns

---

[22] CRAMER, *Ampleforth*, 25; P. GALLIVER, "The early Ampleforth College," *RH,* 28:4 (October, 2007) 512.
[23] DAB, C 103, 28 July 1804, Sharrock to Brewer.
[24] DAB, C 50, 15 November 1803, Sharrock to Brewer.
[25] For details see CRAMER, *Ampleforth,* 68-71.
[26] HOLLINSHEAD, "From Cambrai to Woolton: Lancashire's First Religious House," 461-486.

moved in 1807 to Abbot's Salford in Warwickshire. In 1797 Brewer complained about the nuns' management of the school at Woolton, especially the finances: "I have often told the nuns", he wrote to Bishop Sharrock, "they should endeavour to make the bills as low as possible and be firm in retrenching every useless expense". He asserted: "when I had the management of the school, the average amount of the half year's bills to such as had no masters was £12. But the nuns, contrary to my advice, have raised the pension from 16 to 20 guineas".[27] Yet the school survived and by 1829 there were over twenty girls being educated at Abbot's Salford.[28] The school continued at Stanbrook, after 1838, until early in the twentieth century.

A third English Benedictine school was established at Douai, in northern France, where in 1818, Richard Marsh re-established the community of St Edmund. Four boys went with Marsh in 1818 to found the new school, which by 1823 numbered 28, and by 1850 58. From its first foundations, it was the most distinctive of the English Benedictine schools, for throughout the nineteenth century it took on the character of a minor seminary, as English bishops availed themselves of grants paid by the French government for education in France, in recompense for the properties lost by English Catholics there at the Revolution. Although it also admitted those not destined for ordination, the curriculum at Douai was principally that of a minor seminary, but "the bait of a good French course was designed to lure wealthy lay students from England" to Douai, where "the student may attend exclusively to French...and become a perfect master".[29] Although its location, tucked away behind its high walls in an English enclave in a northern French town, made it somewhat isolated from its counterparts in England, the school proved to be popular with bishops and parents alike, because there students "will be more secluded from the world than they would be at Downside or Ampleforth".[30] Although St Edmund's had the character of a *petit seminaire,* it also educated a number of lay English and French pupils, thus continuing a tradition dating from before the French Revolution.[31]

The organisation of the male Benedictine schools reflected Jesuit influence, indicating the pre-eminence the Society of Jesus had assumed in the eighteenth century in the field of education. Although they had been suppressed by the Pope in 1773 (restored in 1814), the Jesuits became the models for the large number of teaching religious orders and congregations

---

[27] CDA, Bishops' Letter-books, 1797, no.24, 24 March 1797, Brewer to Sharrock.
[28] SAA, box 5, 17 March 1829, President Birdsall to Abbess Chare.
[29] G. SCOTT, "Mariabronn," *DM*, new series, 28 (1977) 8.
[30] DAB, J 418, 14 June 1837, Polding to Brown.
[31] When, in 1790, the monks of St. Edmund's presented their case to the *Comité Ecclesiastique* for the preservation of their monastery, it was asserted that St Edmund's provided facilities for French pupils to learn English. (PARIS, ARCHIVES NATIONALES, D XIX, 30, 430/4, 472, piece 2).

that sprang up in the late eighteenth and early nineteenth centuries, and it is hardly surprising that the structure of the Benedictine schools in this period followed Jesuit lines. The priors took the place of the Jesuit rector, and under him were a number of prefects, usually a prefect of study and a prefect of discipline (at Ampleforth these roles were both the responsibility of the First Prefect). The priors thus had overall responsibility for both spiritual and administrative matters, which worked because of the smallness of the schools. At Douai, the prior acted as the bridge between the community and the college, and would give religious instruction on Sunday evenings and preside at the reading of pupils' reports in the Study at the beginning of each term. The Jesuit "prefect" system was also reflected in the constant surveillance of the pupils by the prefects who were usually the youngest monks in the community and were addressed as 'Sir.' Jesuit influence can also be seen in the nomenclature of the class divisions within the schools, especially at St Edmund's, Douai, where throughout the nineteenth century the divisions of Rhetoric, Poetry and Syntax were retained. Although these divisions were in existence at Douai in the eighteenth century, they were clearly abandoned at Acton Burnell, and not re-adopted at Downside again until 1866, and then abandoned finally in the 1880s. The Benedictine schools greatly differed from the Anglican public schools of the time in that there was no delegation of authority to senior boys, although at Douai in the nineteenth century, there was the custom of the *bon ange*, an older boy appointed to look after a new boy. The system of "fagging" found at the Protestant public schools never seems to have been a feature of the Benedictine schools in this period.

In the eighteenth century the growth of the schools attached to the monasteries had been necessitated by financial concerns, and education became the main source of income for some of the houses exiled in France. Yet in the period after 1795, gaining recruits for the monasteries became a more pressing need and the schools provided an invaluable source of vocations. Almost 70% of the boys educated at Ampleforth and Douai in the first half of the nineteenth century became professed monks, compared to 54% at Downside after 1814 when the community settled there.[32]

School or Cloister?

These figures prompt a question to be posed about the nature and purpose of English Benedictine education in the early nineteenth century. Were the educational establishments at Acton Burnell, Downside, Ampleforth and Douai seminaries or schools? At the outset, the founders of the new schools each independently gave variations of the same answer. Prior Kendal at

---

[32] Figures calculated from DA, MS, *Fasti Gregoriani*, 24-80; "List of Ampleforth pupils, 1830-1850," <http//www.monlib.org.uk> [accessed 5 December 2003]; Scott (ed.), *Douai 1903-Woolhampton 2003*, list of pupils on the enclosed CD-ROM.

Acton Burnell declared that the primary purpose of the school there was: "to obtain the increase of ecclesiastical members".[33] Similarly, President Brewer had declared the purpose of the Ampleforth school to be "for bringing up Youth to a Religious Life, and qualifying them for the discharge of the Ministerial Functions".[34] Richard Marsh likewise described the purpose of the new school at Douai in northern France to make its pupils "good Religious men and good Ministers of Religion".[35] However, it was not long before the English Benedictines began to follow a broader policy of educating lay pupils alongside those destined for the monastic life and the priesthood. By 1812, advertisements for Ampleforth College included the phrase "a limited number of young gentlemen not designated for that state will be admitted".[36] In 1833 the Prior of Douai acknowledged that: "with regard to lay students, we do not refuse to admit them, though it is our full determination never to allow their numbers to preponderate over those of the church".[37] However, an 1836 prospectus for Douai declared it to be

> open for the Education of Lay as well as Ecclesiastical Students. To form them to a solid and enlightened piety, and to give them a thorough knowledge of their religion while they are being initiated in the Languages and Sciences.[38]

The ecclesiastical purpose of Ampleforth College was not mentioned in advertisements after 1815, when an impressive four-page flyer declared:

> It will not be difficult to appreciate the merits of a system which, while it renders the classical part of education more extensive, combines at the same time every principal branch of useful education and enables a young man, on quitting the college, to appear in society with the solid learning of a scholar as well as the elegant accoutrements of a gentleman.[39]

The advertisement was the work of Augustine Baines who, as Prefect of Studies, wanted the College to have a broader constituency than just church students and, as the above quotation emphasises, to prepare boys for life in the wider world. Yet despite this, between 1803 and 1850, Ampleforth

---

[33] DAB, D 34, 29 June 1810, Kendal to Lorymer.
[34] J. McCann, "The Nineteenth Century," in J. McCann and C. Cary-Elwes (eds), *Ampleforth and its Origins*, 218.
[35] Marsh, *Reminiscences*, 24.
[36] *Laity's Directory*, privately printed, 1812.
[37] DAB, I 2, Douay, 7 January 1833, Appleton to Heptonstall.
[38] *The Catholicon*, (1836) 26.
[39] AA, EX01.

produced 31 secular priests and Douai, between 1818 and 1850, 57, achievements of which both communities were very proud.[40]

At Downside, despite Prior Kendall's initial declaration, more lay Catholics came to be admitted into the school. Although over half the number of its pupils between 1814 and 1850 became professed monks, only three of its students became secular priests. Not everyone at Downside was happy about running a school comprised of both lay and ecclesiastical students. In 1827 the future prior and bishop, Joseph Brown declared that "in a large school composed principally of secular students, the remote preparation for a religious state cannot be attended to as it ought among the ecclesiastical students", and "the system of education for secular students is not that which is best adapted to those destined for the ministry". He believed that the "worldly notions and sentiments of lay students" made it "difficult for those destined for the church to the prejudice of their vocation". He wrote candidly to a confrère of the difficulties of educating "spoilt children and puppyish young men" and deplored the fact that "piety is falling off and the sacraments are neglected". He believed that: "the number of boys ought to be reduced to 25 or the vocations of the church boys will be ruined",[41] before advocating a more radical solution:

> There are abundantly other establishments for education and if it cannot be with us more than a secondary object, it should be abandoned if prejudicial to the growth of religious fervour and the education of good missioners....The protection of influential Catholics, though desirable, is not essential to our existence.[42]

Neither was Brown convinced that close bonds between school and cloister were desirable: "our holy rule entirely prohibits young religious from associating with boys. We are compelled to neglect this useful regulation".[43] Such a view differed from the easy informality that characterised relations between monks and boys that was highly regarded at both Ampleforth and Douai. Cramer cites the 1816 diary of Ampleforth pupil Robert Nihell, with its portrait of close interactions between monks and boys as evidence that in this period, Ampleforth was "a seamless garment, from the Prior down to the youngest boy".[44] Galliver observes that "the picture of relationships between boys and masters created in the diary is one far removed from the great Anglican schools of the day," where "before 1850...the public school master

---

[40] For figures, "List of Ampleforth boy pupils,", and for Douai, "The Douai Lists", *DM*, 4 (1898) 218-223; 5 (1899) 143-148.
[41] DAB, G 129, 2 October 1827, Brown to Deday.
[42] DAB, G 157, undated memo.
[43] DAB, G 157.
[44] CRAMER, *Ampleforth*, 61.

was a distant figure to his boys and for the most part indifferent to their extra-curricular pastimes." [45] At Douai:

> The senior boys formed a part of the religious community; they attended the same lectures, observed a certain amount of monastic discipline, rising at the same hour of the monks and being present at the early meditation, assisting at the Conventual Mass, spiritual reading and the rest.[46]

The development of the school buildings in this period at Downside and Ampleforth reflects their differing approaches to the relationship between monastery and school. At Downside, the school buildings that were put up after the monks' arrival were erected at a distance from the monastery, whereas Ampleforth Lodge, the original monastery, lay at the very centre of the estate, and subsequent school buildings were built radiating from it, and were linked to the monastery by a long cloister. In the event, Brown's criticisms of the mixed nature of English Benedictine education led ultimately to fundamental changes in its educational policy thirty years later, when as a bishop, he convinced the Congregation of the need to establish a separate common novitiate at Belmont near Hereford.[47]

Some parents were also opposed to the practice of educating lay pupils alongside church students. Alan McClelland has noted that as the century progressed, several English Catholic aristocratic families increasingly objected to such a practice on social grounds, as church students mainly came from humbler origins and enjoyed free or subsidised education on the understanding that they would offer themselves to the church.[48] Although such social mingling in schools run by religious communities was criticised by some observers later in the century,[49] this does not appear to have had a detrimental effect on the English Benedictine schools in the first part of the nineteenth century: the lists of Ampleforth pupils between 1815 and 1830 boast at least three future peers (Arundell of Wardour, Clifford of Chudleigh and Stafford) together with other notable Catholic gentry such as several Mostyns of Talacre, and Blundells of Crosby Hall, Lancashire. Even in 1830 when Bishop Baines enticed many of Ampleforth's pupils away to Prior Park, the sons of Sir Thomas Massey-Stanley and Blundell of Crosby remained there. At Acton Burnell and at Downside the Catholic gentry were well represented by the Smythe family, several Eystons and the Irish Catholic

---

[45] GALLIVER, *The Early Ampleforth College*, 523, J.A. MANGAN, *Athleticism in the Victorian and Edwardian Public School, The Emergence and Consolidation of an Educational Ideology*, Routledge, London 2000, 113.
[46] DOYLE (ed.), *Tercentenary of St. Edmund's Monastery*, 50-51.
[47] See A. HOOD, "Bishop Thomas Joseph Brown OSB," in A. BERRY (ed.), *Belmont Abbey: Celebrating 150 Years*, 61-71.
[48] MCCLELLAND, "School or Cloister?" 121.
[49] C. CHICHESTER, *Schools*, Burns & Oates, London 1882, 105.

gentry family, More O'Ferrall. The names of several foreign nobles are also well represented: in 1826, Prince Iturbide, the son of the Emperor of Mexico was admitted at Ampleforth, and several European counts are listed among Downside pupils in the 1820s and 1830s, a sign that the Benedictine schools were opening up to a wider world. Because of its location, Douai attracted a number of French students, many from the local area; others came from the Belgian cities of Brussels, Ghent, Bruges and Hainault. There were also pupils from wider afield, including Australia and Mauritius, important English Benedictine missionary fields in the nineteenth century, most of them paid for by the Benedictine bishops appointed to those areas. The first student from the United States was admitted in 1836.[50]

Educational attainment

First and foremost, the English Benedictine schools in the early nineteenth century were blessed with gifted teachers such as the future bishops Joseph Brown and Bede Polding at Downside, and Austin Bury at Ampleforth. Of Brown, his obituarist recalled that:

> Those who studied under him speak of the enthusiasm his energy and depth of reading was able to enkindle in the minds of his pupils…those who had the benefit of being in his class at Downside will greatly remember the spirit and earnestness of his teaching and the peculiar power he evinced in recognising and encouraging the opening abilities of his pupils. Indeed to attend class under him was an enjoyment to them, as he not only commanded their respect and admiration by his learning, but won their affection and put them at their ease by his kind, considerate and genial way of keeping them truly interested in their studies and their own self-advancement.[51]

Of Bede Polding, the future apostle of Australia, it was said:

> [He was] highly esteemed…for his was not only merely the accurate knowledge and scholastic ability of a good professor, but the wise and generous spirit of sympathising and appreciative perception, which knew how to improve every opportunity in the lesson of educating the feelings as well as the mind.[52]

---

[50] Between 1818 and 1850 there were 35 French pupils at St Edmund's, of whom 9 are listed as being from Douai itself. (SCOTT, *Douai 1903, Woolhampton 2003*, CD ROM giving list of pupils.)
[51] "The Rt. Rev Thomas Joseph Brown," *DR*, 1 (1880) 7.
[52] "Memoirs of distinguished Gregorians: II. The Most Rev. John Bede Polding, DD, OSB," *DR*, 1 (1880) 96.

Austin Bury was only eighteen years of age when in 1844 he was appointed to teach French to the last class in the Upper School at Ampleforth. After returning from his studies in Italy in 1848, he taught Greek, French and Geometry. A former pupil recalled:

> As a master, he always came to class with the lesson thoroughly prepared. His patience in demonstrating a difficult problem to a slow student was simply incomparable. Sometimes he would use a variety of illustrations, sometimes he would descend into the student's mind and from what he did know lead him step by step to the solution of his difficulty.[53]

Such gifted teachers were few and far between, and although the Benedictine schools in this period were largely "unpretentious and domestic",[54] yet they offered a curriculum which was broader than that being provided at the great English public schools of the day, where nothing beyond the Classics were taught. The enthusiasm and imagination of the monks' teaching is seen in the broadening of the curriculum beyond the Classics to include history, geography, science and modern languages, but also in their encouraging their pupils to read widely. A good example of this is that of John William Polidori, who gained fame as the physician of the poet Byron and who died prematurely at 25. Polidori was educated at Ampleforth between 1804 and 1810 where "the breadth of his reading" was almost "mythical". After John's death, his father observed: "it seemed impossible that a young man who lived only twenty-five years could have thought and written so much"; a remark which represents "a striking testimonial of a school of a dozen pupils in an isolated Yorkshire valley at a time when Catholic levels of education were very low".[55]

The impressive advertisement for Ampleforth College placed in the *Laity's Directory* for 1815 gives a detailed explanation of the programme of studies, which includes natural history, ornithology and botany. The advertisement concludes by mentioning the author of the programme, a noted educationalist, Gregor Feinagle, a German Cistercian who lectured in London. Feinagle was a proponent of a system of memory training which, although quite a controversial one, appears for a time to have brought Ampleforth College to quite high standards.[56] Several contemporary letters now extant at Downside reveal the notoriety of Feinagle amongst English Benedictines of the period. Prior Augustine Lawson immediately recognised

---

[53] <http://www.monlib.org.uk/obits/smith/bury_a.htm>, [accessed 6 December 2003].
[54] BELLENGER, "Revolution and Emancipation," 211.
[55] P. SMILEY, "Polidori at Ampleforth," *AJ*, 97 (1992) 37.
[56] On the importance of Feinagle, see F.A. YATES, *The Art of Memory,* Penguin, Harmondsworth, 1978, 94.

the advantages of the Feinagle system, which was introduced at Downside,[57] and was still in use some years later when the future bishop, Bernard Ullathorne was in the school. Ullathorne later recorded:

> The College attached considerable importance in those days to Finegle's (sic) System of fixing the chronology of History, using which system, we were taught Goldsmith's English and Roman Histories and Reeve's Church History. I took to the Histories, but mentally discarded Finegle's method as cumbrous and overloaded with contrivances.[58]

At Ampleforth, Feinagle was also responsible for introducing public examinations, and "Exhibition", an open-day and prize-giving, which is still kept at Ampleforth. This had the dual purpose of stimulating the intellects of the boys, and advertising the excellence of the school. Prior Lawson had no intention of following the same practice at Downside, declaring: "as to public exhibitions and show, I condemn them: they will introduce too much of the world amongst us and I fear in the end be detrimental to discipline".[59] Lawson may well have seen and been displeased by a letter sent to a boy at Downside in 1815 which observed:

> no house of education has, within late years, forced itself so much into public notice as the little college at Ampleforth. The gentlemen there have boldly dared to think for themselves, and to leave the beaten track…they profess to make a lad a tolerably good scholar before you at Downside could find time to get him through his horn-book and reading-made-easy; not that your professors are deficient either in learning or abilities, but because they have not been initiated in the magic operations of squares and circles.[60]

Baines' publicity campaign had clearly had some effect, not least in encouraging a spirit of rivalry and competition between the two schools.

The Feinagle system also discouraged corporal punishment. This was a marked contrast with the practice at contemporary Eton where, as Bernard Green observed: "Dr Keate was still capable of flogging the entire school in one session".[61] Corporal punishment was also a feature of life at the Jesuit College at Stonyhurst, where in 1846 the *Preston Guardian* reported that it had learnt "with some surprise, that the practice of flogging is carried on…with a severity, which calls loudly for reprobation. No fewer than six youths were very recently subjected to this degrading punishment in one day". The newspaper grimly added that: "one of the youths has preserved his blood-

---

[57] DAB, D 373, 21 August 1815, Lawson to Lorymer.
[58] *The Devil is a Jackass*, 39.
[59] DAB, D 373, 21 August 1815, Lawson to Lorymer.
[60] ANON, "Journalism at Downside," *DR*, 5 (1886) 95.
[61] B. GREEN, "Augustine Baines, OSB, 1786-1843," *AJ*, 92 (1986) 20.

stained bum to exhibit to his parents".[62] According to Alan McClelland, "the harshness of Jesuit discipline alienated many aristocratic families and was to be objected to increasingly as the nineteenth century advanced".[63] In contrast, in 1833, Prior Francis Appleton at Douai asserted that "corporal punishment is seldom or never had recourse to. The students are ruled with mildness and condescension. They live together like brothers".[64] Birt, in his history of Downside School, makes reference to "rough and turbulent times" there in the 1840s, which brought "a passing element of insubordination". He relates that this was successfully quashed by the two Prefects, nicknamed "the arm", and "the hand and tongue", by whose efforts "the unruly symptoms were suppressed before they had become hurtful".[65]

New building at Downside in the 1820s encouraged an enlargement in the scope of studies and music gained particular prominence there. Sir John Lambert, whose name is closely associated with the revival of plainsong in England in the nineteenth century, was educated at Downside during these years and he later set down his reminiscences of the period when foundations were laid "for the cultivation not only of music for the church, but also of secular music". The newly opened chapel became the focus for a new choir and quickly attracted the talents of several noted contemporary musicians such as C.W. Manners, who also taught piano, and the well-known composer and pianist Joseph (afterwards Count) Mazzinghi, whose music was sung at the coronation of King George IV. Mazzinghi was well connected in the upper echelons of English society, and often played duets with the Prince of Wales. It was Mazzinghi who was appointed to compose the Mass for the opening of the new chapel at Downside, which "was most ably executed, and ravished the audience".[66] Under these musicians, music at Downside went from strength to strength, so that "the Masses of Webbe gave place to the more difficult ones of Casaldi, Baldi and Ricci, and the latter in their turn were ultimately succeeded by those of Haydn and Mozart".[67] Yet despite these advances, Downside could not emulate Stonyhurst, which, even before the opening of its church of St Peter in 1835, had three choirs: the main college choir, a "Congregational Choir" and a smaller Vespers choir, which recruited not only boys but professors and students from its seminary at St Mary's Hall. Thomas Muir's study of the musical repertoire of the Stonyhurst choir reveals that by 1811 it was already tackling the ambitious

---

[62] T.E Muir, *Stonyhurst College, 1593-1993*, James & James, London 1992, 92.
[63] McClelland, 'School or Cloister?' 120.
[64] DAB, I 2, Douai, 7 January 1833, Appleton to Heptonstall.
[65] Birt, *Downside*, 217.
[66] Birt, *Downside*, 189.
[67] J. Lambert, "Music and Musicians at St Gregory's, 1823 to 1831," *DR*, 7 (1888) 12.

choral works of Mozart and Haydn, and that it was one of only 6 English purchasers of the first full score of Mozart's *Requiem* in 1826.[68]

The Benedictine schools in the early nineteenth century were no match for Stonyhurst in other respects too. As well as their small size, when compared to Stonyhurst, the facilities were far less sophisticated. As early as 1808 Stonyhurst enjoyed the benefits of a fully equipped scientific laboratory, the first of its kind in an English school.[69] It was 1857 before another English school, Rugby, possessed anything comparable to it. Another enhancement was the building at Stonyhurst, in 1837, of an observatory, a facility envied by the Benedictine schools, and not acquired by Downside until twenty years later. Likewise, the Benedictine nuns at Woolton and Abbot's Salford were unable to compete with the forward-looking curriculum being offered by the English Canonesses who had migrated from Liège to New Hall in Essex. As early as the 1770s the Canonesses were offering a broad curriculum of subjects that included Italian, double-entry book-keeping, heraldry and the principles of natural history.[70] In the 1830s, both Ampleforth and Downside also suffered from the competition posed by the opening of Bishop Baines' new school at Prior Park. Baines had practically stripped Ampleforth of its teachers and pupils to stock his new school, and its popularity also "gave a serious check to Downside, where the numbers at once fell off appreciably", especially among the parents of some boys who "were attracted…by the glamour of a school presided over by a bishop".[71]

Stonyhurst also pioneered the provision of tertiary level higher education for Catholic lay men, as well as those proceeding to holy orders, which gained academic credence through its affiliation with the University of London in 1839. For some years before this, Stonyhurst had begun to admit "gentlemen philosophers" who pursued a course of higher studies in philosophy.[72] The affiliation with London University enabled students to sit for external London degrees, the first recognised academic qualifications English Catholics were able to gain since the Reformation. Downside followed the lead of Stonyhurst in 1840 in becoming affiliated to London University, but although its students were called philosophers they did not study philosophy, and their numbers were significantly smaller than at Stonyhurst.

---

[68] T.E. MUIR, "Ad *Majorem Dei Gloriam:* Catholic Church Music at Everingham and Stonyhurst," <http://www.bpmonline.org.uk/bpm5-admajorem.html> [accessed 2 December 2003].
[69] T.E. MUIR, *Stonyhurst College,* 81.
[70] M. WHITEHEAD, "'A Prolific Nursery of Piety and Learning," Educational Development and Corporate Identity at the *Académie Anglaise,* Liège and at Stonyhurst, 1773-1803,' in T. MCCOOG (ed.), *Promising Hope: Essays on the Suppression and Restoration of the English Province of the Society of Jesus,* Institutum Historicum Societatis Iesu, London 2003, 137.
[71] BIRT, *Downside,* 204.
[72] See H.J.A. SIRE, *Gentlemen Philosophers: Catholic Higher Education at Liège and Stonyhurst, 1774-1916,* Churchman, Worthing 1988.

The English Benedictine schools may have been no match for Stonyhurst in the first half of the nineteenth century, but in general terms they far exceeded the educational standards found in the English Protestant schools. In an article published in 1848 in *The Tablet*, Bishop Bernard Ullathorne, who was educated at Downside in the 1820s, stated that he "learnt more in a few weeks on first entering a Catholic school than years before" in a Protestant establishment.[73] His detailed description of the studies offered at Downside is illuminating, and reveals the breadth of the curriculum. In 1838 a local Protestant clergyman wrote in glowing terms of the quality of education there:

> the masters, for skill and assiduity and temper, are fully equal to their important functions, and between them and their students there prevails a confidence which is truly exemplary...the situation of the place is entirely healthy, and the comforts of the students truly appropriate and inviting.[74]

At Ampleforth during "exhibition" in June 1831, "the mathematical department drew particular attention and astounding applause. A parson...said the manner in which the problems were gone through would have done credit to either of the universities".[75]

Norbert Birt notes that despite its "spartan simplicity", the fare at early nineteenth-century Downside was superior to that found in contemporary English Protestant schools "for at Downside the food was served on decent household ware, and not on wooden trenchers".[76] At Douai, the amount of bread and milk was "not limited morning and evening and for dinner there is a good soup, a good joint of meat and vegetables".[77] Whilst not quite matching the formidable standards of Stonyhurst, there is a case for concluding that in many respects, when compared with their English Protestant counterparts, the Benedictine schools were at the cutting edge of English secondary education in the first half of the nineteenth century.

One of the fundamental weaknesses of the new Benedictine schools was their small numbers compared to Stonyhurst, which had 50 students on its roll within a few months of the arrival in Lancashire, and within five years this had risen to 90. By 1839 it housed 170 boys. Numbers at Downside had reached 24 by 1818, and remained steady in the period 1830-45 at 36. By 1830 Ampleforth peaked at 80 students, but due to the Baines affair, it did not reach this number again until later in the century. At Douai there were 35 boys in 1832, by mid-century this rose to nearly 60. The school run by the nuns at Abbot's Salford stood at between 20 and 30 by the 1830s. Each of the

---

[73] B. ULLATHORNE, "Catholic and Protestant Education,"*DR*, 7 (1888) 2.
[74] BIRT, *Downside,* 218.
[75] DA, Abbot's Archives, Ampleforth, 22 July 1831, Ullathorne to Birdsall.
[76] BIRT, *Downside,* 211.
[77] DAB, I 2, 7 January 1833, Appleton to Heptonstall.

schools was highly dependent on income from fees, which at the outset seem to have been set lower than those charged by the Jesuits at Stonyhurst, where in 1797 the fees were 40 guineas per annum. It was nearly 20 years before Downside claimed this sum from parents, no doubt spurred on by Ampleforth, which in 1815 set its fees at 50 guineas per year. An 1836 advertisement for Douai promised "distinguished Masters in all the Arts… on much more reasonable terms than in England…" and the terms were highly competitive: "£32 per annum and church students are taken at £30 per annum which covers every expense".[78] By the 1820s, the nuns at Abbot's Salford were charging £30 a year for educating girls.

Money was tight, especially as new buildings were needed to house the expanding schools. At Downside a "begging circular" was sent round the friends of the community in 1817 to procure funds for a "commodious and decent Chapel, as the whole of the community, pupils and servants have at present no other place for the performance of their religious duties than a small room 16 feet square".[79] The early development of the buildings at Ampleforth owed much to the energy and wisdom of Prior Gregory Robinson who added the east wing to the original lodge, but by 1815 the school was rapidly expanding and "needed money badly",[80] no doubt to finance the ambitious educational schemes of Augustine Baines. Financially, St Edmund's College, Douai fared rather better than the Benedictine schools in England. Unlike Downside and Ampleforth, Douai benefited from bursaries paid by the French Government that enabled English bishops to educate their seminarians at Douai. In the words of Richard Marsh, who had refounded the St Edmund community at Douai:

> The French government required that whatever we received for our restored property should be spent on education in France. This was a point that our Brethren in England did not sufficiently consider, but were continually calling for it to be paid to them in England.[81]

Thus, bursaries financed the majority of the students at Douai. In addition to these "bishops' boys" – those destined to be secular priests, there also existed a number of "president's boys" whose finances were settled by the President of the English Benedictines. Augustine Birdsall, for instance, President from 1826 to 1837 financed at least seven boys at Douai including the future Bishop of Mauritius, Adrian Hankinson. Other students were financed by benefactors such as the Stourtons of Allerton, and by monks on the English Mission, who in those days had their own money, known as their *peculium*.[82]

---

[78] *The Catholicon*, (1836) 26.
[79] BIRT, *Downside*, 177.
[80] DAA, Parker letters, no. 30, Woolton, Oct 31 1815, Brewer to Parker.
[81] MARSH, *Reminiscences*, 23.
[82] *Mr Swale's Diary, Rome, 1830-32*, viii.

Supplying the schools with professors was a continual problem for the Congregation in the first half of the century. Most of the communities were overstretched, and suffered from the fact that the President had the power to remove a monk from his monastery to serve on the Mission. Prior Barber at Downside in 1821 warned: "if our worthy President continues to take masters for the mission …we shall never have a learned man in the house".[83] Six years later his successor, Joseph Brown lamented: "in our establishments which are drained to supply the mission, we cannot without imposing great labour on certain individuals conduct a large school".[84] Even when masters were not sent on the Mission, "the strain put upon those engaged in school work by the obligations of choir and by rules which made it impossible for them to devote the energy to teaching required in the modern world was most injurious".[85] A further problem was that many of those employed to teach "had no gifts for that calling",[86] let alone any academic training, which only became possible after 1840 when monks were able to gain external degrees from London University. Little wonder that as late as 1850, the Oxford convert W.G. Ward declared that it was still too generally assumed that if "anyone in the shape of a monk or nun can be converted into a teacher, then all is supposed to be perfect".[87]

Alongside the schools attached to the monasteries, the English Benedictines also had responsibility for elementary schools attached to their missions, which have tended to be overlooked. Before considering these schools in any detail, the broader context of English Catholic elementary education in the early nineteenth century needs to be established.

English Catholic elementary education in the early nineteenth century

Until the early nineteenth century, education in England had almost exclusively been under the control of the established church, but the Industrial Revolution and the subsequent expansion of the major cities and an influx of immigrants to the country created an ever increasing need to supply a system of elementary education, especially for the poor. In 1833 a system of annual grants was established, whereby £20,000 was voted in aid of the erection of schools under the umbrella of two Protestant educational bodies, the National Society and the British and Foreign School Society. In 1847 Catholic schools were permitted to have a share in the grant, and the Catholic Poor School Committee was founded to represent the educational

---

[83] DAB, E 303, 5 February 1821, Barber to Lorymer.
[84] DAB, G 127, memo of 1827.
[85] R. BLENNERHASSETT, "Memories and a forecast," *DR*, 24 (1905) 229-230.
[86] BLENNERHASSETT, 229.
[87] *The Rambler*, 3 (1850) 91f.

interests of Catholics.[88] This body was the successor of the "Catholic Institute", a body of influential laymen intent upon obtaining more widespread educational provision for Catholics. In an era when the clergy were gradually gaining supremacy over the Catholic gentry who had dominated the English Catholic church, it was inevitable that the new Poor School Committee would "in no way be dependent upon the aristocracy" and would come under the jurisdiction of the Vicars Apostolic, whose status would within a few years be raised with the restoration of the English Catholic hierarchy.[89]

One of the most stalwart defenders of Catholic education in England in the mid-nineteenth century was the new bishop of Birmingham, the English Benedictine, William Bernard Ullathorne, who in 1850 issued a pamphlet[90] in response to a bill proposed by the Oldham Member of Parliament, William Johnson Fox, who was a Unitarian minister. Fox argued for the establishment of education committees which would ensure that any new schools built would be non-denominational, and that religious teaching should be separate from secular teaching.[91] In his pamphlet, Ullathorne argued that to divorce secular lessons of all religious content would lead to the de-Christianisation of the country and strongly denied the right of the State to "usurp parental rights by interfering in education." [92] In a subsequent pamphlet, Ullathorne was openly critical of the terms under which Catholic schools had been granted financial assistance from the State in 1847, when it became necessary for Catholic schools to draw up trust deeds that could be used when applying for grants.[93] A later section of this chapter will consider the significance of the trust deed that was selected as a model.

The English Benedictines and elementary education

English Benedictines were already involved in the provision of elementary education long before the middle of the nineteenth century. Reference has already been made to the efforts of Bede Brewer, Gregory Cowley and

---

[88] J.P. MARMION, "The Beginnings of the Catholic Poor Schools in England," *RH*, 17:1 (May, 1984) 67-83; E.G. TENBUS, *English Catholics and the Education of the Poor, 1847-1902*, Pickering & Chatto, London 2010, 29-31.
[89] NORMAN, *The English Catholic Church in the Nineteenth Century*, 167-8; WARD, *Sequel to Catholic Emancipation*, 2: 155.
[90] W.B. ULLATHORNE, *Remarks on the proposed Education Bill*, Burns & Lambert, London 1850.
[91] R. K. WEBB, "Fox, William Johnson (1786–1864)," *ODNB*, <http://www.oxforddnb.com/view/article/10047> [accessed 13 March 2014].
[92] C. HANSEN, unpublished M.A. thesis, *Roman Catholic Education in England in the Nineteenth Century, with special reference to William Bernard Ullathorne*, University of Durham 1998, 57.
[93] W.B. ULLATHORNE, *Notes on the Education Question*, Richardson & Son, London 1857.

Richard Marsh in establishing educational facilities in the Liverpool area in the latter part of the eighteenth century. In 1802 Ambrose Allam had a small school "for eight or ten years" at Stratford-upon-Avon,[94] whilst in 1809 the missioner at Coventry, John Dawber wrote to Richard Marsh:

> with respect to teaching French, I have now acquired a certain celebrity. More scholars have offered themselves than I can possibly attend to...I confine myself to twenty-eight...when you know that the price of teaching French is a guinea per quarter, you may consider my situation very capable of being converted into an academy at very small expense.[95]

Further north, at Liverpool, Thomas Burke noted that: "as was only to be expected from an Order celebrated for its pursuit of learning, the monks were the pioneers of elementary education" in the town, establishing a school in Gerard Street in 1803.[96] Later, in the 1820s, Vincent Glover, whilst assistant priest at St Peter, Seel Street established the Poor Schools near to the church.[97] In March, 1844 this school, which could accommodate 160 boys, was handed over to the care of the Christian Brothers, and a few months later the Brothers were also asked by the monks at St Mary's Church to run their school in Ray Street, which by the following year had an estimated number of 350 boys on the roll.[98] A previous chapter has already noted the active interest taken in the two schools at Bath by Augustine Baines, even going so far as to replace the management committee for one of them.[99] In Cheltenham, Augustine Birdsall opened an elementary school in 1827, which began as a Sunday school but within a year was so successful that it attracted anti-Catholic propaganda from the local Anglican clergyman, Francis Close.[100]

The Kemerton Trust Deed, 1844

When after 1847, it became necessary for Catholic schools to draw up trust deeds that could be used when applying for grants from the State, the trust deed selected as the model for others to follow was that of the school attached to the English Benedictine mission in the tiny village of Kemerton in

---

[94] The mission at Stratford-upon-Avon was not officially founded until 1859 but Allanson notes that Allam "ministered to a few Catholics there and taught a School for eight to ten years," *AB*, 292.
[95] *AB*, 290.
[96] BURKE, *Catholic History of Liverpool*, 32.
[97] *AB*, 362.
[98] W. GILLESPIE, *The Christian Brothers in England, 1825-1880*, The Burleigh Press, Bristol 1975, 101.
[99] WILLIAMS, *Post-Reformation Catholicism in Bath*, CRS (R), 65 (1975) 83-84, 230.
[100] J. BADHAM, "The Development of Catholic Education in Cheltenham 1818-1939," *Journal of the Gloucestershire Catholic History Society*, 48 (2006) 6.

Gloucestershire. Although this trust deed has often been cited in accounts of nineteenth-century English Catholic education, it significance has not been fully appreciated. The trust deed states that on 24 October 1844, land at Kemerton was "set out and appropriated for a school and school-house for the education of poor Roman Catholics belonging to the spiritual care of the Church of Saint Benet's" and that the buildings were to be used "as a Roman Catholic week-day school for the religious and secular education of children and young persons, and, in special cases, adult persons".

What is striking about the Kemerton document is that it expresses a tradition that the new Catholic Poor School Committee was set up to reform, namely the influence of the Catholic aristocracy. According to the trust deed, the priest at Kemerton was to have "the management and superintendence of the religious instruction of all the scholars", but the overall superintendence was in the hands of the committee, on which sat not only the priest but six laymen, all of whom initially were influential local Catholic gentry such as Ferdinand Eyston of Overbury Court and Compton John Hanford of Woollas Hall, who were also benefactors of the church at Kemerton.[101] The Kemerton situation contrasts sharply with that in Liverpool, where in 1844 the Vicar Apostolic of the Lancashire district, George Hilary Brown replaced all lay committees for churches and schools with a district board, which would have no lay members. It is therefore ironic that the Kemerton trust deed became the "model" for other Catholic schools, when its management structure reflected an outdated system that was soon to be replaced.

By 1850 much had been achieved by the English Benedictines in education, despite the inauspicious conditions that greeted them on their arrival in England in 1795. The apostolate of education continued in the years that followed, and important changes were implemented, notably a more focussed concern at Ampleforth and Douai of educating students for the secular priesthood, and a different tradition of a predominantly lay school at Downside. The three schools had each experienced expansion as well as periods of hardship and trial, notably the forces of potential destruction unleashed by one of their own members, Augustine Baines. There was still much to be achieved to catch up with their Jesuit rivals at Stonyhurst and bring their schools into closer competition with the longer established public schools of the land. Nevertheless despite their deficiencies, the English Benedictine schools had begun to provide much needed centres of Catholic education in the land that could co-exist with the seminaries established at Oscott, Ushaw and Ware, even if the distinctive value of a Benedictine education had yet to be formally defined. On the missions, significant work had also been done to provide elementary education, especially in Liverpool. Abbot Snow's eloquent tribute to the educational achievements of the monks

---

[101] W.M. LILLY and J.E.P. WALLIS, *A Manual of the Law Specially Affecting Catholics*, W. Clowes & Sons, London 1893, 107, 230-249.

of St Gregory could just as fittingly be applied to those of all the houses, for early nineteenth-century English Benedictine education was characterised essentially by "much sacrifice, much obedience...much dashing of hopes, much deliberation and zeal for souls in the authorities, much resignation and self-repression in the individual - but there were giants in those days".[102]

---

[102] SNOW, *Sketches of Old Downside*, 26.

Chapter 8

"Sharing treasures throughout a mighty Hemisphere": English Benedictines and the Empire.

Considering the agitated state of Europe, perhaps the interests of the Congregation would be well consulted by the formation of an establishment in a region beyond the storm and where land is cheap enough to encourage an imitation of the eventually stupendous work of our forefathers. Why may not Mauritius have its Alcuin or New Holland and the Cape their Wilfrid and Boniface? [1]

Until the early decades of the nineteenth century, English Benedictine monks understood "mission" purely in terms of their pastoral apostolate in England, yet by mid-century they found themselves labouring in the furthest corners of the British Empire.[2] Like many other Christian bodies in the early nineteenth century, the involvement of English Benedictines in missionary endeavour overseas came as a result of a unique blend of individual romantic pipedreams and practical circumstances which need to be seen within the wider context of Christian missionary activity.

The Missionary Movement of the Nineteenth Century

The nineteenth-century missionary movement was the product and blossoming of a religious revival that manifested itself in all the churches in this period, at the heart of which was the impulse to save souls from damnation and preach the Gospel to all nations.[3] The Evangelical Revival in the Church of England, with its emphasis on sin, conversion and philanthropy gave birth to an impressive clutch of missionary societies such

---

[1] AR, 2: 511, Bishop Slater to General Chapter, 1822.
[2] BELLENGER, "The English Benedictines and the British Empire," in S. GILLEY, *Victorian Churches and Churchmen*, 94-109.
[3] S. BROWN, *Providence and Empire: Religion, Politics and Society in Britain and Ireland, 1815-1914*, Routledge, London 2008; S. GILLEY and B. STANLEY, (eds), *World Christianities, c.1815-1914*, Cambridge University Press, Cambridge 2006; B. STANLEY, *The Bible and the Flag: Protestant Mission and British Imperialism in the Nineteenth and Twentieth Centuries,* Apollos, Nottingham 1990; A. PORTER (ed.),*The Oxford History of the British Empire: Volume III: The Nineteenth Century,* Oxford University Press, Oxford 1999; A .PORTER, *Religion Versus Empire?: British Protestant Missionaries and Overseas Expansion, 1700-1914*, Manchester University Press, Manchester 2004; H.M. CAREY, (ed.), *Empires of Religion,* Palgrave Macmillan, Basingstoke 2008; *God's Empire: Religion and Colonialism in the British World, c.1801-1908,* Cambridge University Press, Cambridge 2011.

as the Society for Missions to Africa and the East in 1799. Of still earlier foundation was the Baptist Missionary Society of 1792.[4]

Within the Catholic Church the principal agents of overseas missionary expansion in the seventeenth and eighteenth century had been the Jesuits, but the suppression of the Society by Pope Clement XIV in 1773 brought to a halt the era of their missionary activity, especially in China and Latin America, much of which had received the enthusiastic support and patronage of imperial governments in Spain and Portugal. It was only after 1814 when the Society was formally revived by Pope Pius VII that it was able to spearhead new missionary initiatives. Paradoxically, although anti-clerical forces in France swept away many of the religious orders, the Catholic missionary revival began with the foundation of several new missionary congregations, beginning in 1805 with the Congregation of the Sacred Hearts of Jesus and Mary (the Picpus Fathers) and continuing with the Oblates of Mary Immaculate in 1816, both in France. In 1822 the Association for the Propagation of the Faith was founded in Lyons; this was to become the most important source of funding for overseas missions in modern times.

In the words of Christopher Dowd, "Having survived the shock of...the ordeal of the French Revolution and the Napoleonic Wars, the Church emerged battered into the nineteenth century to find itself surrounded by a new and unfamiliar world." The Church had a great fear of democracy which had expanded massively by the 1840s, and so Rome "looked to self-defence by tightening its command structures," so that "the entire Church became increasingly centralised at its symbolic heart, papal Rome".[5] This process of centralisation began with Pope Pius VII, who revitalised the Congregation for the Propagation of the Faith and confirmed the status of the new missionary congregations, thus paving the way for further missionary initiatives undertaken under his successor, Pope Gregory XVI, who as Cardinal Cappellari had headed the Congregation of *Propaganda Fide.* The transformation of the Catholic Church into a centralised body under Gregory and Pius IX (after 1846) helped to facilitate a new worldwide missionary strategy. Between 1822 and 1885, 300 new ecclesiastical administrative jurisdictions were established in mission territories, sixteen of which were located in Australia.[6] The enforced return of many English Catholic communities to England after the French Revolution, according to Carey was largely responsible "for the orientation of English Catholicism

---

[4] See A .PORTER, *Religion Versus Empire?* 40.

[5] C. DOWD, *Rome in Australia: The Papacy and Conflict in the Australian Catholic Missions, 1834-1884,* Brill, Leiden 2008, 1: 30-31.

[6] For the background see R. AUBERT, P.J. CORISH and R. LILL, *The Church between Revolution and Restoration,* Burns & Oates, London 1981, 189-205 and R. AUBERT, P.J. CORISH and R. LILL, *The Church in the Age of Liberalism,* Burns & Oates, London 1981 175ff.

away from Europe and towards the fresh fields of the British empire,"[7] into which the English Benedictines somewhat unexpectedly found themselves involved.

English Benedictine missionary concern

Even before the repatriation of many English Benedictines to England in 1795, approaches had been made to the Congregation to make new foundations overseas. In 1794 an invitation was made by the Bishop of Baltimore to make a foundation in Pittsburgh in America, which came to nothing.[8] Five years later came an invitation to make a foundation in Madeira. Richard Marsh volunteered to go there to investigate, but was overruled by the President because of the expense. The initiative was postponed on account of the Napoleonic wars and was never revived. Instead Mauritius and Australia became the two principal overseas mission territories for the Congregation.[9]

Mauritius

Britain had acquired the Cape of Good Hope in 1810, and by 1818 there was a sizeable Catholic population there. Moreover, Britain had also captured the island of Mauritius from the French, which was formally granted to her by the Treaty of Paris in 1814. The island was of strategic importance to Britain because it lay along the sea route used by the British merchants and navy in transit to Asia and India.[10] However the island remained under French episcopal control, a situation that the British Colonial Office found embarrassing and the government urged the Holy See to ensure that the island came under the jurisdiction of an English cleric. As a result of negotiations made through Bishop Poynter, Vicar Apostolic of the London District, who was the link between the British government and Rome, it was agreed that Mauritius should come under the jurisdiction of the new Vicar Apostolic of the Cape of Good Hope, and that the Vicar Apostolic should reside in Port Louis, the capital of Mauritius, as a clear sign of the change of regime. It so happened that Father Bede Slater of Ampleforth was in Rome in 1818 at a time when the Roman authorities were seeking an English priest to become Vicar Apostolic of the Cape of Good Hope. Although Slater was not initially thought of by the Roman authorities as the bishop-elect, he seems to have so impressed Carlo Maria Pedicini, the Secretary of the Congregation of Propaganda that Slater felt

---

[7] CAREY, *God's Empire,* 119.
[8] AH, 2: 382.
[9] F. O'DONOGHUE, "Australia's connections with Mauritius," *Australasian Catholic Record,* 53 (1976) 70-80.
[10] A. JACKSON, *War and Empire in Mauritius and the Indian Ocean,* Palgrave Macmillan, Basingstoke 2001, 15-18.

justified in informing his uncle, Bede Brewer, then President of the English Benedictines that "South Africa was to be given over to the Congregation by way of recognition for the services it has rendered to the church" and that "one of its members' should be sent there".[11] Slater's subsequent consecration as Bishop of Ruspa took place without the Congregation being consulted, but by the end of the year Slater's position was strengthened by an agreement between Rome and the British government that Catholics in British colonies should henceforth be under the jurisdiction of prelates who were the subjects of the Crown.[12] Thus the initial overseas involvement of the English Benedictines came about in a curious marriage of convenience between an otherwise anti-Catholic British government and the Holy See.

In the case of Mauritius, it came to be considered that the Vicar Apostolic of this former French colony should be a French speaker and it is noteworthy that the first five bishops of Port Louis, Mauritius (after this see was founded in 1847) were English Benedictines from St. Edmund's Priory in Douai, the last of the English Benedictine houses to remain in France, and the first four had spent a significant amount of time living in France. Until 1847, Slater's jurisdiction extended over a huge area that took in most of the southern hemisphere, but it was another fourteen years before an English Benedictine, Bernard Ullathorne of Downside, was sent to Australia in 1833.

Throughout the early decades of the nineteenth century the majority of the population of Mauritius consisted of slaves, who had been brought to the island to work in the sugar cane plantations. Although by the time Bishop Slater arrived in 1819, many of these slaves were already Catholics, by the time of Bishop William Bernard Allen Collier's arrival in 1841, tens of thousands of newly-emancipated slaves were still illiterate and unbaptised.[13] There was a marked indifference to the practice of the Faith, particularly among the male Catholic population, few, if any of whom frequented the sacraments.[14] The challenge to Collier was formidable.

Australia

The Benedictine mission to Mauritius occurred largely by accident, as a result of the British attraction to the trading and military potential of the island. Australia was attractive for a different reason: its barrenness and remoteness made it an ideal territory for a prison.[15] The practice of transporting convicts from Britain to the colonies dated from the early seventeenth century,

---

[11] DAB, E 98, 20 June 1818, Brewer to Lorymer.
[12] DAB, E 123, 24 December 1818, Poynter to Slater.
[13] A. NAGAPEN, *Histoire de l'Église: Isle de France – Ile Maurice 1721-1968,* Diocése de Port Louis, Port Louis 1996, 109; A. NAGAPEN, "A Century of English Benedictine Apostolate in Mauritius – 1819-1916," *EBHS,* privately printed, 1998, 15.
[14] DAB, E 426, 22 July 1822, Lorymer to Barber.
[15] N. FERGUSON, *Empire,* Basic Books, New York 2002, 83.

although the practice did not become formally established until 1717. Between 1787 and 1853 an estimated 150,000 men and women were transported to the Antipodes for a variety of crimes.

The first Catholics to reside in Australia arrived with the First Fleet in 1788. They were mostly Irish convicts, together with a few marines. One-tenth of all convicts transported to Australia were Catholic, and half of these were born in Ireland, while a good proportion of the others were English-born but of Irish extraction. Most of the rest were English or Scots. By the year 1803, a total of 2086 Irish convicts, nearly all of whom were Catholic, had been transported to Botany Bay, and by 1820 many of these convicts had served their sentences or had received remission, and the character of the colony began to change. Ferguson observes that "with only one in fourteen ex-convicts electing to return to Britain, by 1828 there were already more free people than convicts in New South Wales "and some of the old lags were fast becoming *nouveaux riches*".[16] By 1820 the British Government deemed it appropriate to appoint the first Catholic chaplains to the colony, and in 1834 the Vicariate Apostolic of New Holland and Van Diemen's Land (Tasmania) was established with its headquarters in Sydney. The Downside monk John Bede Polding was appointed as its first Vicar Apostolic.[17]

English Benedictine Missionary Enthusiasm

The involvement of English Benedictines in overseas mission came about not only through force of circumstances but also by a missionary fervour amongst certain individuals in the Congregation in the early decades of the nineteenth century. An important example was Bede Polding, who came from Liverpool, Britain's second port of empire, and belonged to the merchant class, "one of the chief beneficiaries of empire".[18] Long before his appointment in 1834 as the first Catholic bishop in Australia, Polding was nicknamed by his contemporaries "the Bishop of Botany Bay" as he openly shared with his novices his dream of becoming a missionary in Australia. One of those novices, the future Vicar General of Australia, Bernard Ullathorne, recalled that Polding had spoken to him of the "great want of missionaries in Australia" because of the new opportunities there, and that

---

[16] FERGUSON, *Empire*, 87.
[17] E.M. O'BRIEN, *The Life of Archpriest J.J. Therry, Founder of the Catholic Church in Australasia*, Angus and Robertson, Sydney 1922, but see also the account given in P. COLLINS, unpublished D.Phil. thesis, *William Bernard Ullathorne and the Foundation of Australian Catholicism, 1815-1840*, Australian National University 1989, 95-98.
[18] BELLENGER, "The English Benedictines and the British Empire," 96; J. HOLLINSHEAD, "John Bede Polding: First Catholic Metropolitan of Australia and his Lancashire origins," in J. DAVIES and A. MITCHINSON, (eds), *Obstinate Souls: Essays Presented to J.A. Hilton on the occasion of his seventieth birthday by the North West Catholic History Society*, North West Catholic History Society, Wigan 2011, 48-69.

there was "no part of the world where there was such a field for missionary labour".[19]

Missionary fervour was not, however, found only among English monks. A nun of Stanbrook, Dame Magdalen le Clerc "listened to the voice which has long been calling for the sacrifice of all that was dear on earth". She declared: "the call is from God...to impart to others a share of those spiritual treasures [I have] gathered".[20] She persuaded Polding to allow her to make the journey to New South Wales in 1847 and, together with Scholastica Gregory from Princethorpe, made the first Benedictine foundation for women in Australia two years later. With the help of Polding they founded a monastery and school at Rydalmere.[21] The nuns proved to be more successful in establishing themselves in Australia than the monks, even though their monastery, to quote Terence Kavenagh, came to represent "an island of English tradition in the sea of Irish Australian Catholicism".[22] Their story in Australia has yet to be fully told and is an important part of a larger as yet unwritten narrative of the contribution made by religious women to the social and religious development of the country, a contribution which, in the words of Hilary Carey "made the explosive growth of the British empire possible".[23]

Underpinning this missionary fervour was a strong tinge of romanticism, for as Alberic Jacovone has observed:

> In the debilitated state of monasticism in the early part of the nineteenth century, missionary expansion was thought to provide the hour of grace...wherein to repeat the great achievements of missionary monasticism in the early Middle Ages and so restore the prestige and glory monks had enjoyed in earlier times.[24]

Such sentiments were clearly expressed to the English Benedictine General Chapter at different times by both Slater and Polding: Slater in 1822 in the

---

[19] *The Devil is a Jackass*, 56-7.
[20] Letter of farewell printed in *TJ*, 8 (1974) 19. Also M.G. FORSTER, "Magdalen le Clerc," *TJ*, 8 (1974) 259-336.
[21] Some doubts have been expressed about the sincerity of Dame Magdalen's call to the Australian Mission, seeing in it a response to frustrated ambition, following the abbatial election at Stanbrook in 1846, in which she failed to be elected as the superior of the community. (See FORSTER, "Magdalen le Clerc," 265). However, there is no evidence to support this view. The arrival of these nuns in Sydney is recounted in M.G. FORSTER, "Subiaco: The Arrival of Benedictine Nuns in Sydney," *TJ*, 54 (1998) 21-55.
[22] T. KAVENAGH, "Australia," in W.M. JOHNSON, (ed.), *Encyclopedia of Monasticism*, Fitzroy Dearborn Publishers, Chicago 2000, 1: 109.
[23] CAREY, *God's Empire*, 379.
[24] A. JACOVONE, "Polding-Hope- And the Women of '38'," *TJ*, 16 (1978) 108.

words which introduced this chapter and, by Polding in 1842, when he addressed the General Chapter in a similar vein:

> The mind naturally reverts to the period when men of God…went forth from the Holy City at the bidding of Pope St Gregory the Great, to the barbarous climes of Northern Europe, and established the first Monastery of our holy order in our native land. History has recorded how it spread and…how it provided Pastors for parishes, Bishops for the larger population of Episcopal Sees. We deem ourselves peculiarly favoured by Almighty God, that we have been called upon to imitate the conduct of these heroic Apostles of England…May the Benedictine Order which during so many centuries has produced the fruits of eternal life in England, be transplanted in its native vigour to the far distant South – to a Country in every respect excellently adapted to receive Religious Institutions of a Monastic Missionary character.[25]

Similar sentiments were also expressed by other Benedictines at this time, notably the German Benedictine, Boniface Wimmer who in 1845 was preparing to establish a Benedictine mission in America, declaring that:

> We owe the conversion of England, Germany, Denmark, Sweden, Norway, Hungary and Poland almost exclusively to the Benedictines, and in the remaining parts of Europe Christianity is deeply indebted to them…The Benedictine Order by its Rule is so constituted that it can readily adapt itself to all times and circumstances…Conditions in America today are like those in Europe a thousand years ago, when the Benedictine Order attained its fullest development and effectiveness by its wonderful adaptability and stability.[26]

A third Benedictine with missionary aspirations was the Italian abbot, Pietro Casaretto, a former diocesan priest who, in 1847, established a college for the formation of missionary monks who "would enter the monastery for the purpose of consecrating themselves to God under the rule of St Benedict and to go then and spread the faith of Jesus Christ as workers on the Foreign Missions".[27] Casaretto also was fired with a romantic nostalgia for the missionary monasticism of an earlier age, particularly the mission entrusted by Pope St Gregory to Augustine in the sixth century. Casaretto regarded

---

[25] DA, "Acta Capitulorum Generalium, 1798-1900," no.461.
[26] *Augsburger Postzeitung,* 8 November 1845, quoted in J. OETGEN, "Out of Bavaria. Boniface Wimmer and the American Cassinese Congregation," in C. LEYSER and H. WILLIAMS, *Mission and Monasticism: Acts of the International Symposium at the Pontifical Athenaeum S. Anselmo, Rome, May 7-9, 2009,* Pontificio Atenos S. Anselmo, Roma 2013, 127. On Wimmer see J. OETGEN, *An American Abbot: Boniface Wimmer OSB, 1809-1887,* The Catholic University of America Press, Washington D.C 1997.
[27] ARCHIVES OF SANT'AMBROGIO, ROME, College for the Missions, quoted in G. LUNARDI, "The Missionary Spirit of Abbot Casaretto," *TJ,* 8 (1974) 44.

Pope Pius IX as "another Gregory," now choosing another son of an Italian monastery "to go and establish an order of the Patriarch of the West."[28]

The English Benedictine Congregation and overseas mission, 1822-1850

Although the initial response of the General Chapter of the English Benedictine Congregation had been unfavourable to the proposal to establish a mission in the southern hemisphere,[29] in 1829, the recently elected President of the Congregation, Augustine Birdsall, who was not given to romantic pipedreams, was quick to realise the potential for the Congregation in this new missionary field and wrote to the future Cardinal Wiseman at the English College in Rome:

> Should the affairs of the Mauritius take a favourable turn and be settled...there is no doubt that some of our good young men will be sent on that important mission...involving as it does the interests of Christianity in all that mighty Hemisphere. For our Island is in constant intercourse with all the countries of the East by means of their commercial relations, and might be made a sort of Head Quarters from which the Church would be able to exercise its authority and dispense its blessings to all around us.[30]

Birdsall was to be instrumental in the appointment of Ullathorne as Vicar General in Australia in 1833 and of Polding a year later as the first bishop of the colony. Polding was well known to Birdsall because the former had been appointed as his secretary in 1826. Handling much of Birdsall's correspondence, Polding in turn became known to Bishop Bramston, Poynter's successor as Vicar Apostolic of the London District, who was a regular correspondent. Thus a network was established between the English Benedictines, the London Vicar Apostolic and the Colonial Office, which lasted until 1836, the year that both Bramston and Birdsall died. Birdsall considered the question of missionary involvement overseas "the greatest quest...since the Reformation".[31]

However, Birdsall's initial enthusiasm for the mission overseas waned due to the shortage of manpower in the home mission and within a

---

[28] ASA, 8 May 1853, Casaretto to Grant.
[29] In 1822, the request of Bishop Slater for support for his mission was met with this response: "The Congregation is indeed increasing in numbers and has the most flattering prospects...but the numerous and increasing missions entrusted to its charge amongst our own countrymen who are the first entitled to our services, keep all of our members fully occupied and render it impossible for us to accept for the present of any foreign mission".[29] AR 2: 512.
[30] English College, Rome, Wiseman papers, BEN VII.1, 15 August 1829, Birdsall to Wiseman.
[31] ALLANSON, Records added to the first version of volume 2 of the *Biography*, Ampleforth MS 166, 136.

few years Birdsall informed the bishops in both Mauritius and Australia that they must not expect help from England.[32] The mind-set of General Chapters from 1822, remained, in the phrase of Améde Nagapen, "impassive as marble".[33] Both as Prior of Downside, and later, as Vicar Apostolic of the Welsh District, Joseph Brown was vociferous in encouraging the Congregation to have a policy of non-cooperation with the bishops of the new territories. In 1834 he wrote to Birdsall expressing his concern about the difficulty in recalling monks to England, who had been appointed to the overseas mission, and pointing out that the President General may well be laying up difficulties for his successor in dispatching monks there, for "a President has but a four year interest in the exercise of his office. His successor may in vain endeavour to recover the subject whom his predecessor has sent abroad, but whom his successor wants at home".[34] In 1837, Bernard Collier, the future bishop in Mauritius, contended that the Congregation "must not, in the goal of extending our Congregation abroad, neglect ourselves at home".[35] The view of General Chapter concerning this issue did not change substantially over time.

Inevitably problems arose which led to strained relations between the English Benedictine bishops in the colonies and the officials of the Congregation at home. One particularly controversial issue proved to be the question of providing personnel for the overseas mission, whilst another was the question of autonomy. In 1834 Polding asked General Chapter that his new Vicariate be formed "into a Province of the Congregation under the same Supreme Head – differing somewhat in its internal Government from the other two Provinces by reason of its peculiar circumstances".[36] Chapter refused, and it was another four years before the Congregation, encouraged by *Propaganda Fide* in Rome gave Polding delegated powers. In 1842, Rome issued a rescript allowing for the canonical erection of a Benedictine monastery in New South Wales, independent of the English Benedictine Congregation.[37] In practice, an English Benedictine bishop in the colonies seems to have had jurisdiction over the monks working within his district or diocese, but this jurisdiction seems not to have applied when the monks went back to England for visits. In 1849 Bishop Collier sent his secretary, Stanislaus Giles, home to England to recruit teachers for Mauritius, only to discover on Giles' return, that upon landing in England he had immediately been placed by the English Benedictine Northern Provincial to work in a

---

[32] DAB, J 250, 14 October 1836, Birdsall to Morris.
[33] NAGAPEN, "A Century of English Benedictine Apostolate in Mauritius," 10.
[34] DAB, I 297, 28 September 1834, Brown to Birdsall. As bishop, Brown addressed the 1842 General Chapter on this point; see DAB, L 166, 9 July 1842. See also his letter on the subject to Prior Wilson at Downside, DAB, L 161, 11 June 1841.
[35] AR, 4: 299.
[36] AR, 2: 761-762.
[37] For the text of the rescript see BIRT, *Benedictine Pioneers*, 1: 348ff.

vacant mission in Liverpool. Collier subsequently wrote directly to *Propaganda* to request that henceforth he be formally recognised as the ordinary ecclesiastical superior of all English Benedictines who came to work on the island.[38]

Personnel

Given the shortage of manpower in the Congregation before 1850, it is unsurprising that the number of English Benedictines dispatched to the overseas mission between 1818 and 1850 was very small, especially when compared with the numbers of monks sent to work on the English mission. 21 monks were sent overseas between these years, compared to the 86 in the same period who were sent on the missions at home. Of these 21 monks, one was sent to minister to Catholics on the Cape of Good Hope (Clement Rishton), 9 to Mauritius (these included the three bishops, Slater, Morris and Collier), and 11 to Australia, including the two bishops, Polding and Charles Davis.[39]

Figure 6 - MONKS WHO SERVED IN MAURITIUS, 1819-1850

MONK	HOUSE	DATES SERVED
Bede Slater (Vicar Ap)	St Laurence's, Ampleforth	1819-32
Cuthbert Spain	St Gregory's, Downside	1819-27, 1830-47
Anselm Collyer	St Gregory's, Downside	1819-61
Placid Morris (Vicar Apostolic)	St Gregory's, Downside	1832-40
Austin Clifford	St Laurence's, Ampleforth	1832-43
Bernard Collier (Bishop)	St Edmund's, Douai	1840-63
Stanislaus Giles	St Edmund's, Douai	1840-49
Cuthbert Heptonstall	St Laurence's, Ampleforth	1842-67

---

[38] RSRNC, (Africa, Isole' dell'Oceano, Australe & Capo di Buona Speranza, 3) fol.905; AA, MS 262, 26 October 1850.
[39] See *Figures 6 & 7*.

Figure 7 - MONKS WHO SERVED IN AUSTRALIA, 1833-1850

MONK	HOUSE	DATES SERVED
Bernard Ullathorne	St Gregory's, Downside	1833-40
Bede Polding (Bishop)	St Gregory's, Downside	1835-77
Ambrose Cotham	St Edmund's, Douai	1835-51
Bede Sumner	St Gregory's, Downside	1835-71
Gregory Gregory	Ss Adrian and Denis	1835-61
Denis Tootell	Ss Adrian and Denis	1846-47
Edmund Moore	St Gregory's, Downside	1847-49
Edmund Caldwell	St Edmund's, Douai	1847-49
Bernard Caldwell	St Edmund's, Douai	1847-49
Henry Davis (Bishop)	St Gregory's, Downside	1848-54
Cyprian Hubbersty	St Laurence's, Ampleforth	1848-65

Not all those sent on the overseas mission were suited to the challenge that lay before them. The first two Benedictine bishops in Mauritius, Slater and Morris, were not successful. In fairness to both of them, it was a well-nigh impossible task to govern effectively a huge missionary diocese, which until the appointment of bishops in Australia and New Zealand, covered most of the southern hemisphere. However, there is evidence that Slater was a difficult character, whose fiery temperament and extravagant lifestyle incurred popular displeasure and large debts.[40] It was alleged that he was drowned by his debtors who pursued him on to the ship he used for his escape from the island.[41] His successor, Placid Morris of Downside, was recalled to London after a misunderstanding with *Propaganda Fide,* which led to him being removed from office because of false allegations made against him by a priest on the island.[42] Conversely, Morris was well respected by the Governor and the local people.[43] Others had to be sent home. It was assumed

---

[40] DAB, E 426, 22 July 1822, Larking to Lorymer.
[41] I. CUMMINS, "Bishop Slater OSB, 1774-1832," *AJ,* 37 (1932) 185-191.
[42] *DR,* 1 (1882) 337-339.
[43] On 23 February 1841, in a memo to Lord John Russell in London, Governor Lionel Smith expressed "sincere regret" at the loss of Morris' "valuable services in his sacred office in which he has acquired the respect and regard of his flock, whilst to those of a different creed, his conduct has been marked by a most commendable spirit of tolerance and Christian benevolence". NA, CO 167/228 no. 10.

that those monks who had experience of the English Mission might be suitable for the colonies, but this appeared not to be the case. Father Augustine Clifford, the fifth son of the seventh Lord Clifford of Chudleigh in Devon had spent thirteen years on the English mission where his "fickle character and extravagance in his habits" had already led to conflict with his superiors. In 1832 he persuaded Bishop Morris to take him with him to the Mauritius where "his extravagant habits and heavy debts" again landed him in trouble and led to his early death at the age of 41.[44] Archbishop Bede Polding lamented to his cousin, Paulinus Heptonstall: "We cannot be too careful in our selection. Men who have been once on your Missions get into ways we deem strange. Pious men, zealous men, and so forth, but with too much of their own will for us".[45]

Bernard Collier believed the problem of unsuitable clergy lay with colonial bishops being too dependent upon priests "whom chance may send", and as bishop in Mauritius in the 1840s he was diligent in dismissing unsuitable clergy and in personally recruiting candidates for the priesthood from Europe who would be trained as missionaries by François-Marie-Paul Libermann, whose Congregation du Saint-Coeur de Marie (later to become the Holy Ghost Fathers) was founded in 1840 with Collier as its Protector.[46] Initially, Collier was able to direct only English or Irish seminarians to Libermann's novitiate because the British government would not permit the employment in Mauritius of non-British born clergy.[47] After 1846 this restriction was lifted.

Criticism has been levelled at the English Benedictines for failing to encourage male indigenous vocations, both in Australia and Mauritius. Although in 1848, Polding ordained two native-born white Australians,[48] it was a Spanish, rather than an English Benedictine, Rosendo Salvado, who in 1848 recruited the first aborigines for the Benedictine order.[49] Nagapen criticises the English Benedictines in Mauritius for their short-sightedness in not encouraging indigenous vocations. However in 1848, one young Mauritian, Paul Raynal, did enter the English Benedictines at Downside, much to the annoyance of Bishop Collier who, "notwithstanding [his] attachment to his Congregation", urged the Prior of Downside to encourage the young man to train instead as a priest for Mauritius. Collier asserted:

---

[44] *AB*, 376-378; DAB, L 163, 17 June 1842, Collier to Heptonstall.
[45] DAB, M 105, 24 October 1848, Polding to Heptonstall.
[46] NA, CO 167/245 No. 42, Collier to Gomm, 21 January 1843, NAGAPEN, "Century," 16.
[47] The government did allow a number of exceptions to this policy. See NAGAPEN, "Century,"7.
[48] DAB, M 94, Sydney, 3 July 1848, Polding to Heptonstall.
[49] G. RUSSO, *Lord Abbot of the Wilderness*, Polding Press, Melbourne 1980, 136-147.

> The wants of England may be great, but they can never be put in comparison with those of this island…I cannot bring myself to consider it just to receive into our Congregation subjects from a distant country whose faith is almost extinct for want of labourers in the vineyard and at the same time to forbid them to return to labour in it.[50]

In the event, Collier did not get his way and Raynal went on to enjoy a distinguished English Benedictine career, serving for over twenty years as Prior of Belmont and ending his days as Procurator-in-Curia in Rome.[51]

Financing the English Benedictine Overseas Mission

At least the Congregation did not have to take responsibility for financing those who went to the colonies, for, in contrast to the Catholic missions in England, the British government gave financial support to Catholic clergy in the colonies by paying their salaries and travelling expenses. This seems remarkable in the days before Catholic emancipation, but has to be seen against the background of the situation in Ireland, where the British government had already in 1795 provided funding for the seminary at Maynooth, thereby attempting to gain the loyalty of Irish clergy to the Crown. A further grant was made in 1845.[52] Secondly, the funding of Catholic clergy in the colonies was part of a liberal policy towards Catholicism adopted by the Colonial Office, under Lord Bathurst between 1812 and 1827.[53] Moreover, the particular situation in Mauritius shaped colonial policy towards Catholics. In its policy of preventing the influence of the Archbishop of Paris in the former French colony, the British Colonial Office took on the financial commitments outlined in the French Concordat, which held that clergy were to be paid by the state. The gesture was not an altruistic one, for in paying the salaries of Catholic clergy, the British government was able to maintain control, since "he who pays, usually directs".[54]

According to President Birdsall: "of the Colonies, Mauritius is the one most favoured by the English government: I mean in the allowances they

---

[50] DA, President's Archive, Box 760, 19 April 1849, Collier to Barber.
[51] B. WHELAN, *Annals of the English Congregation of the Black Monks of St.Benedict 1850-1900,* typescript, reissued 1971, 1: 24, 97; Account books for St Edmund's Priory at Douai show that in the early 1850s, indigenous Mauritians and Australians were sent there to be educated on bursaries.
[52] On Maynooth see E.R. NORMAN, *Anti-Catholicism in Victorian England,* Allen & Unwin, London 1968, 27-29.
[53] D.M. YOUNG, *The Colonial Office in the Early Nineteenth Century,* Longmans, London 1961; N.D. MCLACHLAN, "Bathurst at the Colonial Office, 1812-1827: A Reconnaissance," *Historical Studies,* 13 (1969) 477-502.
[54] BIRT, *Benedictine Pioneers in Australia,* 1: 30.

make for the bishops".[55] Certainly, Bishop Slater had enjoyed a salary of £1000 per annum, twice that paid to Bede Polding in Australia, but from 1832 the salary of the Vicar Apostolic of Mauritius was reduced to £720 per annum, and remained at this figure even after Bernard Collier's status was raised from Vicar Apostolic to Bishop of Port Louis.[56] Ullathorne as Vicar General of Australia was paid an annual salary of £200. Ordinary clergy in Mauritius too were paid slightly better than their Australian counterparts; an annual salary of £150 as opposed to £100. Some, such as Ambrose Cotham in Van Diemen's Land (later Tasmania) found it impossible to survive on such a sum, although during his sixteen years in the colony, he managed to amass a fortune.[57]

The missionaries would also have had collections, stipends, stole fees and contributions but in a penal colony like New South Wales these cannot have amounted to very much. An important source of income was the Society for the Propagation for the Faith in Lyons, which, following approaches by Ullathorne, made regular contributions to the mission in Australia (contributions rose steadily from £300 in 1838 to over £1000 in 1841).[58] Assistance was also provided by the Vienna Fund, roughly £1000 provided as a foundation by an Austrian priest to found a mission at the penal settlement on Norfolk Island. Ullathorne obtained grants from this fund through *Propaganda Fide* in Rome.[59] Despite the efforts of Governor Richard Bourke in New South Wales to give financial support to other Christian churches besides the Anglican Church, through the Church Act of 1836, when it came to the distribution of financial resources, Anglicanism continued to receive the larger proportion. By 1840 the Church of England in Australia was granted over £200,000 in funding, whilst the Catholic Church received only £37,000.[60] In Mauritius Bishop Collier complained that he was the victim of discrimination from the colonial government, who paid him a salary of £720 whilst other heads of public departments on Mauritius were paid annual salaries of £1000 each. He had to set up a *Comité chargé de l'oeuvre de la construction de nouvelles églises catholiques au Port-Louis* which organised annual fund-raising activities to provide money used by Collier to purchase

---

[55] AR, 4: 293.

[56] For the correspondence between Bishop Collier and the Colonial Office in this matter see NA, CO 167/321, no.105, 17 June 1850.

[57] NA, CO 201/325, 8 December 1835, Cotham to the Foreign Office; DAA, VIII.A, Cotham papers.

[58] For an outline of the Society's work for Australia see J. WALDERSEE, *A Grain of Mustard Seed: The Society for the Propagation of the Faith and Australia, 1837-1977* Chevalier Press, Kensington, New South Wales 1974, 54.

[59] DAB, K 41, 14 April 1838, Collier to Ullathorne.

[60] P. COLLINS, unpublished D.Phil. thesis, *William Bernard Ullathorne and the Foundation of Australian Catholicism, 1815-1840*, 207.

land and finance building projects.⁶¹ Finance from government societies and continental religious enterprises provided important recognition and enhanced the status of the English Benedictine Congregation, even though the demands of overseas mission remained very contentious.

The character of the overseas mission

Accounts extant of the long journeys by sea to Mauritius and Australia by Bishops Bernard Ullathorne,⁶² Placid Morris ⁶³ and Edmund Moore ⁶⁴ are of interest for the details of the voyages, but the authors of them are remarkably silent concerning their hopes and expectations for the mission that awaited them. The only exception is the diary of Bishop Placid Morris which reveals the author's trepidations as to what would greet him when arriving at Port Louis, the "difficulties, dangers, perhaps even lessons in to which [he] was about to be plunged".⁶⁵

It is beyond the scope of this present work to deal in any significant detail with the activities of individual English Benedictines in the colonies in this period; these are supplied elsewhere.⁶⁶ However, some general comments need to be made about the character of the work undertaken in both Mauritius and Australia.

Firstly, in these new mission territories there was a similar tension as at home between the monastic and missionary impulses within the Congregation. This was true especially in Australia, where Polding had the aim of establishing not only a Benedictine missionary diocese, but also, as seen in an earlier chapter, a monastery in the colony which would be a centre of culture, where "in the monastic church, the liturgy would be carried out in all its solemnity and beauty." Furthermore, no doubt aware of the criticisms that had been made against Bishops Slater and Morris and their fellow monks in Mauritius, Polding was determined to train a new generation of missionary monks who were formed in the regular discipline of the monastic life. Polding's dream was that the monastery would supply priests for the mission who would all be Benedictines and would spread a monastic spirit "from Sydney to other towns and districts in the form of other communities

---

⁶¹ *Le Mauricien,* nos.1747 (16 January 1846) and 1804 (29 May 1846).
⁶² *The Devil is a Jackass,* chapters nine and ten.
⁶³ DA, Box 703.
⁶⁴ Moore's journal was published in *DR,* 32 (1913) 70-92; 197-209; 314-327.
⁶⁵ DA, box 703, Morris diary, 44.
⁶⁶ For Mauritius see NAGAPEN, "Century," 91-113; for Australia see CHAMP, *William Bernard Ullathorne,* 37-86; O'DONOGHUE, *The Bishop of Botany Bay,* 29-99; DOWD, *Rome in Australia,* 1: 77-124; W.T. SOUTHERWOOD, "A Benedictine Pioneer in Van Diemen's Land," *Australian Catholic Record,* 54 (1977) 43-62; R.M. WILTGEN, *The Founding of the Roman Catholic Church in Oceania, 1825-1850,* Princeton Theological Monograph, Wipf & Stock Publishers, Eugene OR 2010.

of monk missionaries as places of prayer, education and ministry and put down deep roots in Australian soil".[67] The idealism inherent in Polding's vision is expressed in a letter where he asserted:

> We shall in our Institute come as near to the form of the Benedictine Institute as it existed in England before the Reformation, blending as it did in perfect harmony Episcopal authority with the Abbatial and producing missionaries who more zealously fulfilled their duties from the habitual renunciation of all things, the consequence of their monastic profession.[68]

Polding's view on the importance of establishing a monastery in missionary territories was shared by the German Benedictine, Boniface Wimmer who in 1846 established a Benedictine presence on the estate in Pittsburgh, Pennsylvania, previously offered to the English Benedictines in 1794. Wimmer contended that "a self-sufficient monastic colony would become a magnet for further settlement".[69]

Secondly, some consideration should be given to how far the new apostolate could be regarded as "missionary", especially since the Catholic Church already had a presence in both these places by the time English Benedictines appeared on the scene. Certainly these colonies were not virgin mission lands in the strict ecclesiastical sense. Nevertheless there is evidence that missionary tactics were still required in both places. Waldersee has asserted that whilst the Irish population in Australia may have been nominally Catholic, the majority were indifferent to their religion, and given the upheaval of transportation and the problems of adjusting to a new existence in an alien land, needed the encouragement of Catholic clergy to return to the practice of their faith.[70] This is borne out by the experience of Ambrose Cotham, monk of Douai, who accompanied Polding to Australia in 1835; he clearly declared that his main objective in Hobart was "to induce those who have forsaken their religion to return to it and to hold out better days to those who though they acknowledge themselves Catholics know no more of their religion than the name".[71]

In Mauritius, Bishop Slater found not only "an extremely limited number of clergymen…for the religious wants" of the island but also a very

---

[67] DOWD, *Rome in Australia*, 1: 17.
[68] Polding to William Leigh, 7 January 1845, quoted in O.THORPE, *The First Mission to Australian Aborigines*, Pellegrini & Co, Sydney 1950, 193.
[69] C. STEWART, "False Alternatives: The Active/Contemplative Dichotomy," in C. LEYSER and H. WILLIAMS, *Mission and Monasticism*, 22. See also the address given by Abbot Primate Notker Wolf on the occasion of the bi-centenary of Wimmer's birth: http://www.bonifacewimmer.org/newsmodule/view/id/82/src/@random4e8c5e5 49192f/ > [accessed 16 May 2014].
[70] J. WALDERSEE, *Catholic Society in New South Wales, 1788-1860*, 186-199.
[71] DAB, J 118, 12 March 1836, Cotham to Polding. For Cotham's work in Tasmania see W.T. SOUTHERWOOD, "A Benedictine Pioneer in Van Diemen's Land," 43-62.

mixed population, descended from "hangers-on, cast-offs from the French army", and "many with ruined healths and fortunes".[72]

Thirdly, although mission overseas represented a significant change in the English Benedictine apostolate, it is striking that once installed in the new mission areas of Mauritius and Australia, the monks reverted to traditional Congregational activities rather than adapting themselves to the local needs that presented themselves when they arrived. In Mauritius, the English Benedictines provided ecclesiastical administrators rather than the missionary priests that were urgently needed. Indeed, it is striking that in Mauritius and Australia, the English Benedictines appeared to demonstrate little commitment to evangelising the non-white population in both places, and were content to leave this work to others.

In Mauritius, Bishop Collier allotted the work of evangelising the population of former slaves to the Holy Ghost Fathers, where Father Jacques Désiré Laval successfully evangelised 66,000 of the community on the island.[73] The pastoral needs of indentured workers from India in the colony were entrusted to the Jesuits.[74] Although in his early years in Australia, Polding undertook a number of long missionary journeys through the bush, and tried to defend the rights of the indigenous population of aborigines by appealing to a Parliamentary Committee on their behalf, from the outset his principal concern was the care and maintenance of the existing Catholic community, principally the convicts.[75] The evangelisation of the aborigines, was entrusted to the Passionist Fathers.[76] As has briefly been mentioned above, it is also noteworthy that among those who worked successfully with the aborigines were the Spanish Benedictines, Benedict Serra and Rosendo Salvado who were recruited by Bishop Brady to work in Western Australia. These monks not only proved to be tenacious and successful in evangelising the aborigines but also in 1847 established a monastery at New Norcia around which many aborigines settled.[77] Whilst their Spanish brethren were working with aborigines in the bush, the English Benedictines in other parts of the country were building new churches and schools, and catechising the white settlers, in many ways continuing the style of work they had been doing in England for generations.

---

[72] RSRNC, (Africa, Isole dell'Oceano, Australe et Capo di Buona Speranza, 2) fol.240.
[73] A. NAGAPEN, *La naturalisation du Père J-D Laval et des missionaires spiritains – Un volet de la politique coloniale britannique à l'Ile Maurice,* Diocése de Port Louis 1992, 82-95.
[74] NAGAPEN, *Histoire de l'Église,* 112, 118-119, 156, 172, 175-176, 185-186, 193.
[75] F. O'DONOGHUE, *The Bishop of Botany Bay,* 36; *The Devil is a Jackass,* 131. Also Ullathorne's printed circular addressed to "the faithful of Britain," 7 July 1834, DAB, I 338.
[76] DAB, L 152, 18 May 1842, Polding to Heptonstall.
[77] RUSSO, *Lord Abbot of the Wilderness,* 125-147; "Bishop Salvado of New Norcia 1814-1900," in R. RIOS, *Benedictines of Today,* Stanbrook Abbey, Worcester 1946, 195-232.

Relationship with the British Government

In both Mauritius and Australia, the English Benedictines succeeded in forging effective relationships between the Church and the colonial government, thereby raising the status of the Catholic Church within the colonies. In dealing with issues such as Catholic emancipation, Ireland, and problems in their colonies, the British government had increasing need to establish good relations with the Holy See. The first port of call for the government was the Vicar Apostolic of the London District, who since 1688 had held faculties for Catholics in the British colonies.

From 1812 to 1827 William Poynter, who seems to have been the first Vicar Apostolic to attempt to deal with the problems of Catholics in the colonies in a systematic fashion, filled this office. His was a particularly difficult task, to be the intermediary between *Propaganda* in Rome and the Colonial Office in London, and to satisfy both these authorities. Poynter quickly realised that it was only by working closely with Colonial Office officials that permission and support could be obtained to appoint clergy to the colonies. Poynter had to try to balance the British government's objectives of maintaining social order and reinforcing social cohesion in the colonies with Rome's aims of expanding the church's mission and, increasingly, under Popes Gregory XVI and his immediate successors, the policy of centralisation to ensure cohesion between the ecclesiastical authorities and the local churches. Thus mission and ultramontanism were intimately connected. Paul Collins clarifies the relationship between the British government and the Holy See by observing:

> The Catholic Church and the English state had evolved a unique working relationship. This was not state support for the church envisaged in the papal doctrine of church-state relations, nor was it a strict separation of the two. Rather it was a realistic recognition by the Colonial Office that the British government had a role to play in the regularisation of the position of Catholics in the colonies.[78]

In its turn, the government, with its inherent erastianism and growing evangelical outlook which held that religion was an important expression of public morality, recognised the need to recruit Catholic bishops and clergy who would be loyal to the Crown and offer effective pastoral leadership to colonial Catholics. Although the policy regarding Catholicism may have been common to all colonies, the government adapted its policy to each place. Whilst Bishop Poynter was able to attempt to establish good working relationships with senior colonial officials in London, it was up to the English Benedictines to do so with officials in London responsible for implementing policy, as well as with local officials in New South Wales and in Mauritius.

---

[78] COLLINS, *William Bernard Ullathorne*, 92.

Increasingly after 1835 the English Benedictines came to rely on the services of Paulinus Heptonstall, cousin of Bede Polding, until 1850 missioner at Acton in Middlesex. He became the mediator between the Congregation and the Colonial Office charged with dealing with financial matters and making practical arrangements of all kinds; initially his role was to obtain payments from the Colonial Office for the salaries and travel costs of the monks and lay teachers who had been approved for service to the Catholic Church in New South Wales. Later, his function seems to have been to arrange for the sending of supplies.[79]

Ullathorne and Collier were particularly successful in establishing a working relationship with colonial officials. Ullathorne, for instance, enjoyed a particularly good relationship with Governor Richard Bourke in New South Wales, who not only increased state support for Catholicism but also allowed Ullathorne considerable independence in governing the church. Ullathorne later recalled that he "always found the heads of departments friendly and considerate and the official dinners at Government House strengthened our good understanding".[80] In contrast, Slater in Mauritius did not enjoy such cordial relations with the Governor, Sir Lowry Cole, and complained that he "was twice invited to dinners at Government House apparently for the purpose of being publicly degraded from the rank assigned to him".[81] Collier seems to have fared rather better, but did occasionally have problems, especially in fighting for Catholic education and the Catholic policy with regard to mixed marriages, as well as the question of his own status.[82]

The English nationality of Ullathorne, Polding and Collier undoubtedly helped them to gain entrée to the social circle of the colonial government, and enabled them to take full advantage of the "marriage of convenience" that had been forged with regard to the colonies, between the British government and the Holy See. The English Benedictine President Birdsall soon realised: "our government do not like to have Irish priests and bishops sent. No, our government wants English priests in her colonies".[83] Indeed, this may partly explain why Irish priests sent to Australia before 1833 had failed to establish effective infrastructures there for the Catholic Church. Another distinct advantage with regard to English Benedictine missioners in Mauritius was that these continentally-trained English monks spoke French, the language of the island. Evidently, some of them, especially

---

[79] Some of such letters have been preserved: NA, CO 201/280, .340ff, Heptonstall to Lord Glenelg, June – December 1838; also DAB, L 163, 17 June 1842, Collier to Heptonstall.
[80] COLLINS, *William Bernard Ullathorne*, 73.
[81] RSRNC, (Africa, Isole dell'Oceano, Australe et Capo di Buona Speranza, 2) fol.242.
[82] For original correspondence between Collier and the Governor of Mauritius on these issues see: NA, CO 167/262/no.192, CO 167/270/no.24; CO 167/302/no.253.
[83] AR, 4: 294.

Collier who had spent twenty years living at Douai, spoke the language most eloquently.[84]

Achievements

It was only after 1850 that many of the initiatives begun in the colonies were consolidated, and English Benedictines continued to maintain a presence in both Mauritius and Australia long after this date. Nevertheless, some assessment needs to be made of their achievements and failures by mid-century. Firstly, in both colonies, English Benedictine monks shaped the church into a more cohesive organisation, bringing both pastoral vision and order into a colonial church that had hitherto been governed unsystematically on an *ad-hoc* basis. Soon after the arrival of Ullathorne in Australia as Vicar General, one of his clergy observed that the Downside monk had "done much in bringing some order to this anomalous mission' that had been served by Irish clergy".[85] To a certain extent the English Benedictines were victims here of their own success: tensions soon sprang up between the monks and the Irish priests, several of whom had laboured in the colony long before the arrival of the Benedictines.[86] Indeed resentment sprang up as "some of the Irish secular clergy felt that while they languished in the bush, the Reverend OSBs were given the plum jobs in Sydney".[87]

Although in Mauritius the English Benedictines were not instantly successful in providing effective ecclesiastical leadership, the first bishop, Bernard Collier, quickly brought order and vision to the diocese of Port Louis. The English Benedictines in this period must be seen as belonging to a new breed of professional clergy that was emerging in the early nineteenth century, and to a more confident body of Catholic clergy, who were beginning to gain greater power and influence as their church became more centralised. The experience gained by Bishop Collier as the English Benedictine Procurator-in-Curia, the Congregation's agent or representative in Rome, and earlier, as Prior of Douai, was of crucial importance in equipping him not only with administrative skills, but with a useful knowledge of the workings of ecclesiastical government. Thus, on his arrival in Port Louis in 1841, Collier was able to articulate quickly a pastoral strategy for the island.[88]

---

[84] J. MAMET, *Le diocèse de Port Louis,* Diocése de Port Louis, Port Louis 1974, 169.
[85] DAB, I 238, 3 June 1834, McEnroe to Morris.
[86] On this point see M. SHANAHAN, *Out of Time, Out of Place: Henry Gregory and the Benedictine Order in Colonial Australia*, Australian National University Press, Canberra 1970, 142-164.
[87] G. HAINES, "Reflections on Polding," unpublished paper, 1976, 19.
[88] NAGAPEN, "Century," 15.

In contrast, Bernard Ullathorne may not have had the benefit of Collier's administrative and pastoral experience before his appointment as Vicar General in Australia, yet he had a clear, confident perception of his professional role, as the following passage demonstrates. Ullathorne recalled that upon his arrival in New South Wales he had no trepidation:

> I do not remember that I had any fears of much sentimentality. The affairs I had to manage... [did not] greatly distress me. I saw a crooked state of things requiring to be put straight, but was not inclined to hurry things before they were ripe for action. But when I struck, the blow was decisive, and it was soon found that I was not to be turned from my path.[89]

Given his relative inexperience and youthfulness (aged only 26 when he arrived in the colony in 1833), Ullathorne's early achievements in bringing order to the church there and establishing an infrastructure for it are remarkable. Commentators have tended to neglect Ullathorne's contribution to the Australian church, preferring to emphasise the achievements of his fellow English Benedictine, Bede Polding, but, as Collins asserts, it was actually Ullathorne who laid the foundations of the Australian Catholic Church.[90] Of the two men, Ullathorne was the more able and, unlike Polding, a more perceptive administrator. Mary Shanahan notes that "everyone who had dealings with Polding in an official capacity complained of his lack of organisation of his want of decision".[91] Even Ullathorne himself voiced criticism of Polding's "penchant for the mission" which made him "neglect business," especially "the Government correspondence" which Ullathorne declared was "in a scandalous state," and Polding's duties towards the clergy and other important issues "done, put off or abandoned according to impulse." Ullathorne concluded that "the Bishop is a continued prey to his own acute and morbid feelings".[92] Ullathorne's departure from Australia in 1841 deprived Polding of an able and adroit lieutenant.

Ullathorne was also one of the few English Benedictines to have returned to England from Australia,[93] and use his Australian experience for the benefit of the English Catholic Church: For instance, having been involved in the establishment of the Catholic hierarchy in Australia, he was to prove particularly helpful to English Catholics as a principal negotiator with the Holy See in the years immediately preceding the re-establishment of

---

[89] *The Devil is a Jackass*, 93.
[90] COLLINS, *William Bernard Ullathorne*, 406-407; J. CHAMP, *A Different Kind of Monk: William Bernard Ullathorne*, 37-86.
[91] SHANAHAN, 68.
[92] BIRT, *Benedictine Pioneers*, 1: 438.
[93] Another notable English Benedictine to do so was Ambrose Cotham, who returned from Tasmania in 1851 and built a new church at Cheltenham.

the English Catholic hierarchy in 1850.[94] It was Ullathorne who helped to bring to public attention the conditions experienced by convicts who were sent to Australia through his book, *The Horrors of Transportation*.[95] After his return to England in 1841, Ullathorne recycled sermons he had preached in Australia to the convicts and delivered them to English Catholic congregations "just emerging from the catacombs". Ullathorne "thus colonised urban, industrial England by means of sermons" that had been preached "in the Australian backwoods, his most famous, "The Drunkard" being first heard in Australian public houses but now enthusiastically adopted by the English temperance movement". [96]

Ullathorne's departure from Australia marked the beginning of a decline in Polding's fortunes and by 1850 there were indications that the English Benedictine mission to Australia was destined to fail. The most significant problem was the shortage of manpower; although the monastery Polding had established in 1843 boasted 45 monks, it was simply not large or efficient enough to supply competent and well-trained missioners. Not only did Polding have a very limited number of Benedictine students, but very few of the Irish seminarians and priests who volunteered for the Australian mission demonstrated any interest in becoming monks.[97] In March 1851, the Irish secular priest, Archdeacon John McEnroe asserted in a letter to Bishop Goold of Melbourne that "the 'infant' Benedictine Monastery CANNOT…supply New South Wales with priests".[98] In other words, Polding's Benedictine vision for Australia was doomed "because it lacked the essential ingredient needed to maintain it – Benedictines".[99] Furthermore, by 1849 there were destructive forces at work within the monastic community itself as a result of poor discipline and dissension in the ranks. [100]

Polding's monastery served as his seminary, and the shortage of trained men meant that leadership and teaching roles were often given to

---

[94] THE RT.REV B. ULLATHORNE, *History of the Restoration of the Catholic hierarchy in England*, Burns, Oates & Co, London 1871; *The Devil is a Jackass*, 308-67.

[95] W.B. ULLATHORNE, *The horrors of transportation*, R Coyne, Dublin 1838.

[96] G. SCOTT, "Sermons in British Catholicism, 1689-1850," in K.A. FRANCIS and W. GIBSON, (eds.), *Oxford Handbook of the British Sermon, 1689-1901*, Oxford University Press, Oxford 2012, 143.

[97] Livingston notes that when Polding invited the first priest from All Hallows College, Dublin to come to Sydney and join his order, the priest bluntly replied that he preferred "the Order of St Peter," K.T. LIVINGSTON, *Emergence of an Australian Catholic Priesthood, 1835-1915*, (Studies in the Christian Movement, 3), Catholic Theological Faculty, Sydney, Sydney 1977, 20, n.99.

[98] BIRT, *Benedictine Pioneers*, 2: 166-167.

[99] J. MOLONY, "The Australian Hierarchy and the Holy See, 1840-1870," *Australian Historical Studies*, 13 (1968) 177.

[100] A flavour of such an atmosphere can be gleaned from letters written by one of the community, Edmund Moore, to a former confrere, Alphonsus Morrall, at Downside, between 1848 and 1849, DAB M 71, M 129 & M 138.

those who were unsuited for them. Polding's new Vicar General, the Downside monk Henry Gregory Gregory was appointed as Prior and Novice master of the monastery, despite the fact that his own monastic training had by all accounts been superficial. He had been ordained before the canonical age without having completed his own studies for ordination, and added to these he had certain defects of character that made him abrasive and inflexible. There were also non-Benedictine professors in Polding's monastery/seminary who have been described as "an eclectic, transient group of priests," who were simply not capable of fulfilling the task entrusted to them. [101] Added to these problems were the frequent and often prolonged absences of Polding and Gregory either on missionary journeys or overseas trips, absences that in the words of Birt "were detrimental to the discipline of the house," for "half-trained religious, who had never had experience of monastic life in an old-established house, living in the midst of the hurry and bustle of an active colonial town, easily lost the bloom of first fervour and recollection".[102]

In 1848, the arrival of another Downside monk, Charles Henry Davis, as Bishop of Maitland and Polding's co-adjutor in Sydney seemed to provide a solution to many of these problems. Polding soon entrusted him with the running of the seminary, where Davis won hearts and minds due to his character, spirituality and administrative ability. In the event the solution proved to be short-lived, for six years later in 1854, Davis died of heart-failure at the early age of 39.[103] This proved to be a significant loss for both Polding and his Benedictine dream, since in the mind of one commentator, "the loss of Davis gave the last push to the tottering edifice of colonial monasticism".[104]

Polding has been sharply and sometimes unfairly criticised for chasing a Benedictine dream that was "out of time, out of place," and "for never seeming to understand that at the very core of Benedictine monasticism stood the concept of stability that bound a monk to live within a monastic community".[105] The trouble was that Polding was too absorbed in his own ideal to accept that it was unworkable. In particular he underplayed the importance of a stable monastic life lived in common. Indeed, one might

---

[101] These issues are explored in K.T. LIVINGSTON, *The Emergence of an Australian Catholic Priesthood*, 18-26.
[102] BIRT, *Benedictine Pioneers*, 2: 368.
[103] SHANAHAN, 51; K.T. LIVINGSTON, *The Emergence of an Australian Catholic Priesthood*, 23-24; R.A. DALY, "Davis, Charles Henry (1815–1854)," in Australian Dictionary of Biography, National Centre of Biography, Australian National University,<http://adb.anu.edu.au/biography/davis-charles-henry-1963/text2367> [accessed 29 June 2014].
[104] BIRT, *Benedictine Pioneers*, 2: 368.
[105] M. SHANAHAN, *Out of Time, Out of Place*, 13; J.N. MOLONY, *The Roman Mould of the Australian Catholic Church*, Melbourne University Press, Melbourne 1969, 11.

argue that like Pietro Casaretto, Polding, "turned missionary activity into one of purely personal endeavour" rather than of the experience of his Benedictine community.[106] Polding took until 1843, eight years after arriving in New South Wales, before establishing a monastery. This fact stands in stark in contrast to Boniface Wimmer in the United States a decade later. From the outset of his Benedictine mission, Wimmer asserted that:

> Benedictines are men of stability; they are not wandering monks, they acquire lands and bring them under cultivation and become thoroughly affiliated to the country and people to which they belong…Benedictine monasteries of the old style are the best means of checking the downward tendencies of our countrymen in social, political and religious matters.[107]

In giving first priority to founding a monastery, Wimmer realised that the success of a Benedictine mission depended upon the establishment of a stable monastic community at its heart. [108]

In receiving permission in 1842 for the establishment of the Sydney monastery and the creation of an Australian episcopal hierarchy, Polding's star seemed to be in the ascendant, and the Roman authorities appeared to be satisfied with his plans. By 1845, Polding's reputation in Rome began to be tarnished by complaints forwarded to Propaganda from superiors of other religious orders, especially the Passionists, the Christian Brothers, the Sisters of Charity and the Marists who resented Polding's attempts to control the missionary activities of their subjects in Australia, and assert Benedictine supremacy over them.[109] As a result of these complaints, Polding's standing in Rome entered a long period of decline from which it never really recovered. The death in 1846 of the monk-Pope, Gregory XVI, who had been favourably disposed towards Polding, and the election of Pope Pius IX, who had been a secular priest with a more pragmatic approach to pastoral strategies, also signalled a change in Polding's fortunes.[110]

In fairness to Polding, many of the reasons for the failure of his Benedictine vision for Australia lay outside his control. In the words of his twenty-first century successor as Archbishop of Sydney, "Polding's Benedictine dream was shattered less by incompetence than by its incompatibility of the Benedictine vocation with Australian missionary

---

[106] LUNARDI, "The Missionary Spirit of Abbot Casaretto," 54.
[107] B. WIMMER, Über die Missionen," *Augsburg Postzeitung,* 8 November 1845, translated in J.T. ELLIS, (ed.), *Documents of American Catholic History,* Bruce Publishing, Milwaukee 1962, 283, 288.
[108] See note 69.
[109] For the detail on these squabbles see DOWD, *Rome in Australia,* 1: 97-123
[110] MOLONY, *The Roman Mould of the Australian Catholic Church,* 39-55.

conditions".[111] The Benedictine mission in Australia was hampered by being sandwiched between two powerful empires: "the British empire at the beginning of its rise to pre-eminence, and also the empire of Catholicism whose metropolitan influence was split between Rome and Dublin".[112] In addition were the attendant complications posed by Ireland and the handful of Irish clergy who had been labouring in the colony long before the English Benedictines arrived. By the middle of the century, there was an explosion of the population of the colony, mainly through immigration which affected the Catholic community in Australia, and by 1850 there was only one priest per 1500 people. Furthermore, the Catholic population was made up of a diversity of national and ethnic backgrounds, but the predominant group were first or second generation Irish. The composition of Catholic clergy in Australia also reflected ethnic differences but was also predominantly Irish, and there was almost continual friction between the English monks and Irish priests, who had been labouring in the colony long before the English Benedictines arrived. As early as 1838, Ullathorne had surmised that Australia "would become an Irish mission…" and that "to do anything Benedictine in the colony" was "now out of the question". Even by 1838 Ullathorne had realised that the Australian Mission was "Hibernicised and will not be Benedictinised".[113] Ullathorne, unlike Polding, shared Bishop Collier's ability to read correctly the signs of the times.

Although Polding's vision of a vibrant Australian Benedictine monastery and mission failed to take root, it has been asserted that, paradoxically a Benedictine tradition and spirituality did endure there, "through a line of strong individuals who outlived the collapse of their weak community".[114] Despite a number of unsympathetic and critical assessments of his work in Australia, notably by one of his successors, Cardinal Patrick Moran, Polding's memory is still revered there to this day. His most recent successor as Archbishop of Sydney, George Pell, acknowledges that "with his vast energy and pastoral zeal and his weaknesses," Polding "still made a profound contribution" to the Australian Church. The website of the Sisters of the Good Samaritan, founded by Polding in 1857 laud him for his "passion

---

[111] G. PELL, "Archdiocese born from 'mission' to Aborigines," 19 July 2009, <http://www.catholicweekly.com.au/article.php?classID=3&subclassID=66&articleID=5867&&sub> [accessed 3 July 2014].
[112] P. CUNICH, "Archbishop Vaughan and the Empires of Religion," in H.M. CAREY (ed.), *Empires of Religion,* Palgrave Macmillan, Basingstoke 2008, 137-160.
[113] DAB, K 77, 11 July 1838, Ullathorne to Heptonstall; K 85, 2 August 1838, Ullathorne to Heptonstall. On the Irishness of the Australian Catholic Church in this period see C. KIERNAN, "The Irish Character of the Australian Catholic Church," in J. JUPP (ed.), *The Australian People: An Encyclopedia of the Nations, Its People and their Origins,* Angus & Robertson, Sydney 1988, 569-573.
[114] K.T. LIVINGSTON, "Anselm Curtis: First Sydney-born Benedictine priest of St Mary's Monastery," *TJ*, 8 (1974) 206.

for the reign of God and compassion for the people of God. He spoke out about injustices in society and gave a voice to those who had no voice: the poor, the convicts, the Aborigines and women". Furthermore, "when Polding died in 1877, his funeral was the largest ever held in Australia. More than 100,000 people joined the funeral procession through the streets of Sydney".[115]

Another English Benedictine whose spirit and legacy is remembered is Polding's short-lived co-adjutor, Bishop Charles Henry Davis, of whom "everyone spoke well, both in his lifetime and for years afterwards" as "one of the worthiest prelates that ever trod Australian soil", one who not only made a significant contribution to the life of the Sydney monastery and seminary, but also to the University of Sydney.[116]

By 1850, the English Benedictines were well established in both Australia and Mauritius, despite the difficulties mentioned above. Collier and Polding had gained recognition for their endeavours, both in Rome and elsewhere. It is significant, for instance, that Pietro Casaretto's idea to found a College for missionary monks in Genoa in 1846 was partly inspired by the work Polding was doing in the Antipodes.[117]

The English Benedictine colonial adventure had begun in 1819, and was not to attain its centenary. Polding's beloved monastery was suppressed soon after his death by his successor, Bede Vaughan, also a monk of Downside.[118] The last monk of the Congregation to work in Australia, the Edmundian, Francis Barry, died at Kerang near Melbourne in 1896, whilst another Douai monk, Romanus Bilsborrow, the last Benedictine bishop of Port Louis, left Mauritius in 1916. Considering its scant human and material resources in the early decades of the nineteenth century, and the early

---

[115] G. PELL, "Archdiocese born from 'mission' to Aborigines," 19 July 2009, <http://www.catholicweekly.com.au/article.php?classID=3&subclassID=66&articleID=5867&&sub> [accessed 3 July 2014]. Moran's criticisms of Polding are outlined in J.H. CULLEN, *The Australian Daughters of Mary Aikenhead: A Century of Charity 1838-1938*, Pellegrini, Sydney 1938, 102. See also J. HOSIE, "1859: Year of Crisis in the Australian Catholic Church," *Journal of Religious History*, 7:4 (1973) 342-361; *Challenge: The Marists in Colonial Australia*, Allen & Unwin, Sydney 1987; For the Sisters of the Good Samaritan on Polding's legacy, see <http://www.goodsams.org.au/who-we-are/history/john-bede-polding/> [accessed 4 July 2014].
[116] R.A. DALY, "Davis, Charles Henry (1815-1854)," ; BIRT, *Benedictine Pioneers*, 2: 205; Mr. Graeme Pender, a doctoral student in Australia is currently working on a study entitled: "Bishop Charles Henry Davis, OSB: His contribution to the early Australian church,"shortly to be submitted for the award of the degree of Doctor of Theology at Melbourne College of Divinity.
[117] The archives of the Subiaco Benedictine Congregation at Sant' Ambrogio in Rome contain several letters from Polding to Casaretto. See also G. LUNARDI, *La Congregazione Subiancense OSB*: 1, Noci Abbey 2004.
[118] T. KAVENAGH, "Vaughan and the monks of Sydney," *TJ*, 25 (1983) 147-233.

failures of Bishops Slater and Morris, it is remarkable that the English Benedictine Congregation was able to provide bishops and clergy for such a vast area of the globe. It was also striking that in the midst of change, in the form of these new colonial opportunities, it was continuity that became the order of the day, especially in Australia, where the monks reverted to type and chose to take up their traditional apostolates rather than grasp the nettle of innovation. Nevertheless, in its two little corners of the rapidly expanding British empire, the English Benedictine Congregation was sowing seeds that would in time yield important fruit: Ullathorne and Collier established in Australia and Mauritius the infrastructure upon which others were able to build in later generations. Although the English Benedictines can be criticised at one level for their failure to evangelise the indigenous population of both those colonies, their energies in building new churches, presbyteries and schools ensured that the Catholic Church had the resources it required in order to establish itself in the colonies.

English Benedictine superiors may well have resented the loss of much-needed manpower at home in order to supply the overseas mission, but it was a sacrifice that would ultimately benefit the English Catholic Church. The experience gained by Bernard Ullathorne in founding the Australian Catholic Church proved also to be of benefit to its English counterpart, for Ullathorne went on to be one of the architects of the English Catholic hierarchy that was established in 1850. Although English Benedictine influence in the colonies was not to endure, the Congregation could pride itself that it had, at least for a time, shared its treasures throughout a mighty hemisphere.

CONCLUSION

By 1850 the English Benedictines could look back with some satisfaction on their achievements of the previous half-century for, having been threatened with extinction following the damage inflicted by the French Revolution on their personnel, property and finances, all the surviving houses of the Congregation had settled down in their respective new locations, and were about to embark on new buildings to house their increasing numbers and expanding apostolates. The most significant development had taken place on the Mission, not just in terms of the Catholic population or even the priests that served it, but in terms of the numbers of new churches, schools and presbyteries that were built, especially in the new urban centres such as Liverpool. The English Benedictine contribution to the growth of the English Catholic Church was valued and appreciated, notably by Cardinal Henry Manning, Archbishop of Westminster, who in 1889 in a letter to the ailing Bishop Bernard Collier: "You and your brethren broke the ground and sowed the seed".[1]

The status of the Congregation had been enhanced by its dealings with the Colonial Office and by Rome's regard for it as a nursery for future bishops in the new missionary territories overseas. This latter work offered the Congregation new challenges and opportunities. For the first few decades after their repatriation to England the English Benedictines had little opposition from other religious orders due to the slow recovery of the Jesuits after their revival and the virtual extinction in England of the mendicant orders such as the Dominicans and the Franciscans. Especially on the Mission, be that at home or overseas, the early nineteenth century was for the monks a time of vibrant activity that stimulated energy and courage that showed the Congregation at its best.

However, there was no time for complacency. New challenges for the Congregation had recently appeared in England with the new religious congregations such as the Rosminians, the Redemptorists and the Passionists, whose missionary activity in the towns and cities was threatening the monopoly the monks had hitherto enjoyed there. These religious, unlike the monks, were willing to be compliant and co-operative with the bishops, who by the 1850s were actively welcoming them into their dioceses. The Jesuits had not initially posed a threat to the monks, but by the 1840s the Society had not only built up a successful school at Stonyhurst, but had also shown that it was more successful than the Benedictines in marshalling the laity to support its educational and pastoral enterprises.

The restoration of the English hierarchy in 1850 presented a number of issues for the Congregation. Although it could boast having two of its

---

[1] DAA, Collier papers, Box 1, 25n, 6 June 1889, Manning to Collier.

members, Brown and Ullathorne, on the new bench of bishops, the Congregation had failed to secure for itself either new spheres of influence or the restoration of its ancient privileges. Although both were proud of their Benedictine roots, Brown and Ullathorne had already fired warning shots across the bows that the Congregation needed to reform itself, especially with regard to its policies concerning formation and the character of the English Benedictine Mission. The Congregation was warned that it might not have the luxury it had hitherto enjoyed of independent jurisdiction of its missions, should the bishops adopt a policy of appointing secular clergy to new missions and preventing regulars from serving them. It was, therefore, little wonder that many English Benedictines did not welcome the restoration of the hierarchy. Athanasius Allanson, soon to be appointed annalist and Provincial, spoke for many when he described the restoration of the hierarchy as having been "made at the expense of the Congregation" and furthermore, that those English Benedictines who had written to congratulate Cardinal Wiseman on the event had "signed the death warrant of the E.B.C".[2] But if the English Benedictines were to maintain their missions, then they needed to work with, rather than against, the bishops.

It is striking that even in the midst of their changed circumstances after 1795 and the achievements that had been made up to 1850 with regard to the monasteries and the new initiatives on the home and overseas missions, the overall theme of early nineteenth-century English Benedictinism was continuity rather than change. In their new locations, whether in rural England or on the other side of the globe in New South Wales, the monks chose to replicate their well-tried traditions and attitudes, as can be seen in their tenacious grasp of liturgical rituals, house customs and pastoral strategies. It was ironic that the same conservative mind-sets that preserved continuity and tradition both ensured the survival of the Congregation and endangered its future, through resistance to change, particularly concerning attitudes towards the Mission and the Vicars Apostolic. "Out of time, out of place" was the phrase Mary Shanahan used to describe the English Benedictine mission in colonial Australia,[3] and by 1850 the English Benedictines had demonstrated that they were not wholly "out of place" in the landscape of mid-nineteenth century Catholic Britain; they showed that they had a very real contribution to make to the pastoral mission and the educational apostolate, but it is certainly true that the English Benedictines were in danger of being "out of time", imprisoned in a time-warp where change was resisted and the *status quo* was maintained. The combination of the restoration of the English hierarchy, the centralising policies of Rome, and the reforming winds of the continental Benedictine

---

[2] WHELAN, *The Annals of the English Benedictine Congregation 1850-1900,* 1: 34.
[3] M. SHANAHAN, *Out of Time, Out of Place.*

revival threatened to destroy the independence and character of the English Benedictine Congregation.

This study has made significant contributions to the debate concerning the role of the religious orders in nineteenth-century English Catholicism. It is the first to have explored in any significant detail the plight of English Benedictine men and women in the half-century following the French Revolution. It has drawn attention to the accomplishments of English Benedictine missioners at a time of transition and change not just for the Catholic Church in England, but the nation as a whole. It has shown that for one particular group of English religious the early nineteenth century was not an "intertestamental age" characterised by stagnation and listlessness, but an era of new hope, new energy and important foundations.

Secondly, this book has thrown into sharp relief the fragile relationship that existed in the early nineteenth century between the English Vicars Apostolic and the religious engaged in pastoral work, a relationship that has tended to be neglected by historians of the English Catholic Church in this period. Chapters three and four have demonstrated the important role played by the Benedictines in challenging the authority of the Vicars Apostolic, but also in provoking Rome to overhaul the rickety structure of the English Catholic Church. The names of Wiseman, Newman and Manning are well-known nineteenth century Catholic figures, but this study has shown that there were other significant achievements made by English Benedictines such as Ullathorne, Polding and Brown.

Little has so far been written about the English Catholic contribution to the Missionary movement in the early nineteenth century. This study has underlined the significance of the English Benedictine Congregation in providing bishops and clergy who laid important foundations for the growth of Catholicism in the colonies of Mauritius and Australia. Missionary experience gained in these places was used to benefit the English Catholic Church, and this is a topic worthy of further research. The work of Bernard Collier in Mauritius also merits more detailed consideration.

This volume has also opened up other avenues for future research that were not able to be fully explored within the limited scope of this present work. It would be helpful, for instance, to consider the continuities and changes in the English Benedictine Congregation within the broader perspective of religious life in nineteenth-century Catholicism. Although some reference has been made to the plight of English Benedictine nuns in this period, more research is needed to assess the contribution made to Catholic life in England and in Australia by the these women, whose contemplative life counterbalanced the active apostolate of the monks. This study furthermore has outlined the contribution of the Benedictines to Catholic Education in England, but whilst the schools attached to their monasteries became well-known, there is scope for more research on the

Benedictine contribution to elementary education in England, especially in Liverpool.

As the year 1850 drew to its close, the death occurred at Stanbrook on 29 December of President Bernard Barber. He was the first English Benedictine President to be clothed and professed in England and yet he was untypical of his generation, never having had the care of souls on the Mission, but having lived the conventual life at Acton Burnell, Downside, and latterly, for twenty years, in the shadow of the convents at Abbot's Salford and Stanbrook. Barber's *curriculum vitae* and outlook on his Congregation could not have been more different from that of Athanasius Allanson, whose harsh criticisms of the President stemmed from the simple fact that they belonged to opposite camps, the monastic and the missionary.[4] These two wings of the Congregation had been brought together in 1795 and had hitherto co-existed amicably, but now began to draw increasingly apart after 1850 as the Congregation sought to define itself anew in the face of the new threats to its existence from Roman policies of centralisation and new pastoral structures in England. Continuity had been the dominant impulse in the English Benedictine Congregation in the first half of the nineteenth century but after 1850 it would be necessary for continuity to give way to change if the Congregation was to be guaranteed a role in a more settled and increasingly self-confident English Catholic Church.

---

[4] *AB*, 426-428. For a defence of Barber see J.A. MORRALL, "The Right Rev. Dom Luke Bernard Barber," *DR*, 11 (1891) 1-17.

APPENDIX 1

Officials and Superiors of the English Benedictine Congregation, 1795- 1850[1]

A. The Presidents General.

1. 1794   Dom Gregory Cowley   L[2]
2. 1799   Dom Bede Brewer   L
3. 1822   Dom Richard Marsh   L
4. 1826   Dom Augustine Birdsall   D
5. 1837   Dom Richard Marsh   L
6. 1842   Dom Bernard Barber   G
7. 1850   Dom Alban Molyneux   L

B. The Provincials of the South (Canterbury)

1. 1777   Dom Bernard Warmoll   G
2. 1895   Dom Dunstan Garstang   E
3. 1806   Dom Ralph Ainsworth   L
4. 1814   Dom Bernard Barr   G
5. 1822   Dom Bernard Hawarden   G
6. 1822   Dom Augustine Birdsall   D
7. 1826   Dom Benedict Deday   G
8. 1834   Dom Bernard Barber   G
9. 1842   Dom Dunstan Scott   G
10. 1846   Dom Jerome Jenkins   G

C. The Provincials of the North (York)

1. 1785   Dom Michael Lacon   G
2. 1806   Dom Richard Marsh   L
3. 1822   Dom Henry Lawson   G
4. 1822   Dom Gregory Robinson   L
5. 1837   Dom Anselm Brewer   L
6. 1846   Dom Alban Molyneux   L
7. 1850   Dom Ignatius Greenough   L

---

[1] Extracted from B. WHELAN, (ed.), *A Series of Lists relating to the English Benedictine Congregation,* Stanbrook Abbey, Worcester 1933, 12-27.

[2] In these lists the house of profession of the monks is indicated by the following letters: G. St Gregory's; L. St Laurence's; E. St Edmund's; D. Ss Adrian and Denis.

D. Priors of St Gregory's

1.	1781	at Douai	Dom Jerome Sharrock
2.	1808	at Acton Burnell	Dom Peter Kendal
3.	1814	at Downside	Dom Augustine Lawson
4.	1818		Dom Bernard Barber
5.	1830		Dom George Turner
6.	1834		Dom Joseph Brown
7.	1840		Dom Peter Wilson

E. Priors of St Laurence's

1.	1789	at Dieulouard	Dom Richard Marsh
2.	1802	at Ampleforth	Dom Anselm Appleton
3.	1806		Dom Bede Brewer
4.	1810		Dom Gregory Robinson
5.	1815		Dom Clement Rishton
6.	1818		Dom Lawrence Burgess
7.	1830		Dom Adrian Towers
8.	1834		Dom Bede Day
9.	1838		Dom Anselm Cockshoot
10.	1846		Dom Ambrose Prest
11.	1850		Dom Wilfrid Cooper

F. Priors of St Edmund's

1.	1789	at Paris	Dom Henry Parker
2.	1823	at Douai	Dom Richard Marsh
3.	1826		Dom Bernard Collier
4.	1833		Dom Francis Appleton
5.	1841		Dom Placid Burchall

G. Superiors of the monastery of Ss Adrian and Denis

1.	1762	at Lamspringe	Dom Maurus Heatley
2.	1802		Dom Placid Harsnep
3.	1810		Dom Augustine Hatton
4.	1828	at Broadway	Dom Augustine Birdsall
5.	1837		Dom Francis Kershaw

H. Abbesses of the convent of Our Lady of Consolation

1.	1792	at Cambrai	Dame Lucy Blyde
2.	1802	at Woolton	Dame Teresa Shepherd
3.	1806		Dame Agnes Robinson
4.	1814	at Abbot's Salford	Dame Augustina Shepherd
5.	1818		Dame Agnes Robinson
6.	1822		Dame Christina Chare
7.	1830		Dame Gertrude Westhead
8.	1846	at Stanbrook	Dame Scholastica Gregson

APPENDIX 2

Chapels, Chaplaincies and Missions
served by the English Benedictines between 1795 and 1850.[1]

A list of missions already established before 1795 (and continuing). Missions established after 1795 in **bold**.

1.	Aberford, Yorkshire	
2.	Acton, Middlesex	1825-50
3.	Acton Burnell, Salop	
4.	**Aigburth, Lancashire**	**1838**
5.	Allerton Park, Yorkshire	1808-34
6.	**Ashton-le-Walls, Northamptonshire**	**1849-52**
7.	Baddesley, Warwickshire	1803-4
8.	**Barton-on-Humber, Lincolnshire**	**1848**
9.	Beaufront, Northumberland	until 1796
10.	Bath	
11.	Beckford, Gloucestershire	1831-5, 1838-41
12.	Biddlestone, Northumberland	until 1839
13.	Birtley, Durham	
14.	**Bodmin, Cornwall**	**1846-48**
15.	Bonham, Wiltshire	
16.	**Bosworth Hall, Leicestershire**	**1828**
17.	Brambridge, Hampshire	to 1815
18.	**Brandsby, Yorkshire**	**1805**
19.	Brindle, Lancashire	
20.	**Broadway, Worcestershire**	**1828-50**
21.	Brownedge, Lancashire	
22.	**Bungay, Suffolk**	**1821**
23.	**Calehill, Kent**	**1827-1838**
24.	**Cannington, Somerset**	**1807-36**
25.	**Cheltenham, Gloucestershire**	**1809**
26.	**Chipping Sodbury, Gloucestershire**	**1838**
27.	**Clayton Green, Lancashire**	**1822**
28.	Coughton, Warwickshire	
29.	**Coventry, Warwickshire**	**1803**
30.	**Cowpen, Northumberland**	**1838**
31.	Crosby Hall, Lancashire	
32.	Easingwold, Yorkshire	
33.	Felton Park, Northumberland	

---

[1] Extracted from B. WHELAN, (ed.), *A Series of Lists relating to the English Benedictine Congregation,* 114-45.

34.	Flixton Hall, Suffolk	to 1826
35.	Foxcote, Warwickshire	to 1848
36.	**Goosnargh, Lancashire**	**1833**
37.	**Grassendale, Lancashire**	**1835**
38.	**Great Haywood, Staffordshire**	**1834**
39.	Hazelwood, Yorkshire	1807-32
40.	Hesleyside, Northumberland	to 1797, 1803-33
41.	Hetherop, Oxon	to 1796
42.	Hindley, Lancashire	
43.	Holme Hall, Yorkshire	
44.	Horsley, Gloucestershire	
45.	Horton, Gloucestershire	1795-1823
46.	Houghton Hall, Yorkshire	to 1805
47.	**Ince Blundell, Lancashire**	**1826**
48.	**Kenilworth, Warwickshire**	**1820-22, 1840-5**
49.	**Kemerton, Gloucestershire**	**1841**
50.	**Knaresborough, Yorkshire**	**1797**
51.	Lawkland, Yorkshire	to 1796
52.	**Leyland, Lancashire**	**1845**
53.	Lindley, Salop	to 1807
54.	**Little Crosby, Lancashire**	**1836**
55.	**Little Malvern, Worcestershire**	**1826**
56.	**Liverpool St Anne**	**1843**
57.	**Liverpool St Augustine**	**1849**
58.	Liverpool St Mary	
59.	Liverpool St Peter	
60.	London [2]	to 1832
61.	Longhorsley, Northumberland	to 1832
62.	Lytham Hall, Lancashire	to 1804
63.	Marnhull, Dorset	to 1802
64.	**Maryport, Cumbria**	**1841**
65.	Middleton Lodge, Yorkshire	
66.	**Midford Castle, Somerset**	**1820-41**
67.	**Monmouth**	**1840**
68.	Morpeth, Northumberland	
69.	Netherton, Lancashire	
70.	**Newport, Salop**	**1796-1800**
71.	Ormskirk, Lancashire	
72.	**Pershore, Worcestershire**	**1799-1805**

---

[2] No specific location is known, other than that three monks were active in the capital in this period: The Gregorian, Bede Bennet, (resident 1759-1800), Father Dunstan Garstang of St Edmund's (who was stationed at the Portuguese Chapel from 1767 until his death in 1814) and the Gregorian, Anselm Lorymer. (BIRT, *Obit Book of the English Benedictines*, 123, 129, 138; *CRS (R)*, 12: 123, 20: 59; AH, Appendix, 487.)

73.	Plowden Hall, Staffordshire	to 1802
74.	**Pocklington, Yorkshire**	**1803-07**
75.	**Poole, Dorset**	**1839-44**
76.	**Redditch, Worcestershire**	**1834**
77.	Richmond, Yorkshire	to 1814
78.	**Rixton, Lancashire**	**1831**
79.	**Saltwellside, Durham**	**1816-22**
80.	**Sawston Hall, Cambridgeshire**	**1824-6**
81.	**Scarisbrick, Lancashire**	**1824**
82.	**Shaftesbury, Dorset**	**1797-1803**
83.	**Shottery, Warwickshire**	**1831-2**
84.	**Shrewsbury, Salop**	**1822-4**
85.	Swinburne Castle, Northumberland	
86.	**Talacre, Flint**	**1827-31**
87.	Tixall, Staffordshire	to 1798
88.	**Twysog, Denbighshire**	**1824-5**
89.	**Wappenbury, Warwickshire**	**1830**
90.	Warrington St Alban	
91.	Warwick Bridge, Cumbria	
92.	Welshpool, Montgomery	to 1801
93.	**Weobley, Herefordshire**	**1834**
94.	**Westby Hall, Lancashire**	**1821**
95.	Weston Underwood, Buckinghamshire	to 1837
96.	**Weymouth, Dorset**	**c.1823**
97.	Whitehaven, Cumbria	
98.	**Wingerworth, Derbyshire**	**1841-43**
99.	Woollas Hall, Worcestershire	to 1806
100.	Woolston, Lancashire	to 1831
101.	Woolton, Lancashire	
102.	**Wootton Hall, Warwickshire**	**1806**
103.	**Wootton Wawen, Warwickshire**	**1806**
104.	**Workington, Cumbria**	**1810**
105.	**Wrightington Hall, Lancashire**	**1806**

BIBLIOGRAPHY

A. Manuscript sources

Ampleforth Abbey Archives, Yorkshire:

MSS 155-56 Allanson, A., *A History of the English Benedictine Congregation, 1558-1850.*

MSS 160-4 Allanson, A., *A Collection of Records and Letters referred to in the History and   Biography of the English Benedictines.*

MSS 238-240, 243, 260, 261, 263, 267-8 (Letters and Documents).

BX26 Baines, P.A., *Diary.*

MS 284 McCann, J., *The Mission Funds.*

EX01-10 Nihell, R., *Diary.*

6U68 Turner, J., *Sunday Afternoon Lectures* (3 volumes).

MC147, 150, 151, 152 Turner, J., *Sermons for Sundays and Feasts* (2 volumes).

Archives of the Archbishop of Westminster, London:

III.C.vii - Griffiths papers, correspondence from Bishops Augustine Baines and Thomas Joseph Brown.

A53 Douglass, *Diaries.*

Wiseman and bishops box, 1-71.

Birmingham Archdiocesan Archives:

P.127/1/1 Baptismal registers for Coughton, 1795-1850.
P.140/1-4 Baptismal registers for Coventry, 1803-1850.
R.244 MS *Short history of the Bath Mission and troubles with Bishop Baines.*
B.973, 1002, 1224, 1242, 1243, 1607, 1847, 1927, 1928, 1941, 1982 (letters to Bishop William Bernard Ullathorne).

CLIFTON DIOCESAN ARCHIVES, BRISTOL:

Bishops' Letter Books, 1795- 1809.

Baines Box Files, 1-7.

COVENTRY ARCHIVES, WARWICKSHIRE:

PA/101/153/1-4 Contracts for the construction of St Osburg's Church, 1843.

DOUAI ABBEY ARCHIVES, UPPER WOOLHAMPTON, BERKSHIRE:

III.B1, VII.A.3.F, Bishop Collier papers.
IV.B.1.1 Correspondence between Bishop Thomas Joseph Brown and Father Randal Lythgoe S.J. relating to the dispute between the Vicars Apostolic and the Regulars, 1842-1844.
IV.C.XI.1 Papers of Father Augustine Birdsall relating to the Cheltenham Mission.
IV.C.XI.2 Scrapbook of newspaper cuttings collected by Father Ambrose Cotham whilst in Australia.
IV.C.XI.3 BIRDSALL, J.A., MS, *History of the Cheltenham Mission*.
VII.A.1.1 Letters to Prior Henry Parker from various members of the English Benedictine Congregation, 1795-1817.
VII.A.2.[1], "Materials for the annals of St Edmund's from its restoration in 1818".
VIII. A. COTHAM, J.A., *Diary, 1846-1851*.

DOWNSIDE ABBEY ARCHIVES, STRATTON-ON- THE-FOSSE, SOMERSET:

II.A *Acta Capitulorum Generalium, 1798-1900*.
VII.D.250 (BIRDSALL, J.A., *Diary*).
VIII.A Birt papers, 1795-1850. (references B 77 – M 80).
MS, *Fasti Gregoriani*.
Box 703 (MORRIS, P., *Diary*).
Boxes 748, 760 (Presidential papers).
Box 756 (Ullathorne papers).
IV.B (iv) MSS 12, 31, 46, 69, 100, 106, 165, 173, 176, 180, 191, 192, 424. (Account Books relating to the North and South Provinces of the Mission).
MS I.A 450 (President Birdsall's *Report*).
MS 295. VII.A.f (Bishop Baines' *Statement*, also known as *Dr Baines's Defence*).
MS 386, BIRDSALL, J.A., *The Contest between the Abbot of the EBC Monastery of Lambspring and the President of the EBC, 1801-2*.
VII.A. 3f TIDMARSH, B., *Diaries, 1839-1841*.

ENGLISH COLLEGE, ROME:

BEN III.71.2, IV.71.3, 71.6, V.2, VII.3a, 72.2, 72.39, 72.6, VIII. 71.8 (Wiseman papers).

LEEDS DIOCESAN ARCHIVES:

Briggs papers nos 5, 108, 621, 650, 651, 662, 673, 832, 1018, 1026, 1045, 1069, 1208, 1217, 1444, 1661, 1834.

LIVERPOOL RECORD OFFICE:

282 ANN/ 1/1 Baptismal registers, St Anne, Overbury Street.
282 AUG/1/1 Baptismal registers, St Augustine, Great Howard Street.
282 HIG/ 1/1-3 Baptismal registers, St Mary, Highfield Street.
282 PET/1/1-2 Baptismal registers, St Peter, Seel Street.
282 PET/3/1 Seel Street Notice Book, 1845-51.
282 PET/6/1 Register Book of Confraternities, 1841-1912.
D'Andria papers (listed under 942 DAN).
St Anne, Ormskirk, *The Tolerated Religion, 1690-1850* (typescript, no date).

NATIONAL ARCHIVES, KEW, LONDON:

Colonial Office Papers:
CO 167/228 no.10; 167/245 no.42; 167/262 no.192; 167/270 no.24; 167/302 no.253; 167/321 no.105 (Original correspondence relating to Mauritius).
CO 201/280: 340ff; 201/325 (Original correspondence relating to New South Wales).

NATIONAL LIBRARY OF WALES, ABERYSTWYTH:

Archdiocese of Cardiff archive, Bishop Thomas Joseph Brown's unsorted papers are contained in 15 Box Files. The following files were consulted: boxes 2, 4-9, 10, 11-15.

PROPAGANDA FIDE, HISTORICAL ARCHIVES, ROME:

Scritture Riferite nei Congressi: Anglia: volumes 5-12.
Africa, isole dell'Oceano Australe, Capo di Buona Speranza: volumes 1-4

STANBROOK ABBEY ARCHIVES, CALLOW END, WORCESTER:

Annals.

Box 4 (Abbot's Salford).
Box 5 (Presidential letters).
Box 6 (Conferences of Abbess Chare).
ANSTEY, B., MS *Life of Dom Laurence Shepherd* (1897).
SHEPHERD, L., MS *My personal souvenirs of the Abbot of Solesmes.*

SUBIACO CONGREGATION CURIAL ARCHIVES, SANT' AMBROGIO, ROME:

Archivium Subiacensis III, Inizi Congregazione (1842-1880), Casaretto correspondence, principally from Archbishop Bede Polding and Father Paulinus Heptonstall.

USHAW COLLEGE, DURHAM:

Lingard correspondence, 1805-1851.
Wiseman correspondence, 1819-1850.

B. Printed primary sources

Association of Prayer...in honour of the Immaculate Heart of the Blessed Virgin Mary...established...at St Peter's, Seel Street, and affiliated to the Arch-Confraternity of Our Lady of Victories at Paris, privately printed, Liverpool 1845.

BAINES, P.A., *A Letter to Charles Abel Moysey, Archdeacon of Bath,* H. Gye, Bath 1821.

_____, *A Defence of the Christian Religion...in a second letter to Charles Abel Moysey...,* H. Gye, Bath 1822.

_____, *A Remonstrance, in a third letter to Charles Abel Moysey...,*J.A. Robinson, Manchester 1824.

_____, *Course of Studies and Methods of Instruction...with the rules and regulations followed in the colleges at Prior Park,* privately printed, Prior Park, Bath 1838.

BIRDSALL, J., *Christian Reflections for Every Day in the Month,* G.A. Williams, Cheltenham 1822.

_____, *Christian Reflections on the Advantages of Poverty, intended principally for people in Humble Life,* W.E. Andrews, London 1834.

(CALDERBANK, J), *Bath Chapel Prayers,* privately printed, Bath 1816.

CHALLONER, R., *The Garden of the Soul: or, A Manual of Spiritual Exercises, and Instructions, for Christians, by…Dr Richard Challoner,* Catherine Finn, Kilkenny 1779, J.P. Coghlan, London 1781, 1800 , J. Smart, Wolverhampton 1801, Rockcliff & Duckworth, Liverpool 1832, Thomas Bolland, York 1839, Rockcliff, & Ellis, Liverpool 1840.

_____, *Llyfr Gweddi y Catholig; Nou Ymarfrion Bywd Cristionogol, yn ol Arthawiaethau Gwir Eglwys Jesu Crist, ac yn ol Egwyddorion ac Yspryd Ei Efengyl Ef,* Edward Metcalfe, Lle'rpwll 1837.

Congregationis Anglo-Benedictinae, in Missione Laborantis Gubernatio, privately printed, Liverpool 1813.

Constitutiones Congregationis Anglicanae Ordinis Sancti Benedicti: Formularium E.B.C. Ritualis Compendium E.B.C., privately printed, Paris 1764.

Elements of French Grammar as taught at Vernon Hall, Liverpool, J. McCreery, Liverpool 1797.

GLOVER, E.B., *An Explanation of the Prayers and Ceremonies of the Holy Sacrifice of the Mass in familiar discourses addressed to a congregation,* Ambrose Cuddon, London 1825

GOBINET, C., *Instruction of Youth in Christian Piety,* F. Needham, London 1741, Newcastle-upon-Tyne 1783, R. Coyne, Dublin 1824.

HAINES, G., FORSTER, M.G., and BROPHY, F., *The Eye of Faith: The Pastoral Letters of John Bede Polding,* Lowden, Kilmore 1978.

HOOKE, L.J., *Religionis naturalis et reveletae principia,* Berton, Paris 1774) [ed. J.B.Brewer].

À KEMPIS, T., *The Imitation or Following of Jesus Christ,* Thomas Meighan, London 1744, J. P. Coghlan, London 1779, R. Cross, Dublin 1786, L.B. Seeley, London 1826, 1829.

Laity's Directory, 1812.

Lancashire Registers: Brindle and Salmesbury, CRS (R), 23 (1922).

Le Mauricien, no. 1747 (16 January, 1846); no.1804 (29 May, 1846).

MACDONALD, A.B., *The Layman's Afternoon Devotion,* Walker & Kay, Preston 1778, 1793, 1820.

_____, *Select Discourses on the Gospels for all the Sundays and Holydays throughout the Year,* J. McCreery, Liverpool 1801.

MADIGAN, L., (ed.), *The Devil is a Jackass: Being the dying words of the autobiographer William Bernard Ullathorne,* Downside Abbey, Bath 1995.

MANNOCK, J.A., *The Poor Man's Controversy,* published by his friends, London 1769, R. Cross, Dublin 1794, B. Dormin, J. Robinson, Baltimore 1815, J. Booker, Liverpool 1843.

MARSH, R., *Fr Marsh's Escape from Dieulouard,* St Laurence Papers, Ampleforth 1994.

_____, *Reminiscences 1794-1828,* St Laurence Papers, Ampleforth 1995.

Mr Swale's Diary: Rome 1830-1832, St Laurence Papers, Ampleforth 1995.

PEMBRIDGE, M.P., *A Manual of Prayers and Duties of a Christian,with Historical Lessons from the Old and New Testaments, very useful for Children,* C. Pugh, Hereford 1777.

POLDING, J.B., *The Life and Letters of John Bede Polding,* 2 volumes, Glebe, Australia 1994-1996.

The Rambler, 3 (1850).

Regulae ab omnibus Congregationis Anglo-Benedictinae in Missione Laborantibus Observandae, privately printed, Liverpool 1817.

RODRIGUEZ, A., *The Practice of Christian and Religious Perfection,* 3 volumes, J. Reynolds, Kilkenny 1806.

SCUPOLI, L., *The Spiritual Combat,* F. Needham, London 1742, T. Holliwell, Birmingham 1769, Keating & Brown, London 1816.

The Authenticated Report of the discussion...in the chapel of the Roman Catholic College of Downside near Bath on the 25th, 26th, 27th of February and the 5th, 6th and 7th of March 1834. Subjects 'The Rule of Faith' and 'the Sacrifice of the Mass', Protestant Speakers: Rev Edward Tottenham, Rev John Lyons. Roman Catholic Speakers: Rev T.J. Brown etc. Rev. T.M. Macdonnell...Rev Francis Edgeworth, J & F Rivington, J. Booker, London 1836.

The Benedictine Church Directory for the Laity and Catholic Lady's and Gentleman's Annual Remembrance for the Year 1828, privately printed, London 1827.

The Catholicon, 1836.

The Tablet, 9 August, 1845.

ULLATHORNE, W.B., *The Catholic Mission in Australia,* Rockliff & Duckworth, Liverpool 1837.

―――――――, *The horrors of transportation,* Richard Coyne, Dublin 1838.

―――――――, *Sermons with Prefaces,* T. Jones, London 1842.

―――――――, *The Lenten indult of William Bernard OSB, Bishop of Hetalonia and Vicar Apostolic of the Western District, for the year 1848,* H.C. Evans, Bristol 1848.

―――――――, *A Pastoral Letter addressed to the faithful of the Western District,* H.C. Evans, Bristol 1848.

―――――――, *Notes on the Education Question,* Richardson & Son, London 1857.

―――――――, *The Holy Mountain of La Salette,* Richardson, London 1854.

―――――――, *History of the Restoration of the Catholic hierarchy in England,* privately printed, London 1871.

―――――――, "Catholic and Protestant Education," *DR,* 6 (1888) 1-8.

―――――――, *From Cabin-Boy to Archbishop: The Autobiography of Archbishop Ullathorne with an introduction by Shane Leslie,* Hollis & Carter, London 1941.

WALMESLEY, C., *Charles, Bishop of Rama, Vicar Apostolic to all the faithful, clergy and laity in the Western District,* privately printed, Bath 1796.

Weekly Orthodox Journal, 18 December 1841; 29 July 1843; 30 August 1845.

C. Secondary Sources

AGIUS, D., "The Lambspring Council Book, 1715-1802," *DR*, 104 (1986) 58-165.
_____, "Everyday life in Eighteenth-century Lambspring," *EBHS*, privately printed 1995, 28-35.

ALLANSON, P.A., *Biographies of the English Benedictines*, St Laurence Papers, Ampleforth 1999.

ALMOND, C., *History of Ampleforth Abbey*, R & T. Washbourne, London 1903.

_____, "Ampleforth v. Bishop Baines," *AJ*, 23 (1917) 1-18.

ARNSTEIN, W.L., *Protestant versus Catholic in Mid-Victorian England: Mr Newdegate and the Nuns*, University of Missouri Press, Columbia, Missouri 1982.

ASPINWALL, B., "Changing Images of Roman Catholic Religious Orders in the Nineteenth Century," in SHEILS, W., (ed.), *Monks, Hermits and the Ascetic Tradition, Studies in Church History*, 22, Blackwell, Oxford 1985, 351-364.

ATKIN, N. and TALLETT, F, *Priests, Prelates and People: A History of European Catholicism since 1750*, Oxford University Press, Oxford 2003.

AUBERT, R., CORISH, P.J. and LILL, R., *The Church Between Revolution and Restoration*, Herder & Herder, London 1981.
_____, *The Church in the Age of Liberalism*, Burns & Oates, London 1981.

AVELING, H., "The Education of Eighteenth-Century English Monks," *DR*, 79 (1961) 135 – 152.

AVELING, J.C.H.,"'The Eighteenth Century English Benedictines," in DUFFY, E. (ed.) *Challoner and his Church*, Darton, Longman & Todd, London 1981, 152-173.

_____, *The Handle and the Axe*, Blond and Briggs, London 1976.

_____, "Some aspects of the eighteenth-century EBC," *EBHS*, privately printed 1984, 3-12.

BADHAM, J., "The Development of Catholic Education in Cheltenham 1818-1939," *Journal of the Gloucestershire Catholic History Society,* 48 (2006) 3-22.

BEALES, D., *Prosperity and Plunder: European Catholic Monasteries in the Age of Revolution, 1650-1815,* Cambridge University Press, Cambridge 2003.

BECK, G.A., (ed.), *The English Catholics, 1850-1950,* Burns & Oates, London 1950.

BELLENGER, A., "The exiled clergy and religious of the French Revolution and the English Benedictines," *EBHS,* privately printed 1984, 14-30.
_____, "A Standing Miracle: La Trappe at Lulworth, 1794-1817," in SHEILS, W., *Monks, Hermits and the Ascetic Tradition: Studies in Church History,* 22, Basil Blackwell, Oxford 1985, 343-50.
_____, *The French Exiled Clergy in the British Isles after 1789,* Downside Abbey, Bath 1986.
_____ (ed.), *The Great Return – The English Communities in Continental Europe and their Repatriation, 1793-4,* Downside Abbey, Bath 1994.
_____, "France and England: The English Female Religious from Reformation to World War," in TALLETT, F. and ATKIN, N., (eds), *Catholicism in Britain and France since 1789,* Hambeldon Continuum, London 1996, 3-12.
_____, "Benedictine Responses to the Enlightenment," in ASTON, N., (ed.), *Religious Change in Europe: Essays for John McManners,* Oxford University Press, Oxford 1997, 149 – 160.
_____, "Revolution and Emancipation," in REES, D., (ed.), *Monks of England,* SPCK, London 1997, 199-212.
_____, *Three Centuries of English Presence at Douai,* Downside Abbey 1997.
_____, '"The Normal State of the Church," William Bernard Ullathorne, first Bishop of Birmingham,' *RH,* 25 (2000) 325-334.
_____, "Religious Life for Men," in MCCLELLAND, V.A. and HODGETTS, M., (eds), *From Without the Flaminian Gate: 150 years of Roman Catholicism in England and Wales,* Darton, Longman & Todd, London 1999, 142-166.
_____, "The English Benedictines and the British Empire," in GILLEY, S., (ed.), *Victorian Churches and Churchmen: Essays presented to Vincent Alan McClelland, CRS (M),* 7, Trowbridge 2005, 94-109.
_____, *Downside Abbey: An Architectural History,* Merell, London 2011.

BENEDICTINES OF STANBROOK, *In a Great Tradition: Tribute to Dame Laurentia McLachlan,* John Murray, London 1956.

BIRT, H.N., *Downside: A History of Downside School*, Kegan Paul, Trench, Trubner, London 1902.
_____, *Obit book of the English Benedictines*, privately printed, Edinburgh 1913.
_____, *Benedictine Pioneers in Australia*, 2 volumes, Herbert & Daniel, London 1911.

BOSSY, J., *The English Catholic Community 1570-1850*, Darton, Longman & Todd, London 1975.

BOWDEN, C., & LUX-STERRIX, L., (eds), *English Convents in Exile, 1600-1800*, volume 2, Pickering & Chatto, London 2012

BRIGGS, C. AND WHELAN, B., "The Archives of the Venerable English College in Rome," *Catholic Archives*, 7 (1987) 3-11.

BROWNE, M., AND Ó CLABAIGH, C., *The Irish Benedictines: A History*, Columba Press, Blackrock 2005.

BURKE, T., *Catholic History of Liverpool*, C. Tinling, Liverpool 1910.

BUTLER, C., '"Record of the Century," *DR*, 33 (1914) 18-91.
_____, "Literary output of the century," *DR*, 33 (1914) 181-196.
_____, *Benedictine Monachism: Studies in Benedictine Life and Rule*, Longmans, Green, London 1919.
_____, *The Life and Times of Bishop Ullathorne*, 2 volumes, Burns, Oates & Washbourne, London 1926.
_____, "Prior Park and Bishop Baines," *DR*, 50 (1932) 333-349.

CAREY, H.M., (ed.), *Empires of Religion*, Palgrave Macmillan, Basingstoke 2008.
_____, *God's Empire: Religion and Colonialism in the British World, c.1801-1908*, Cambridge University Press, Cambridge 2011.

CARLETON, F., "Monastic Books: The Sydney Benedictine Collection," *TJ*, 44 (1993) 87-91.

CHAMP, J., *A Different Kind of Monk: William Ullathorne (1806-1889)*, Gracewing, Leominster 2006.

CHARLES, C., "The Origins of the Parish Mission in England and the Early Passionist Apostolate, 1840-50," *JEH*, 15 (1964) 60-75.

CHINNICI, J.P., *The English Catholic Enlightenment: John Lingard and the Cisalpine Movement, 1780-1850*, Patmos Press, Shepherdstown 1980.

COLLINS, C., *St Benet's Church, Kemerton 150th anniversary: a brief history* privately printed 1993

CORNWELL, P., *Prior Park College: The Phoenix, an Illustrated History*, Halsgrove, Tiverton 2005.

CRAMER, A., "Peter Athanasius Allanson, Monk, Missioner, Historian," *Northern Catholic History*, 40 (1999) 35-46.
_____, *Ampleforth: The Story of St Laurence's Abbey and College*, St Laurence Papers, Ampleforth 2001.
_____, "The Librarie of this Howse: Augustine Baker's community and their books," in HOGG, J., (ed.), *Stand up to Godwards: Essays in Mystical and Monastic Theology in honour of the Rev John Clark on his 65th birthday*, Institut für Anglistik und Amerikanistik, Universität Salzburg, Salzburg 2002, 103-110.
_____, (ed.), *Lamspringe: An English Abbey in Germany*, St Laurence Papers, Ampleforth 2004.

CRICHTON, J.D., "Popular devotion in Victorian England," *The Month*, 267 (1996) 322-327.

CROUZET, E., *Slender Thread: Origins and History of the Benedictine Mission in Bungay, 1657-2007*, Downside Abbey, Bath 2007.

CUMMINS, I., "Bishop Slater OSB, 1774-1832," *AJ*, 37 (1932) 185-191.

CUNNINGHAM, A.E., "Henry Norbert Birt's Sins of Omission: The Polding Correspondence, a partial appraisal," *TJ*, 46 (1994) 43-56.

CURTIS, S.A., *Educating the Faithful: Religion, Schooling and Society in Nineteenth Century France*, Northern Illinois University Press, Illinois 2000.

DAVIES, J., "Liverpool Libraries: Sources for Catholic History," *NWCH*, 27 (2000) 107-109.

DEVLIN, J., *The Superstitious Mind – French Peasants and the Supernatural in the Nineteenth Century*, Yale University Press, Yale 1987.

DOBSON, F., *George Silvertop of Minsteracres*, Browne, Burton & Associates, Gateshead 2004.

DOWD, C., *Rome in Australia: The Papacy and Conflict in the Australian Catholic Missions, 1834-1884*, 2 volumes, Brill, Leiden 2008.

DOYLE, F.C. (ed.), *The Tercentenary of St Edmund's Monastery*, R & T Washbourne, London 1917.

DOYLE, P., "Lancashire Benedictines: The Restoration of the Hierarchy," *EBHS*, privately printed 1983, 4-21.
_____, *Mitres and Missions in Lancashire: The Roman Catholic Diocese of Liverpool 1850-2000*, Bluecoat, Liverpool 2005.

EDWARDS, E., "Salford Hall or 'The Nunnery,'" *Worcestershire Recusant*, 27 (1976) 2-21.
_____, "The Influence on the EBC of Dom Guéranger's Revival," *EBHS* privately printed 1985, 31-36.
_____, *Home at Last*, Stanbrook Abbey Press, Worcester 1999.

EDWARDS, E., and TRURAN, M., "Dom James Laurence Shepherd," *EBHS*, privately printed 1985, 37-59.

EDWARDS, F., *The Jesuits in England from 1580 to the present day*, Burns and Oates, Tunbridge Wells 1985.

FERGUSON, N., *Empire*, Basic Books, New York 2002.

FLETCHER, J., "The Library of St Patrick's College, Manly," *The Book Collector*, 29 (1980) 179-200.

FORSTER, M.G., "Magdalen le Clerc," *TJ*, 8 (1974) 259-336.
_____, "Subiaco: The Arrival of Benedictine Nuns in Sydney," *TJ*, 54 (1998) 21-55.

FOSTER, S., "Bernard Ward: Edmundian and Historian," in GILLEY, S., (ed.), *Victorian Churches and Churchmen: Essays presented to Vincent Alan McClelland*, CRS (M), 7, Trowbridge 2005, 163-182.

GIBSON, R., A *Social History of French Catholicism, 1789-1914*, Routledge, London 1989.

GILBERT, P., *The Restless Prelate: Bishop Baines (1786-1843)*, Gracewing, Leominster 2006.

GILLESPIE, W., *The Christian Brothers in England, 1825-1880*, The Burleigh Press, Bristol 1975.

GILLEY, S. "The Roman Catholic Church, 1780-1940," in GILLEY, S., and SHEILS, W., A *history of religion in Britain*, Oxford University Press, Oxford 1994, 346-62.

_____ (ed.), *Victorian Churches and Churchmen: Essays presented to Vincent Alan McClelland CRS (M)*, 7, Trowbridge 2005.

GILLOW, J., *A Literary and Biographical History of the English Catholics, or Bibliographical Dictionary of the English Catholics*, 5 volumes, Burns & Oates, London 1885.

GREEN, B., *The English Benedictine Congregation*, Catholic Truth Society, London 1980.

HALDANE, J., "Thomism and the Future of Catholic Philosophy," *New Blackfriars*, 80 (1999) 158-171.

HANLEY, L., *A History of St. Anne's, Ormskirk*, Causeway Press, Ormskirk 1982.

HAYES, D AND DEFOS DU RAU., (eds), *In a Great and Noble Tradition: The Autobiography of Dom Prosper Guéranger*, Gracewing, Leominster 2009

HEIMANN, M., *Catholic Devotion in Victorian England*, Oxford University Press, Oxford 1995.

HEMPHILL, B., *The Early Vicars Apostolic in England*, Burns & Oates, London 1954

HENDERSON, A., *The Stone Phoenix: Stonyhurst College 1794-1894*, Churchman, Worthing 1986.

HILTON, B., *The Age of Atonement: The Influence of Evangelicalism on Social and Economic Thought 1785-1865*, Clarendon Press, Oxford 1988.

HOLLINSHEAD, J.E., "From Cambrai to Woolton: Lancashire's First Religious House," *RH*, 25 (2001) 461-486.

_____, "John Bede Polding: First Catholic Metropolitan of Australia and his Lancashire origins," in DAVIES, J and A. MITCHINSON, A., (eds), *Obstinate Souls: Essays Presented to J.A. Hilton on the occasion of his seventieth birthday by the North West Catholic History Society*, North West Catholic History Society, Wigan 2011, 48-69.

HOOD, A., "Fever in Liverpool," *NWCH*, 20 (1993) 12-30.

_____, "Belmont and Further Studies," *EBHS*, privately printed, 1997, 52-72.

_____, '"Stirring up the pool," Bishop Thomas Joseph Brown OSB (1798-1880) and the dispute between the hierarchy and the English Benedictines,' *RH*, 25 (2000) 304-324.

_____, "Douai, 1808-1903," in SCOTT, G (ed.), *Douai 1903 - Woolhampton 2003: A Centenary History*, Stanbrook Abbey Press, Worcester 2003, 61-97.

_____, "The Throckmortons Come of Age: Political and Social Alignments, 1826-1862," in MARSHALL, P and SCOTT, G, (eds), *Catholic Gentry in English Society: The Throckmortons of Coughton from Reformation to Emancipation*, Ashgate, Farnham 2009.

_____, "Bishop Thomas Joseph Brown OSB (1798-1880)," in BERRY, A., (ed.), *Belmont Abbey: Celebrating 150 Years*, Gracewing, Leominster 2012, 61-71.

JEBB, P., "The Archives of the English Benedictine Congregation kept at St Gregory's, Downside," *DR*, 93 (1975) 208-225 and *DR*, 113 (1995) 284-288.

JONAS, R., *France and the Cult of the Sacred Heart – An Epic Tale for Modern Times*, University of California Press, Berkeley 2000.

JONES, E., *John Lingard and the Pursuit of Historical Truth*, Sussex Academic Press, Brighton 2001.

KAVENAGH, T., "Polding and 19th century monasticism," *TJ*, 8 (1974) 163-194.

_____, "Vaughan and the monks of Sydney," *TJ*, 25 (1983) 147-233.

_____, "Romanticism and Recrimination: The Boy Postulants at St Mary's, Sydney," *TJ*, 46 (1994) 21-42.

_____, "The Polding Correspondence: Norbert Birt's "Sins" revisited," *TJ*, 47 (1994) 45-62.

KNIGHT, F., *The Church in the Nineteenth Century*, L.B. Tauris, New York 2008.

KNOWLES, D., *The Historian and Character and Other Essays*, Cambridge University Press, Cambridge 1963.

KOLLAR, R., *A Foreign and Wicked Institution? The Campaign against Convents in Victorian England*, James Clarke, Oregon 2011.

KOWALSKY, N. AND METZLER, J., *Inventory of the Historical Archives*, Pontificia Universitatas Urbania, Roma 1983.

KSELMAN, T., *Miracles and Prophecies in Nineteenth-Century France*, Rutgers University Press, New Jersey 1983.

LENNER, U.C., *Enlightened Monks: The German Benedictines 1740-1803*, Oxford University Press, Oxford 2011.

LEETHAM, C., *Luigi Gentili: Sower for the Second Spring*, Burns & Oates, London 1965.

LEYSER, C and WILLIAMS, H. *Mission and Monasticism: Acts of the International Symposium at the Pontifical Athenaeum S. Anselmo, Rome, May 7-9, 2009*, Pontificio Atenos S. Anselmo, Roma 2013.

LILLY, W.M., and WALLIS, J.E.P., *A Manual of the Law Specially Affecting Catholics*, W. Clowes & Sons, London 1893.

LITTLE, B., *Catholic Churches since 1623*, Robert Hale, London 1966.

LIVINGSTON, K.T., *The Emergence of an Australian Catholic Priesthood, 1835-1915*, (Studies in the Christian Movement, 3), Catholic Theological Faculty, Sydney, Sydney 1977.

LUNARDI, G., *La Congregazione Sublancense OSB: L'abate Casaretto e gli inizi (1810-1878)*, La Scala, Noci 2004.

LUNN, D., "The English Benedictines in the XIXth century," *TJ*, 8 (1974) 25-32.
_____, *The English Benedictines, 1540-1688: From Reform to Revolution*, Burns & Oates, London 1980.

MAIDLOW DAVIS, L., "Some notes towards an assessment of Abbot Cuthbert Butler's monastic and spiritual outlook," *EBHS*, privately printed, 1984, 23-28.
_____, "An English Benedictine Novitiate: from Douai to Downside," *EBHS*, privately printed, 1991, 19-29.

MANGION, C.M., *Contested Identities; Catholic Women Religious in Nineteenth Century England and Wales*, University of Manchester Press, Manchester 2008.

MARRETT-CROSBY, A., *A School for the Lord's Service: A History of Ampleforth*, James & James, London 2002.

MCCANN, J., *English Benedictine Missions: A survey*, Alden Press, Oxford 1940.
_____, *Annals of the English Benedictine Congregation, 1840–1901*, typescript, 1942.

McCann J. and Cary-Elwes, C. (eds), *Ampleforth and its origins,* Burns, Oates & Washbourne, London 1952.

McClelland, V.A., "From Douai to Dublin: Four Hundred Years of Educational Endeavour," *Studies* 59 (1970) 40-52.
_____, *English Roman Catholics and Higher Education, 1830-1903,* Oxford University Press, Oxford 1973.
_____, '"School or Cloister?" An English Educational Dilemma,' *Pedagogica Historica,* 20 (1980) 108-128.
_____, "School and Studies," in Cramer, A., (ed.), *Lamspringe: An English Abbey in Germany,* St Laurence Papers, Ampleforth 2004, 103-120.

McCoog, T., (ed.), *Promising Hope: Essays on the Suppression and Restoration of the English Province of the Society of Jesus,* Institutum Historicum Societatis Iesu, London 2003.

Memorials of Father Augustine Baker, and other documents, CRS (R), 33 (1933).

Milburn, D., *History of Ushaw College,* Ushaw bookshop, Ushaw 1964.

Moore, E., "With Dr Polding to Australia," *DR,* 32 (1913) 70-92, 197-209, 314-327.

Moore-Rinvolucri, M.J., "The Catholic Contribution to Liverpool Education in the Eighteenth Century," *The Dublin Review,* 228 (1954) 283-286.

Morrall, J.,"The Right Rev. Dom Luke Bernard Barber, D.D., Cathedral Prior of Canterbury, Abbot of Westminster and President General of the English Benedictine Congregation," *DR,* 11 (1891) 1-17.
_____, "The Davis Memorial," *DR,* 11 (1891) 124-28.

Muir, T.E., *Stonyhurst College, 1593-1993,* James & James, London 1992.

Mursell, G., *English Spirituality from 1700 to the Present Day,* SPCK, London 2001.

Nagapen, A., "A Century of English Benedictine Apostolate in Mauritius 1819-1916," *EBHS,* privately printed, 1998, 91-133.

Newsome, D., *The Victorian World Picture,* John Murray, London 1997.

Nockles, P.B., '"The Difficulties of Protestantism", Bishop Milner, John Fletcher and Catholic Apologetic against the Church of England in the era from the First Relief Act to Emancipation, 1778-1830,' *RH,* 24 (1998) 193-236.

NORMAN, E., *The English Catholic Church in the Nineteenth Century*, Oxford University Press, Oxford 1984.

O'BRIEN, E.M., *The Life of Archpriest J.J. Therry, Founder of the Catholic Church in Australasia*, Angus and Robertson, Sydney 1922.

O'BRIEN, S., "Terra Incognita: The Nun in Nineteenth-century England," *Past and Present*, 121(1988) 110-140.

_____, "Religious Life for Women," in MCCLELLAND, V.A., and HODGETTS, M., (eds), *From Without the Flaminian Gate: 150 years of Roman Catholicism in England and Wales*, Darton, Longman and Todd, London 1999, 108-141.

O'CONNOR, T., *Luke Joseph Hooke: An Irish Theologian in Enlightenment France, 1714-96*, Four Courts Press, Dublin 1995.

O'DONNELL, R., "Benedictine building in the Nineteenth Century," *EBHS*, privately printed, 1983, 38-48.

_____, "Pugin in France: Designs for St Edmund's College, Douai (Nord), 1840," *Burlington Magazine*, 125 (1983) 607-611.

O'DONOGHUE, F., "Researching Dr Polding," *Footprints*, 2 (1975) 16-17.

_____, "Australia's Connection with Mauritius," *The Australasian Catholic Record*, 53 (1976) 70-80.

_____, *The Bishop of Botany Bay: The Life of John Bede Polding, Australia's First Catholic Bishop*, Angus & Robertson, Sydney 1982.

OLIVER, G., *Collections illustrating the History of the Catholic Religion in the Counties of Cornwall, Devon, Wiltshire, Somerset and Gloucester*, Charles Dolman, London 1857.

PADBERG, J.W., *Colleges in Controversy: The Jesuit Schools in France from Revival to Suppression, 1815-1880*, Harvard University Press, Cambridge MA, 1969.

PHILLIPS, P., (ed.), *Lingard Remembered: Essays to mark the Sesquicentenary of John Lingard's death*, CRS (M), 6, London 2004.

REARDON, B.M.G., *Religious Thought in the Nineteenth Century*, Cambridge University Press, Cambridge 1966.

REES. D., "The Benedictine Revival in the Nineteenth Century," in FARMER, D.H. (ed.), *Benedict's Disciples*, 2nd edition., Gracewing, Leominster 1995, 324-349.

ROCHE, J.S., *A History of Prior Park College and its Founder Bishop Baines*, Burns & Oates, London 1931.

ROE, W.G., *Lammenais in England. The Reception of Lammenais's Religious ideas in England in the Nineteenth Century*, Oxford University Press, Oxford 1966.

ROWELL, B. "Baker's influence on Benedictine nuns," in WOODWARD, M., (ed.), *That Mysterious Man: Essays on Augustine Baker*, Three Peaks Press, Abergavenny 2001, 82-91.

RUSSO, G., *Lord Abbot of the Wilderness: The Life and Times of Bishop Salvado*, Polding Press, Melbourne 1980.

SCHIEFEN, R.J., *Nicholas Wiseman and the Transformation of English Catholicism*, Patmos Press, Shepherdstown 1984.

SCHOFIELD, N and SKINNER, G., *The English Vicars Apostolic 1688-1850*, Family Publications, Oxford 2009.

SCOTT, G., "'The Times are Fast Approaching", Bishop Charles Walmesley OSB (1722-1797 as Prophet,' *JEH*, 36 (1985) 590-604.
_____, "The English Benedictine Confraternity," *DR*, 105 (1987) 143-63.
_____, *Gothic Rage Undone: English Monks in the Age of Enlightenment*, Downside Abbey, Bath 1992.
_____, "English Benedictines and the Revolution: The Case of Dom John Turner, Guardsman and Grammarian," in BELLENGER, A., (ed.) *The Great Return: The English Communities in Continental Europe and their Repatriation, 1793-4*, Downside Abbey 1994, 38-43.
_____, "Fr Richard Marsh: his importance in the English Benedictine Congregation," *EBHS*, privately printed, 1994, 27-43.
_____, "The English Benedictine Mission and Missions," in FARMER, D.H, (ed.), *Benedict's Disciples*, 2nd edition, Gracewing, Leominster 1995, 302-323.
_____, "Dom Joseph Cuthbert Wilks and English Benedictine involvement in the Cisalpine stirs," *RH*, 23 (1996) 318-340.
_____, "The Image of Augustine Baker," in WOODWARD, M., (ed.), *That Mysterious Man: Essays on Augustine Baker*, Three Peaks Press, Abergavenny, 2001, 92-122.
_____, (ed.), *Douai 1903- Woolhampton 2003: A Centenary History*, Stanbrook Abbey Press, Worcester, 2003.
_____, "Library and Publications," in CRAMER, A., (ed.), *Lamspringe: An English Abbey in Germany*, St Laurence Papers, Ampleforth 2004, 49-72.
_____, "Baker's critics," in SCOTT, G., (ed.), *Dom Augustine Baker (1575-1641)*, Gracewing, Leominster 2012, 191-192.

_____, "Something of the Struggle for Belmont's Soul," in BERRY, A., (ed.), *Belmont Abbey Celebrating 150 Years,* Gracewing, Leominster 2012, 72-109.

_____, "Sermons in British Catholicism to the Restoration of the Hierarchy," in FRANCIS, K.A AND GIBSON, W, (eds), *Oxford Handbook of the British Sermon, 1689-1901,* Oxford University Press, Oxford 2012, 136-151.

SHANAHAN, M., *Out of Time, Out of Place: Henry Gregory and the Benedictine Order in Colonial Australia,* Australian National University Press, Canberra 1970.

SHARP, J., *Reapers of the Harvest: The Redemptorists in Great Britain and Ireland, 1843-1898,* Veritas, Dublin 1989.

SIRE, H.J.A., *Gentlemen Philosophers: Catholic Higher Education at Liège and Stonyhurst 1774-1916,* Churchman, Worthing 1988.

SMITH, R.J., *The Gothic Bequest: Medieval Institutions in British Thought 1688-1863,* Cambridge University Press, Cambridge 1987.

SNOW, ABBOT B., *Sketches of Old Downside*, Sands & Co., London 1902.

SOUTHERWOOD, W.T., "A Benedictine Pioneer in Van Diemen's Land," *The Australasian Catholic Record,* 54 (1977) 43-62.

TENBUS, E.G., *English Catholics and the Education of the Poor, 1847-1902,* Pickering & Chatto, London 2010.

THORPE, O., *The First Mission to the Australian Aborigines,* Pellegrini & Co, Sydney 1950.

TOTAH, M.D., OSB (ed.), *The Spirit of Solesmes*, Burns and Oates, Tunbridge Wells 1997.

TRURAN, M., "Spirituality: Fr Baker's Legacy," in CRAMER, A., (ed.), *Lamspringe: An English Abbey in Germany,* St Laurence Papers, Ampleforth 2004, 83-96.

VIDLER, A., *The Church in an Age of Revolution,* Penguin, Harmondsworth 1961.

VIDMAR, J., *The Catholic Church Through the Ages: A History*, Paulist Press, New York 2005, 266-286.

WALDERSEE, J., *A Grain of Mustard Seed: The Society for the Propagation of the Faith and Australia, 1837-1977,* Chevalier Press, Kensington, New South Wales 1974.

WALLS, A.F., *The Missionary Movement in Christian History: Studies in the Transmission of Faith,* Orbis Books, New York 1996.

WALSH, B., *Roman Catholic Nuns in England and Wales 1800-1937: A Social History,* Irish Academic Press, Dublin 2002.

WARD, B., *The Dawn of the Catholic Revival in England, 1781-1803,* 2 volumes, Longmans, Green, London 1909.
_____, *The Eve of Catholic Emancipation: being the History of the English Catholics during the first 30 years of the 19th Century,* 3 volumes, Longmans, Green, London 1911-1912.
_____, *The Sequel to Catholic Emancipation,* 2 volumes, Longmans, Green, London 1915.

WHELAN, B., *Annals of the English Congregation of Black Monks of St. Benedict, 1850- 1900,* 2 volumes, typescript, 1932.

WHITEHEAD, M., "The English Jesuits and Episcopal Authority: The Liverpool Test Case, 1840-43," *RH,* 18 (1986) 197-219.
_____, '"In the Sincerest Intentions of Studying": The Educational Legacy of Thomas Weld (1750-1810). Founder of Stonyhurst College,' *RH,* 26 (2002) 169-193.
_____, '"A Prolific Nursery of Piety and Learning", Educational Development and Corporate Identity at the *Académie Anglaise,* Liège and Stonyhurst,' in MCCOOG, T., *Promising Hope: Essays on the Suppression and Restoration of the English Province of the Society of Jesus,* Institutum Historicum Societatis Iesu, London 2003, 127-150.
_____, '"Education and correct conduct": Randal Lythgoe and the Work of the Society of Jesus in Early Victorian England and Wales,',' in GILLEY, S., (ed.), *Victorian Churches and Churchmen, CRS (M) 7,* Trowbridge 2005, 75-93.
_____, *English Jesuit Education: Expulsion, Suppression and Restoration, 1762-1803,* Ashgate Publishing, Farnham 2013.

WILLIAMS, J.A., *Post –Reformation Catholicism in Bath, CRS (R)* 65 & 66, 1975, 1976.

WILLIAMS, M.E., *The Venerable English College, Rome, A History, 1579-1979,* 2nd edition, Gracewing, Leominster 2008.

WILTGEN, R.M., *The Founding of the Roman Catholic Church in Oceania, 1825-1850*, Princeton Theological Monograph, Wipf & Stock Publishers, Eugene OR 2010.

YATES, F.A., *The Art of Memory*, Penguin, Harmondsworth 1978.

YOUNG, D.M., *The Colonial Office in the Early Nineteenth Century*, Longmans, London 1961.

D. Unpublished papers and theses

BADHAM, J.R., unpublished M.A. thesis, *The Symbolic Landscapes of Nineteenth and Early Twentieth Century English Catholic Public Schools*, University of Gloucester 2004.

CASHMAN, J., unpublished M.Litt thesis, *Bishop Baines and the Tensions in the Western District, 1842-43*, University of Bristol 1989.

COLLINS, P., unpublished D.Phil thesis, *William Bernard Ullathorne and the Foundation of Australian Catholicism, 1815-1840*. Australian National University 1989.

DOWD, C., unpublished Ph.D. thesis, *Papal Policy towards conflict in the Australian Catholic Missions: The relationship between John Bede Polding, OSB, Archbishop of Sydney, and the Sacred Congregation* De Propaganda Fide, *1842-1874*. Australian National University, Canberra 1994.

DUFFY, E., unpublished Ph.D thesis, *Joseph Berington and the English Catholic Cisalpine movement, 1772-1803*, University of Cambridge 1972.

GALLIVER, P.W., unpublished Ed. D. thesis, *The Development of Ampleforth College as an English Public School*, University of Leeds 2000.

HANSEN, C., unpublished M.A. thesis, *Roman Catholic Education in England in the Nineteenth Century, with special reference to William Bernard Ullathorne*, University of Durham 1998.

NELSON, G., unpublished Ph.D. thesis, *Charles Walmesley and the Episcopal Opposition*, University of Tulane, USA 1977.

RICHARDSON, P.A., unpublished Ph.D. thesis, *Serial Struggles: English Catholics and Their Periodicals, 1648-1844*, University of Durham 2003.

INDEX

Acton Burnell	17, 33-34, 45, 49-50, 52-54, 58-59, 63, 65, 87, 107, 118-19, 128, 133, 140, 152, 156-57, 159, 163-64, 166, 210, 215	Bakerism	69-70
		Barber, Bernard	19, 41, 60, 70-71, 78, 88, 96, 99, 102, 112, 146, 174, 210-12
Aigburth	96-97, 99, 107, 132, 215	Bath	32, 40, 73, 75, 79-80, 83, 90-91, 93-94, 105, 107, 109, 115, 118, 120, 122, 124, 129-31, 133, 143, 159, 161, 176, 215
Allanson, Athanasius	19-21, 33, 37-38, 48, 96-97, 102, 112-13, 120, 125, 130, 132-33, 152, 176, 186, 208, 210		
		Beales, Derek	15, 25
Ampleforth	17-18, 20-22, 31, 34-35, 38-41, 44-45, 48-49, 51-52, 56-58, 67-69, 71, 76, 78-79, 90-91, 93, 96, 112, 118, 120, 123, 132-34, 139, 141-43, 149-51, 154, 157-69, 171-73, 177, 188-89	Bellenger, Aidan	14, 16, 29
		Birdsall, Augustine	34, 39, 43-44, 48, 50, 55, 75, 89, 95, 97, 118, 124, 129-30, 132, 173, 176, 186-87, 197, 211
		Bolas, Anselm	158
		Brewer, Anselm	98-99, 111-12, 125-26, 130, 134
Appleton, Francis	35, 59, 122, 129, 144, 170	Brewer, John Bede	32, 43-45, 48, 138, 160-62, 164, 182
Australia	17-18, 20, 27, 39, 45, 51, 55, 57, 71, 77, 117, 126, 141, 153, 167, 180-84, 187-90, 192-200, 202-5, 209	Briggs, John	97-98, 100-101
		Brindle	17, 107, 114, 156, 215
		Brindle, Jerome	93-94, 133
Australian Mission	131, 184, 200, 203	Bristol	120
		British government	58, 182-83, 190-91, 196-97
Baines, Peter Augustine	12, 20, 28, 40, 44, 46, 79-80, 83, 88-98, 101, 110, 112, 120-22, 124, 129, 141-43, 161, 164, 166, 169, 171, 173, 176-77	Broadway	18, 37, 44, 48, 50, 54, 70, 107, 215
		Brown, Joseph	93, 101, 118, 140-41, 146, 148-49, 154, 165, 174, 187
		Burgess, Laurence	34-35, 40, 93, 143
Baker, Augustine	55, 69-70, 151		

INDEX

Bury, Austin — 56, 149-50, 154, 167-68

Butler, Cuthbert — 21-22, 68, 93-94

Cambrai — 4, 17-18, 30-33, 38, 49-50, 52, 55, 57, 69, 158, 161

Cambridge University — 147-48

Cape of Good Hope — 181, 188

Casaretto, Pietro — 15, 27, 185, 202, 204

Cassinese Congr. — 27

Chaplin, Maurus — 43

Chare, Christina — 55, 65-66, 78

Cheltenham — 75, 107, 118-19, 124-25, 129-30, 132, 153, 176, 199, 215

Clement XIV — 86, 146, 180

Cockshoot, Anselm — 71, 112, 134, 149, 154, 212

Collier, Bernard — 96, 98, 101, 144, 151, 182, 187-88, 190-92, 195, 197-99, 204-5, 209

Collingridge, Peter Bernardine — 88, 90-91

Colonial Office — 186, 191-92, 196-97, 207

Commune Depositum — 128, 130-31

Congregation of *Propaganda Fide* — 84-85, 94, 98, 101-2, 110, 180, 187-89, 192, 196, 202

Cooper, Maurus — 94, 152-53

Cooper, Wilfrid — 123, 212

Cotham, Ambrose — 153, 189, 192, 194, 199

Coughton — 107, 116, 118-19, 131, 215

Coventry — 51, 78, 107, 110, 112, 114, 117-18, 120, 126-27, 129, 176, 215

St Osburg's — 126-27

Cumbria — 107-8, 216-17

Davis, Charles Henry — 57, 118-19, 201, 204

de Maistre, Joseph — 63, 139, 151

Dieulouard — 4, 17, 19, 31-33, 57, 70-71, 138, 151, 156, 158-60

Dorset — 29, 41, 108, 216-17

Douai — 4, 17-22, 31, 33-35, 38, 40-42, 45, 47, 49, 51-54, 57-58, 65, 68-70, 77, 87, 116, 122, 137-42, 144-45, 151-52, 157-60, 162-67, 170, 172-73, 177, 182, 189, 191, 194, 198

Downside — 16-17, 19-22, 29-34, 39-41, 45-54, 56-60, 70, 90-94, 96, 117-20, 125-26, 128, 139-42, 145-46, 148-49, 152, 157, 159, 162-63, 165-74, 177, 182, 187, 189-90, 198, 201, 204, 210

Dublin — 153, 203

Durham — 107, 140, 145, 157, 215, 217

English Benedictine Congregation — 1, 3-4, 7, 16, 19, 21-23, 25, 27-28, 37, 42, 44, 56, 60, 63, 69, 76-77, 84-85, 88, 92, 102, 105, 123, 129, 135, 140, 153-54, 186-87, 191, 193, 205, 209-11

Constitutions — 43, 48, 53, 69, 85-86, 132, 138

General Chapter	4, 34, 42–43, 48, 57, 63, 85, 88, 90, 111, 114, 129, 135, 158, 184–87		Guéranger, Prosper	15, 27, 56, 76–77, 150
North Province	130–31, 133		Hansom, Charles	126
South Province	94, 128, 131, 133, 159		Heatley, Maurus	43–44
			Heptonstall, Paulinus	131
English Benedictine Mission	23, 92, 113-14, 135, 208		Holden, Gregory	128
English Mission	83–84, 86, 105, 132, 147, 173, 189		Jesuits	13, 15, 26, 86, 89, 98–100, 102, 109–10, 124–25, 145–46, 157–59, 162–63, 173, 180, 195, 207
Enlightenment	3, 7, 15, 63, 69, 138–40			
Feinagle, Gregor	168–69		Kemerton	107, 115, 125, 176–77, 216
France	1, 3, 9, 18, 25–26, 30–33, 38, 40, 42, 45, 47, 50, 52, 58–59, 61, 63–65, 81, 87, 91, 120, 139, 144, 152, 158–59, 162–63, 173, 180, 182		Kendal, Peter	59, 128, 164
			Lamspringe	4, 15, 18, 31, 34–35, 37, 39–40, 42–44, 48, 55, 70, 138, 144, 151–52, 158, 160–61, 211–12
Government	58–59, 162, 173			
Revolution	1, 3, 7–8, 15, 17, 21, 23, 25–30, 32–35, 38, 42–43, 47–48, 50, 55, 57, 60–64, 70, 76, 87, 91, 93, 105, 137, 139, 144–46, 151–52, 157–59, 161–62, 180, 207, 209		Lancashire	12, 14, 31, 38, 107–8, 110, 114, 120, 133, 146, 156, 166, 172, 215–17
			Lawson, Augustine	65, 168
			Leo XII	89
			Liverpool	12–14, 31, 39, 48, 51, 64, 73, 83, 87, 96, 100–101, 105, 109–10, 112, 115, 118, 121–23, 125–26, 129, 132, 135, 158, 160, 176–77, 183, 188, 207, 210
Gentili, Luigi	78, 102, 143, 154			
Gérardot, J-B	160			
Gloucestershire	107, 176, 215–16			
Glover, Benedict	73–75		St Anne's	98, 100–101, 126
Goodridge, H.E.	46-7		St Francis Xavier	99–100, 110
Gregory I the Great	86, 185		St Mary's	112, 115, 125
Gregory XVI	9, 27–28, 81, 180, 202		St Peter's	78, 81, 115, 122–23, 129, 134, 176

London	10–11, 33, 44, 65, 98, 100, 107, 109–10, 124, 131, 149, 153, 155, 168, 181, 186, 189, 196, 216	Paris	4, 17, 31–34, 38, 57, 64–65, 68, 70, 81, 86, 137–38, 144, 151, 158, 181, 191
University	148, 171, 174	Sorbonne	69, 138, 140–41
Louvel, Père	117	Parker, Henry	32, 34, 37, 65, 87, 151
Lulworth	29, 41	Parma	71, 149–50, 154
		peculium	59-60, 131–34, 176
Macdonald, Archibald Benedict	64, 74–75	Pembridge, Benedict	53, 62–63
		Penswick, Thomas	97, 145, 147
Manning, Henry	207, 209	Pius IX	28, 150, 180, 186, 202
Mannock, Anselm	73		
Marsh, Richard	18, 28, 31, 34, 57, 91, 93, 95, 144, 151, 154, 159–62, 164, 173, 176, 181, 211	Pius VII	26–27, 89, 93, 180
		Polding, Bede	17, 20, 39, 45, 51, 55–56, 77, 122–23, 131, 141–42, 153, 167, 183–90, 193–95, 197, 199–204, 209
Maurist monks	140–41		
Mauritius	90, 167, 173, 179, 181–82, 186–88, 190–98, 204–5, 209		
		Port Louis	181–82, 192–93, 198, 204
Milner, John	11–12, 87–89, 118, 157	Poynter, William	11–12, 181, 186, 196
Mount Saint Bernard	30, 41	Prest, Ambrose	39, 78–79, 96–97, 99, 116–17, 132, 142, 212
Napoleon	26, 33, 42, 62	Princethorpe	50–51, 117, 184
Newman, John Henry	148, 209	Prior Park	20, 40, 79, 91, 142–43, 161, 166, 171
Newsham, Charles	145		
New South Wales	183–84, 192, 196–97, 199, 202, 208	Prussia	42, 44, 158
		Pugin, Augustus Welby	47, 125–26
Northumberland	60, 107–8, 215–17		
Ormskirk	108, 114, 125, 132–33, 216	Redemptorists	110–11, 207
		Regulae Missionis	113–14, 130, 132–33
Oscott	157, 177	Robinson, Gregory	97, 134, 147, 173, 211–12
Oxford			
Movement	80	Rodriguez, Alfonso	67–68
University	147–48	Rome	9–10, 21, 56, 76, 79–80, 84–85, 87–89, 91–93, 95–102, 110, 114, 116, 128, 137,
Parbold	17, 38, 159–61		

143, 145–48, 180–82, 187, 191, 196, 198, 203–4, 208

Venerable English College 21, 147

Rosminians 77–79, 102, 110, 117, 143, 207

Salford Hall 31, 38, 45, 57
Scarisbrick 108, 110, 217
Scholes 159–60
Scott, Geoffrey 3–4, 21–22, 70, 81, 114, 130
Sedgley Park 155
Sharrock, Gregory 88, 90, 161
Sharrock, James 28, 63
Shepherd, Laurence 16, 56, 71, 76–77, 149–50, 154
Shropshire 107, 215–17
Slater, Bede 90, 181–82, 184, 188–89, 197
Smythe, Edward 31, 33, 59, 133, 145
Solesmes 27, 77, 150
Spencer, George Ignatius 79–80
Staffordshire 107, 111, 117, 216–17
Stanbrook 17–18, 20, 38, 49, 51, 57–58, 70–71, 76–77, 150, 162, 184, 210
Stockeld Park 108, 116–17
Stonyhurst 13, 89, 99, 146, 148, 157, 159, 169–73, 177, 207
Suffolk 107, 215–16
Sydney 17, 39, 45, 51, 56, 77, 122, 141, 143, 183, 193, 198, 201–4

St Mary's monastery 45, 51, 56

Talbot, Oswald 133
Tate, Robert 145
Throckmorton family 115–16
Tidmarsh, Benedict 56, 149
Towers, Adrian 41
Trappists 29, 41–42
Turner, John 64, 75–76

Ullathorne, William Bernard 12, 16, 18, 49, 51, 65–67, 70–72, 76, 78–79, 117–19, 126–27, 135, 141–42, 153, 169, 172, 175, 182–83, 186, 192, 197–200, 203, 205, 208–9
Urban VIII 84
Ushaw 109, 120, 144–48, 157, 177

Vernon Hall 17, 87, 159–60

Waldersee, James 194
Wales 80, 101, 170
Walmesley, Charles 62–63, 74, 86, 88, 138
Walsh, Thomas 12, 89, 111
Warmoll, Bernard 158–59
Warwick Bridge 31, 108, 112, 125, 217
Warwickshire 107–8, 115–16, 118, 215–17
Wilks, Cuthbert 86–88, 138
William IV, King 58, 148
Wimmer, Boniface 185, 194, 202
Wiseman, Nicholas 79–80, 147, 209
Woolhampton 17–18

Woolton	14, 17, 31, 38–39, 45, 48–50, 52, 55, 96, 108, 158, 161–62, 217
Worcester	31, 45, 48–49, 101, 117
Worcestershire	48, 54, 107–8, 215–17
Yorkshire	31, 107–8, 119, 142, 215–17